DON'T LET YOUR IDEA OR PRODUCT ATROPHY IN YOUR MIND. ASK YOURSELF THE HARD QUESTIONS TO OVERCOME YOUR FEAR AND SUBJECTIVITY MAKING YOUR DREAM A REALITY. JOHN PARKIN HAS BROUGHT OVER 50 PRODUCTS TO MARKET. HE SHARES HIS TECHNIQUES AND TACTICS FOR SUCCESS WITH THOUGHT PROVOKING QUESTIONS AND CRITICAL INSIGHT ON THE PROCESSES TO BRING YOUR PRODUCT FROM THE THOUGHT PROCESS TO REALITY.

TAKE IT TOO REALITY

AN ENTREPRENEURS GUIDE TO EVALUATING A NEW IDEA AND THE STEPS REQUIRED TO TAKE IT TO REALITY!

By John Parkin

Take It To reality

Copyright © 2015 by John E Parkin

ISBN (9781543113174)

Printed in the USA by

Dedication

This workbook is dedicated to professionals and amateurs alike who have an idea for a product or service but don't understand the steps to "Take it too Reality". I have had a great deal of success taking an idea from just that, an idea to reality. It is not for everyone but if you want to take the steps to better understanding how to take a product or service from an idea to reality, I believe that this workbook will be a valuable tool.

About the Author

John Parkin has always been a fighter. His roots can be traced from a poor to low middle class income family where both parents worked in sweat shops; John wanted better for himself. His first year out of high school he got decisive about his life's ambition and made more money in one year than his parents had made in many of the years of their working lives; he would not live his life the way his parents had.

While he was growing up John was always a standout. He strived to be the best he could in everything he undertook whether it was fighting in school to prove his manhood, getting good grades when required, excelling in athletics or understanding people and how far to push without appearing to be too aggressive. John is a type "A" personality which meant that he hated failure within himself. Although he demanded so much of himself, John also knew that he had a duty to his fellow human beings too so he always tried to help others be successful whether it be in business or athletics.

John's Story

John graduated from high school, and although not with honors, with more tenacity than most. He actually had gained enough credits to have five periods of PE the last semester of his senior year so technically he was done with high school in his junior year. He had good enough grades to enter a university but he wanted to play football. He was interviewed by a coach but much to his disappointment, because he had previously broken his back, he wasn't allowed the risk of a walk on tryout. John scrapped the idea of a university education and went to a Junior College thinking he wanted to work with the under privileged. During his stent at the college his Sociology professor found him a job working with Special Needs people but when John went to apply, he found out that they just closed shop; another door closed but this small missed window actually opened up a world to John that he hadn't anticipated.

Data Processing was the up and coming white collar industry at the time John found his life path changing. Back then if you worked for IBM it was like working for Microsoft, Apple or Google today; both desirable and prestigious. John saw the future and was willing to risk college to enroll in one of the first of its kind data processing training schools specializing in board wiring for IBM accounting machines. He graduated out of the first class and secured a job sorting cards and wiring boards, something vastly different than he had originally seen for himself. He soon got married and applied to Boeing because, in Washington State, when you have a technical education that's what you did….you applied for Boeing. John was immediately hired and advanced through the ranks quickly to become the highest paid non-engineering worker on the floor. Boeing immediately saw John's potential and sent him to over 30 specialized courses on everything from programming, operating systems, management, EEO, time management, space utilization and much more. It would appear at this time that John may have found his nitch but it wouldn't last….John needed more.

After six years John soon got bored with Boeing. He was recruited to manage a service bureau but soon got bored there as well so a friend recommended him to Honeywell. He found new challenges at Honeywell and ended up working there for 10 years. John started out as the low man on the totem pole and was somewhat intimidated by the degrees everyone had but he had his street smarts and logic working for him; he remembered all he had ever learned and applied it to the real time environment. John advanced rapidly and gained a lot of respect. His clients were often surprised to discover that he did not at least have a Masters while many of those he worked with actually thought he had a PHD.

Honeywell sent to him to over 40 specialized classes and he was honored for outstanding achievement, not only in his branch, but nationally for Systems and Personnel Management. At that point he was managing the people who had hired him. He was pleased years later when several employees who had left, came back because they liked his management style and the success the branch achieved through his team's reign. John was sent to MIT and Harvard for special studies and Honeywell selected John as a special study to learn why his branch was so successful in installing over 250 systems on time and why his people were the longest tenured in the company.

John earned industry consultant certificates in accounting, distribution, manufacturing and health. He headed up design teams and consulted at the highest levels of the industry. He was a guest speaker at several universities speaking to graduates entering the field of data processing and he advised them on career paths. John even got the opportunity to recommended new curriculum to the universities as the old curriculum did not address the real world job market requirements.

At this point John had achieved all that he could in the Systems world. He longed to move on into marketing and sales so Honeywell offered him a National Systems Managers position. While he appreciated the offer, John turned it down and ultimately became the first Systems Manager to be promoted to a Marketing Manager with sales quota responsibilities; he was literally writing his own ticket. The first thing he did was to request Boeing as an account. No one had ever sold into Boeing since IBM, NCR and Univac had a tight hold on the business requirements and Honeywell had never been able to make any inroads other than some ruggedized small processors; John aimed to change that.

John knew the systems side of Boeing very well and he approached them from a position of strength because of his previous experience. He asked the systems people what they needed in order to save time, increase productivity, and reduce costs. He soon got a hit on a high speed printing requirement that Honeywell had a potential solution for. This was brand new technology and after extensive testing and negotiations, John convinced Boeing to purchase the printers. He sold over 15 printers at a cost of over $300,000 a piece, not counting the recurring revenue on paper and other supplies. In addition, he sold a record 11 new name company's during his first year in sales; a record that has never been broken. During this time John obtained new respect and made President's Club as well as receiving other honors; he appeared to have finally arrived. But....John got bored again.

John decided at that point that he needed to go out on his own. He figured that if he could sell that amount for a company like Honeywell, he could do it for himself if he had his own company. Why not make substantially more for his effort? At Honeywell he came up with a revolutionary festival seating program, and an octal to decimal and hexadecimal conversion wheel....he needed to ensure that his successes were just that...his.

John was soon recruited by his prior manager who was successfully selling the revolutionary PICK System on Microdata Reality. He accepted the position and was assigned a territory consisting of eastern Washington, Oregon, and Idaho. He too would be selling the revolutionary PICK; the first English based relational data base programming language on Microdata Reality computers. He was quite successful and began taking flying lessons to lessen the time to get from one locale to another. He had three apartments, one in Spokane, Seattle and Boise and was seeing less and less of his family.

Soon John's reputation gained major recognition. He was asked by Piper, Jaffrey and Hopwood, a stock brokerage firm that was pushing Microdata stock, if he would put on a seminar to sell Microdata stock in Boise, Idaho. John agreed and they invited major clients in the region. He jumped at the chance and ultimately sold several systems in the area. Once again John was proving that he could do anything he set his mind to. While working on this project John had a chance encounter with one of the richest families in Boise. One of the sons was enchanted with an idea John had to use the revolutionary PICK operating System on Microdata to put buyers and sellers together using the computer. This was prior to E-bay and all of the on-line businesses using the internet so the concept was revolutionary. John did some research and discovered that two other associates originally had the idea, but they couldn't put it together; now, he would attempt it.

Soon John closed down the PICK/ Microdata distributorship to concentrate on his new venture. He named the new company "The Connection" and put all of his money into the venture attracting the best PICK computer analysts and programmers in the US to work for stock options.

John knew that the son from the rich family was excited about the technology and Business Plan for "The Connection". At this point the son already had a few failures under his belt but his father saw that he finally had a chance to be successful through this venture. After opening the company things started out great. A local newspaper was purchased to advertise "The Connection", John reorganized the paper and increased the want ads from 200 to 2,000 and he also designed the first automated MLS with instant Hot Sheets and computer access from your car. These things had never been done before so John was receiving national attention for the automated MLS and was even invited to be on local/national TV and radio. It is important to note here that there were other firsts as well including designing satellite communications to communicate in burst mode info from one location to another when they expanded. They were also designing purchasing from your TV with a special interface; things were really taking off.

As they set up their new company and with opening day fast approaching, 60 operators were set online to take calls for anything you could purchase in a newspaper and then some. Local Realtors sold more homes than ever before, car dealers sold more cars; there were movie listings, information on where your local Amway distributor was, garage sales, antiques, boats, job listings, etc. etc. The concept was so unique that the television news show 60 Minutes even flew a crew out to interview John about the greatest new advertising company in the United States. He added Arbitron/Nielson type surveys to gage the reception a program or news story received from a TV showing. Things were going great but John didn't know that it was all about to change.

A few months in John heard rumor that the Mafia was interested in purchasing "The Connection". They wanted it as a front company and they got wind of the company via the son who had come on board as a partner. The son was also part owner of a local bank that funded casinos in the Nevada area so to say that his connections were questionable wasn't a reach. While John wasn't okay with doing business with unsavory characters he was excited by the prospect of selling the company for a profit however, it wasn't to be.

The president of the bank met with John and informed him that several meetings had taken place and the final vote was not to purchase the company since it had not been in business long enough. Success is rewarding but it can also be fleeting. Nine months after the launch, success was looming and the business was booming. In fact, it was booming so much that the Statesman, Boise's newspaper owned by Gannett News, had to lower the price of want ads by almost 40% in order to compete with "The Connection". The Business Plan called for expansion when the concept had been proven and it had been proven…in spades. Within a few months the business would be profitable in a way that John hadn't imagined. What John didn't see coming was that JR, the son's father, would soon apply pressure to his son to pull out of the business. It was rumored that, because of the pressure that JR's cronies were applying to him, he needed his son to get out. John walked into his office one day, was pulled aside and told that the business would be shut down. Over 100 people were affected by this decision. The people with the most invested did not receive any payment other than expenses and were betting that when an IPO was offered, their stock would be worth a fortune; John's company was unraveling because of the greed of a few.

John didn't handle it well; he went berserk, smashed the Xerox to pieces with his fist and threw the son up against the wall making a few threatening remarks. He was not a violent man and realizing that his anger was getting him nowhere, he composed himself and drove back to his apartment. The more he thought about it the more he regretted how he had handled the situation. He called and apologized and then headed back to the office. On his way back fate would deal him yet another blow and he was rear ended at a stop sign. His car was totaled and he was unconscious at the scene. He had to be extracted out of the car with the Jaws of Life but when he was taken to the hospital it was discovered that he only had a minor concussion. Once again the Universe had stepped in and taken care of John but he wasn't out of the woods yet…now he would have to deal with the fallout of the business.

Table of Contents

MARKET INFORMATION GATHERING

SALES AND ACCOUNT MANAGEMENT

BUSINESS CASE DEVELOPMENT

RAISING MONEY

PERFORMANCE MEASUREMENT CRITERIA

PRODUCT CERTIFICATION

Forward

Wanna be entrepreneurs are a dime a dozen. Everyone, at some time or another, has thought of a great idea but didn't have a clue about how to make it happen. The goal of this book is to pass along some real life experiences of an entrepreneur. I want to teach people not to make the same mistakes that I did. Your idea has the right to not atrophy in the back of your mind. I will explain how to take your idea through the test of reasonableness and beyond without spending a fortune. All you really need is your time and just maybe, you too, will become a successful entrepreneur.

Individuals and businesses of all sizes tend to overlook the obvious when evaluating or making a decision on developing a new product or idea. Overlooking the obvious can be the difference between profit beyond your wildest dreams or complete devastation. Devastation means different things but can include losing money, being embarrassed, and loss of family or any number of other things. I wrote this book to serve as a guideline and a reminder to ask yourself the hard questions when assessing the market and sales potential of a new idea or product. I want to save you the heartache of devastation.

As the author of this book I bring a lifetime of experience. I have had many real life successes and failures associated with bringing over 50 new products to market. Early in my career, I was always the pioneer that marketed and executed sales strategies to penetrate new markets that were previously thought to be the domain of a large and established incumbent. All of my efforts were successful even if they were not always monetarily profitable. I have been successful to the extent that I have learned some things and have endured many a hard lesson related to control along the way.

Many of my ideas were ahead of their time and required a conceptual sell based on theory or where technology was heading. The key to my success was to have my associates, employees, marketing,

Navigating Points:

Throughout this book you will discover snippets of information designed to help you define what you are learning. These "Navigating Points" are set throughout the text to showcase some of the points that will help you.

There is no better advice than from those who have been there, done that.

Throughout the book look for these boxes for quotes from those who have been successful in business.

sales, support, channel partners, support and end users take ownership of what I was trying to sell them. If you have a significant other they need to buy into your chosen life style as an entrepreneur. It is a 24 hour, 7 days a week, 365 days per year effort. You will need a very understanding significant other because entrepreneurs are usually "A" type personalities and their relationships can suffer as a result of their drive.

Most of the world's most successful people are not the best educated. What most do have in common are excellent street smarts, intuition, they are great out of the box thinkers, they are fearless, hardworking and able to ask the hard questions and then wait for an answer. As the saying goes, "He who speaks first is usually the loser".

It is important to remember that when you ask a question, every answer is a good answer. Even if it is not the answer you asked for, it is an answer. I sometimes will ask a question I know the answer to already. Sometimes, based on a person's perception, a question could garnish a different answer than you were expecting...always keep an open mind. Negatives are also a part of the process. Negatives are great though since you now have an opportunity to address the negative and turn it into a positive. Negative situations are always a learning experience and great opportunities.

You can also be the smartest person in the world but if you can't find a way to secure funding or sell your idea to someone, or a company, you still have nothing. If you have a solid idea and it has passed the test of reasonableness, functionality and is perceived to fulfill a need, you have crossed over the first hurdle. The second hurdle is to prove your idea with a solid marketing study that identifies the demographic of your potential sellers and more importantly your buyers or end users. If you can successfully cross this hurdle, the third hurdle is to write a

Throughout this book we will offer some advise from the author himself. Years of vast experience allows Author John Parkin to pass on some of the wisdom he has obtained through learning and having made some mistakes of his own. Watch for the "What Would John Do" boxes for valuable insight.

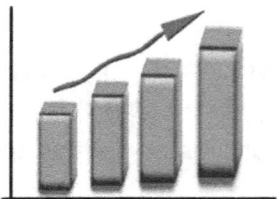

Business Plan that will make sense to a potential investor.

Don't expect to have majority control or ownership every time but is prepared to stand your ground and get a reasonable offer for your idea and the work you have put into the process. Where you can potentially go from here is farther than 99% of where people get to with a viable idea.

The goal of this book is to get you over these three hurdles. Depending on your position, the rest of the book will give you direction on product development, product certification, testing, marketing, sales, management and support.

Many of my efforts were started with an idea but many were pioneering new products with innovative marketing and executing successful sales strategies. Existing products were page printers, personal, mini, main frame and specialized computer applications such as make to order manufacturing, distribution, financial and hospital appointment scheduling. I also sold the first relational data base software and encrypted message processors. Other ideas that materialized into a product were a MIDI recording device that could record any digital sound from an instrument with a MIDI interface, a PC backup device, the first ever computer based advertising linking buyers and sellers, a universal call accounting system that interfaced with any telephone system and the first ever DSP based telephone system. My other project included a first of its kind festival seating program, MIDI recording device, PC backup, computer based training, MLS, and computerized advertising connecting buyers and sellers. Ideas that became products and supported a new business were a state of the art call accounting system, the first DSP based telephone system, computerized advertising, printing company a nonprofit serving Special Needs, wrote novels and this text to name a few. I also started a printing, computer sales, grocery chain, and door manufacturing companies in the Middle East.

Navigating Points:

Don't expect to have majority control or ownership every time but is prepared to stand your ground and get a reasonable offer for your idea and the work you have put into the process. Where you can potentially go from here is farther than 99% of where people get to with a viable idea.

To say that I have a world of experience to offer would not be an understatement.

When there was an existing product, I was asked to prove the concept through developing and executing a marketing plan. In some instances, many millions were spent on developing the idea into a prototype and I was asked to validate the product after the development. What an engineer thought to be beneficial to a market, could be proven to be invalid because of being too costly or the market not large enough to justify the development. Ultimately a product can be written off causing the engineer to leave and form his own company because he/she thinks they know better; often times these types of decisions ignoring the research can lead to large financial losses. I have had products that were highly successful and partially funded with government grants, venture capital and in some instances go to the stock exchange under an Initial Public Offering (IPO); my experiences here are invaluable to beginners. In the case of a new idea, what I learned through experience was the importance of marketing and funding. Without proving the market and having a subsequent channel to market, you are wasting your time. If you do not have adequate funding or a source for funding, the window will close quickly. If you have to lose majority control, do you have the personality to handle taking the credit but with a lesser role in bringing your product to market? Can you handle losing control? If the answer is no you may want to rethink things because sometimes this is a necessary part of doing business.

All of the products I was involved with required specific disciplines with tests of reasonableness against the Window of Opportunity, available market, potential market share, cost to develop, channel to market and most of all, funding sources. You will have to consider all of these things too.

What Would John Do

All of the products I was involved with required specific disciplines with tests of reasonableness against the Window of Opportunity, available market, potential market share, cost to develop, channel to market and most of all, funding sources. You will have to consider all of these things too.

This book is broken into 5 sections with 32 chapters directing you to ask the hard questions about every logical phase of product development from thinking of the idea and performing the initial "test of reasonableness", through fund raising, marketing, development, sales and support. Each step has 9-20 questions with my editorial comments. My comments after each question, paraphrasing my thought processes and what went through my mind when this question arose for me, is intended to stimulate your thought process about a specific issue that you might ordinarily overlook.

I advise you to brainstorm or solicit input from colleagues, family, consultants, investment partners, engineers, competition, potential channel partners and end users. When finished with the fact and information gathering phase, you should be able to make a logical decision on the approach and viability of your idea in a given marketplace. Ideas as it is so often said, "are a dime a dozen." It is true, ideas are cheap and when a business or entrepreneur embarks on the development of an idea without first doing a thorough market study, results could be devastating. If you take the time to think through the questions and exercises contained in this book it will help you through the new product decision process and improve your chances of making a business success of your new idea. You too can **"Take it too Reality"**.

Navigating Points:

Ideas as it is so often said, "are a dime a dozen." It is true, ideas are cheap and when a business or entrepreneur embarks on the development of an idea without first doing a thorough market study, results could be devastating. If you take the time to think through the questions and exercises contained in this book it will help you through the new product decision process and improve your chances of making a business success of your new idea.

Chapter 1 - Hole in the Market

"Boldly going where no one has gone before," to borrow a phrase from "Star Trek" is a good explanation of finding a "Hole in the Market". The antithesis of this would be finding a "Hole in the Market," spending all of your money for development, only to find out that your product, service or technology is out of date, to far advanced, someone else you beat you to the market, it's too costly to make or your market is too small. To find the "Hole in the Market" you will need to;

- Offer a benefit solution to a customer need

- Develop a need

- Have an idea for a breakthrough technology

- Create a fad or seasonal item

- Get lucky.

To find a "Hole in the Market" you need to:

Offer a benefit solution to a customer need

Develop a need

Have an idea for a break-through technology

Create a fad or seasonal item

Get lucky.

But when you find the hole be prepared to act because the market only has a small Window of Opportunity that will last for a finite or limited time before competition rears its ugly head. Also, do not let the greed factor take over your emotions; this is the single biggest obstacle to taking your product to reality. I have seen so many ideas atrophy because the person wanted the whole pie when a piece of the pie would, at the very least, put some money in their pockets.

Greed is the major cause and/or obstacle to ever getting your good idea developed and into a revenue generating position. For your idea to come to fruition, whether you are a new entrepreneur or an existing business, when trying to sell the idea to your management it is important to remember that you are dealing with personalities. Each personality is made up of its own intrinsic value system so you have to understand your own intrinsic values and determine if you are capable of taking and coping with criticism and/or possibly taking a lesser role, or even no role, in your ideas development. This is a huge consideration if you find an investor willing to take a chance on your idea with their company or if you find a family member, venture capitalist or angel investor willing to back your idea. If you find you can't cope, get out or you will become a very cynical and unhappy individual. You will think people are taking advantage of you, taking credit for your idea, out to get you and all you become is a very unhappy individual that bitches about life and everything around you; sometimes attitude is key to being successful. Your family and your job will suffer as well as your mental and physical health if you aren't mindful of your ability to cope.

Everyone has intrinsic values. When you understand, and can cope, with yours then you be able to understand and discover those values in other people. It is important that you are able to do this with those you are trying to get to back or invest in your idea for a product or service. The intrinsic values of entrepreneurs are those that back new ventures and tend to be wide ranging and varied. If your idea is a technology driven product, than you need the intrinsic values of the investor you are seeking to be driven by being involved in leading or cutting edge technology related products. Your idea could be orientated to the kitchen, household, clothes, exercise related, weight loss, beauty, tool, toy, fad, composite, green, teaching, vitamin, stamina, or any of a million other possible new ideas. But remember that the majority of new ideas do not make you an overnight millionaire.

The "Window of Opportunity" is phrase that is used often. It is sometimes overlooked or not totally understood by the erstwhile entrepreneur. Sometimes even an established company looking to

Navigating Points:

Everyone has intrinsic values. When you understand, and can cope, with yours then you be able to understand and discover those values in other people. It is important that you are able to do this with those you are trying to get to back or invest in your idea for a product or service. The intrinsic values of entrepreneurs are those that back new ventures and tend to be wide ranging and varied. If your idea is a technology driven product, than you need the intrinsic values of the investor you are seeking to be driven by being involved in leading or cutting edge technology related products.

launch a new product or service doesn't really understand the concept of their being a "Window of Opportunity". The window needs to be closely examined relative to;

- The market size

- Potential competitors

- Your market share to be successful

- Your cost to develop

- What channel to market you are going to pursue

- Regulatory issues

- Promotional requirements

- Training

- Margin life expectancy

- Price erosion

- Enhancement criteria

- Sales and support.

As you go through this examination process to determine if you or your company has the resources to develop and launch a new product, carefully consider, do you have the resources available to fill the "Hole in the Market?" Would you be willing to take a lesser piece of the pie such as a lump sum buy out, royalties, a position in the company and or a percentage of the profits?

All of these steps take time, resources and money and if any are overlooked, you will probably fail. As you go through this examination process to determine if you or your company has the resources to develop and launch a new product, carefully consider, do you have the resources available to fill the "Hole in the Market?" Would you be willing to take a lesser piece of the pie such as a lump sum buy out, royalties, a position in the company and or a percentage of the profits? Before you make decision, ask the following questions of yourself and if possible, ask for input from trusted friends and colleagues. This is what I call a brainstorming time. We will take a moment to discuss the "Test of Reasonableness" to better understand if you should take the idea through the phase of determining if there is a "Hole in the Market" for your idea.

Make sure that the people in your trusted circle vary depending on whether you are launching a new product for your company or is an entrepreneur trying to validate an idea to take to market. If you are an entrepreneur, make sure to have a non-disclosure signed by those that you are bringing into your inner circle to discuss your idea. If you are thinking about launching a new product for an existing company, solicit input from potential end users and resellers to validate that there is a market for your product or service and have your non-disclosure signed by these people as well.

The input you request should come from potential end user demographics and resellers in order to establish potential need, uses, and sales volumes this way your answers will not to be skewed with subjectivity. I make this statement based on experience where there have been estimates of sales made by the "Ivory Tower" without first conducting a market survey to confirm the potential sales estimate only to fall flat on their face and lose a ton of money in the process. The "Ivory Tower" are those executives or engineers that sit in the big offices and make decisions based on past successes and do not consult the real world to validate their decision. Companies that are engineer driven often fail to do a thorough market study and sometimes rely on the judgment of an engineer that a product is great for the market only to find out that the product is too costly, specific to a market and/or too difficult to use and maintain.

Be introspective of yourself and ask your friends and colleagues the following nine questions. If you do this exercise, your chances for successfully entry into a given market will be greatly

Navigating Points:

Make sure that the people in your trusted circle vary depending on whether you are launching a new product for your company or is an entrepreneur trying to validate an idea to take to market. If you are an entrepreneur, make sure to have a non-disclosure signed by those that you are bringing into your inner circle to discuss your idea.

enhanced. If you come up with a conclusion that does not support your original thoughts about the validity of the market potential, you will be a winner because you did not waste your time and money on a product or service that was doomed for failure. Here are your questions;

- Who is or could be your competitor? - List your competitors having a similar technology or could deliver a similar product with greater features and benefits than yours. If your idea is a fad or fashion item, who could imitate or come up with a fac-simile and erode your market?

- Why are these potential competitors significant? Competitors are significant because they have, national distribution, large development organizations, alliances with other manufacturers or distributors, good financial strength, major market share or manufacturing capability, understand your strengths because they have hired your ex-employees, customers have vendor and product loyalty, can respond quickly to changing market requirements or have huge multi-level distribution organization.

- What are current competitor's products targeting your market demographics? Are their products direct competition? Are their products synergistic or complimentary? What stage of the life cycle are their products in? Are their new products fore-casted that will potentially compete with your idea? Are their products supported well?

- What are the channels of distribution for your competitors?

- What customer need is not now being met with the product offerings that are currently available? If your idea is a service or manufactured product, you need to go through the test of rea-

Why are these potential competitors significant? Competitors are significant because they have, national distribution, large development organizations, alliances with other manufacturers or distributors, good financial strength, major market share or manufacturing capability, understand your strengths because they have hired your ex-employees, customers have vendor and product loyalty, can respond quickly to changing market requirements or have huge multi-level distribution organization.

sonableness. What makes your idea saleable? Why would someone or a company want to purchase your idea?

- Is it technically feasible to meet the needs of "The Hole in Market"?

- Is the technology and are raw materials available to manufacturer your product faster, less expensive, smaller and in quantities necessary?

- If you are offering a service ask yourself if you have a niche market or greater, such as a global market? Depending on your market is it feasible to capture the market with local resources.

- Will you or should you look at partners? Should you sell your idea or ask for a royalty?

If you have a feasible and marketable service or product with a niche, fad or seasonal market you have a better chance of capturing immediate market share than if you have a market that is millions or billions in potential revenue. That is always a good problem to be confronted with.

What expertise is required? Think of the cost to manufacture equation. If you have a product that will sell for less than $5.00 as an example, you will probably have to go off shore to manufacture the product. An example would be a flying disc. You would have to have an injection mold built and the mold would probably build 500,000 discs. The mold might cost $300,000 to build and each product would cost $1.00. You would then need to ship the product back to a warehouse for packaging and distribution. What sort of experts will you need to hire?

Do you have the funds for such expenditures and do you have the distribution channels in place to sell a low priced product Is it economically feasible to plug "The Hole in the Market"?

"Life is a series of experiences, each of which makes us bigger, even though it is hard to realize this. For the world was built to develop character and we must learn that the setbacks and grieves which we endure help us in our marching onward."

—-Henry Ford

Where would you go to raise money for the new product

There are a number of funding sources you could consider such as;

- Venture capital

- IPO/Stock market

- Private investors

- Competitors

- Angels

- Family

- Internal

Navigating Points:

How much are you willing to give up of your idea to secure the funds? Is the window wide enough to write a Business Plan, fund, market, develop, manufacture, sell and make the revenue projections of your Business Plan? Is the market large enough to sustain your projected growth? Are you developing a product for a niche market where the window may be open longer or are you developing a product for a market that has universal appeal that may have many competitors vying for your customers?

How much are you willing to give up of your idea to secure the funds? Is the window wide enough to write a Business Plan, fund, market, develop, manufacture, sell and make the revenue projections of your Business Plan? Is the market large enough to sustain your projected growth? Are you developing a product for a niche market where the window may be open longer or are you developing a product for a market that has universal appeal that may have many competitors vying for your customers? If you are trying to compete in a universal market where there is significant business to be done and you don't have the capability to ramp up quickly, your entry will be late and your market share will be less than anticipated.

If the potential for your product is in the hundreds of millions of dollars, unless you are extremely lucky like the Face Book guys, Google, Apple, Microsoft, the Frisbee or Hula Hoop, you will probably have to settle for something less. Why you may ask? The big players will not want an upstart to start whittling away at market share and they can buy you out, put on advertising campaigns that will place doubts in your potential customers and distributors, and put pressure on potential investors in a variety of ways to not invest with you.

If your product is a onetime purchase you have a different set of circumstances to deal with than if you are wanting to manufacture a product that can be enhanced and evolve. Other possibilities are to develop an enhancement product, extend the life of a product or be a tie breaker to purchase a larger item. Your potential competitor could be your major customer by being an OEM (Original Equipment Manufacturer) and have your product in their catalog and/or be a line item that has to be erased on an invoice. If you can accomplish this task with your product, you will be a success and gain name, loyalty and product recognition for future endeavors.

You have to ask yourself, is your product evolutionary and not necessarily revolutionary. By that I mean will your product sustain life cycle enhancements? If it is, you will get imbedded in the incumbent and their customer's distribution channels. You also need to consider the history of your benchmark competitors? How long have they been in the market? Are they successful? How will they respond to your new product? Will your competitors be proactive or reactive? In other words, will your competitors lead the way with new products and respond quickly to the market trend or do they follow?

If you have a new idea with new technology, you may not have any direct competitors but when your competitors realize that you may be a threat, what will their impact be to your market if they decide to ramp up? If you're perceived competitors are successful, are they successful in niche markets or global markets?

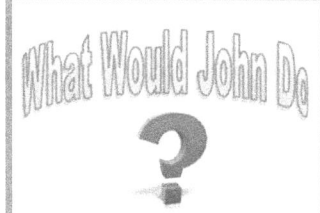

If your product is a one-time purchase you have a different set of circumstances to deal with than if you are wanting to manufacture a product that can be enhanced and evolve. If you can accomplish this task with your product, you will be a success and gain name, loyalty and product recognition for future endeavors.

Are your competitors actively launching or getting ready to launch a similar or new product? These are important questions. Established companies can come out with a bare bones product similar to yours but with fewer benefits and features and your potential customers will purchase from your competitors because they are the incumbent in your demographic market. Patents and copyrights are sometimes hard to defend unless you have something very unique.

Your competitors will probably respond quickly if they perceive you as a player that could potentially take significant market share or become a second alternative to their primary product. Think about your marketing and advertising campaign. Sometimes holding back on advertising during development is a blessing and does not raise red flags with your competitors and you can catch them by surprise when you are fully ramped. I have seen so many companies advertise and then have to postpone or be delayed entry due to raw materials shortages, strikes, regulatory delays, sickness of a key person, disasters and probably the main cause is lack of sufficient documentation and testing when the product is due scheduled to be released.

At this point you must ask yourself who are your benchmark competitor's and potential key business alliance partners and would they be willing to add or change over to your product? Cost to bring a new product to market directly is very expensive if you are using a direct sales and support personnel. Ideally, it is wise to have resellers or distribution channels sell your product as you perform new product development and support. Channels can be retail outlets, national distribution chains, manufacturer's representatives or companies that integrate or use your product to compliment theirs. This is not a 100% statement for reasons that your product may not support the margin for single or multiple tiers of

Navigating Points:

Your competitors will probably respond quickly if they perceive you as a player that could potentially take significant market share or become a second alternative to their primary product. Think about your marketing and advertising campaign. Sometimes holding back on advertising during development is a blessing and does not raise red flags with your competitors and you can catch them by surprise when you are fully ramped.

distribution.

There are a number of places you can find alliances such as:

- Private Label - A company that takes your product and places their name on it and may ask you to repackage and or change the product to differentiate in the market.

- OEM (Original Equipment Manufacturer) - A manufacturer that will integrate, interface or sell your product separately as an integral part of their solution. Your name may or may not appear anywhere on the equipment. An OEM usually uses this type of alliance for fast development and deployment of new features to stay abreast or ahead of the competition. Large companies can't ramp up very quickly so they have suppliers that may have state-of-the-art technologists that are adept at developing to their standards and provide quality products that adhere to their standards.

- Local, Regional, National or International Distribution Channels - These channels are ones that have built in sales and support and may take your product into inventory under consignment or purchase directly with clauses for replacement depending on price fluctuations.

You must ask yourself who are your benchmark competitor's and potential key business alliance partners and would they be willing to add or change over to your product?

- Manufacturers' Representatives - These companies or individuals are usually regional and have select accounts that purchase specific products for select industries such as fashion, fad, telecommunications, software applications, building materials, medical supplies, copiers, beauty supplies, etc.

- MLM (Multi-Level Marketing) - Fad products, security or health products use MLM companies to sell their products.

- Telemarketing/Call Centers - This methodology is used to sell hospitality related products such as timeshare properties, magazines, insurance, clubs for health, cleaning, etc.

- Direct Major Accounts - Typically this type of account is a major channel to market partner that sells direct or has access to your target customers. Many firms have alliances because of quality, support, technology or just because they like the people. If the incumbent competitor has a like product or is coming out with a similar product and the price is close, you will have a hard time replacing the incumbent. You have to be different in technology, feature, benefit, and priced where the reseller can see significant revenue potential. As the new supplier, you will have to do things that the incumbent does not because they have proven themselves. You may not think that this is fair but this is the way that the game is played in the corporate boardrooms.

- ASP's (Application Software Providers) Firms that will sell your product over the internet.

- Web Based companies that sell your product over the internet such as QVC, HSN and E-Bay. Using links to other synergistic web sites is also an excellent way to attract traffic to your web site.

- Your own web page and links to other like websites.

Your channel to market is crucial to your success so choose it wisely. The biggest mistake that new companies make is not allowing enough time and money for the product to ramp up through the various channels. If you are using other than direct channels and your product is not a flagship that brings in significant revenue to the channel, they will not always promote your product the way that you would. Channels do not have the vested interest in your product that you do, they were successful before

Navigating Points:

Your channel to market is crucial to your success so choose it wisely. The biggest mistake that new companies make is not allowing enough time and money for the product to ramp up through the various channels. If you are using other than direct channels and your product is not a flagship that brings in significant revenue to the channel, they will not always promote your product the way that you would.

you arrived so you will have to be patient and have many irons in the fire to sell your product. This ramp up should be well documented in your Business Plan and just because a firm says they will purchase thousands of products, there are many factors that could delay or reduce the number significantly. Have contingency plans for product delays, competition entering the market sooner than expected, price erosion and technology advancements.

Chapter 2

12 Keys for Success in Bringing New Products to Market

1. **A Sharp Focus on the Customers' Needs** -

Focusing on the customers' needs requires intuition, accurate market demographics, and knowledge of the ever changing economic environment. The best way to find out if your idea or product has any market potential is to take it to the potential end user or to a distributor that would sell into your market. Most people will give you input on your idea or product and perhaps input on how to enhance and sell your product.

You can invent and develop a new product to meet a need or you can analyze technology and look for ways to incorporate it into an innovative solution. You can also catch a fad and feed on the frenzy. If you are new in product development, watch those who are successful and analyze how they became successful. The opposite is also true for knowing when to get out of a market. The key is to watch competitors' movements associated with advertising and pricing.

I have been involved in several technologies that were thought to solve customer needs in large and growing markets and most, proved to be winners. All of my experience has been in bringing new technology into a market either as an entrepreneur with the idea, or in a marketing role seeking to define the market and subsequently define and implement a sales plan as well as develop a sales execution

What Would John Do?

Focusing on the customers' needs requires intuition, accurate market demographics, and knowledge of the ever changing economic environment. The best way to find out if your idea or product has any market potential is to take it to the potential end user or to a distributor that would sell into your market.

strategy to capitalize on the marketing.

Some of those products that were before their time were the first computerized advertising system that brought buyers and sellers together and a festival seating system for entertainment and sporting events. The telecommunications products that I was involved in were a Call Accounting System, Voice Mail and first DSP based telephone system with universal application. In each instance, except for the page printer and message processor system where I was the most successful salesperson, I had to conduct extensive marketing research to determine the need, pricing and channel to market. There were many steps to this process. The key steps that I used to determine customer needs were:

Applying the *test of reasonableness* - This simply means that you brainstorm the idea from every conceivable aspect. You look at the size of the potential market, who might your competitors be, what technology you would use, what resources are required and are they readily available? How would you bring the product to market? What is the Window of Opportunity? What type of sales and support are required and finally, what requirements for funding are necessary to make your idea come to reality?

If you have passed the *test of reasonableness*, you are ready to embark on the next phase, which is outside contact. You will talk to potential end users and distribution/sales partners that can give you feedback on your idea. Before you embark on this adventure, understand what it is that you are trying to accomplish. If

Navigating Points:

Applying the *test of reasonableness* - This simply means that you brainstorm the idea from every conceivable aspect. You look at the size of the potential market, who might your competitors be, what technology you would use, what resources are required and are they readily available? How would you bring the product to market? What is the Window of Opportunity? What type of sales and support are required and finally, what requirements for funding are necessary to make your idea come to reality?

you are simply trying to determine if the idea is viable, talk in generalities and do not reveal technology secrets or the potential size of the market. If you want more specific feedback, have product descriptions or a model or prototype and have a non- disclosure agreement signed before discussing your product with an outside source.

Copyright, patent and trademark filing should be done immediately in order to protect your product from possible infringement.

When you begin talking to potential customers or anyone with a possible interest in your idea, have them sign a non-disclosure agreement. This document stipulates that they will not reveal to any other source, the information they are about to receive and it ensures that they will not disclose or duplicate the product in any form. This is a legally binding agreement.

The final phase of your marketing will determine the size of market. Are there any crossover markets? Look at music as an example; country crosses over into pop which makes that market possibly twice as large. Examine the competition and the *Window of Opportunity*. Is this window opening or just closing? If it is opening, there could possibly be less competition and price is not foremost and the demand could be growing. If the window is closing, competition has entered and margin is eroding. Look at the price threshold, development, manufacturing and the methodologies to bring your product to market and well as the tiers of distribution before it gets to the end user, promotion, support and the all-

A supportive culture promotes the vision, embraces teamwork and promotes the opportunity to be a leader in a given market. You need people who do not look for excuses for not getting things done on time; they embrace the moment and look forward to accomplishing the objective.

important funding and ownership.

2.   Supportive Corporate Culture

A supportive culture promotes the vision, embraces teamwork and promotes the opportunity to be a leader in a   given market. You need people who do not look for excuses for not getting things done on time; they embrace the moment and look forward to accomplishing the objective. This type of company culture starts from the top and works its way down; it has to be continually enforced.

3.   A Teamwork Approach to New Products

Teamwork takes many forms but ultimately a team   works together to accomplish or work towards a common goal. My experience has shown that when you empower your employees to work towards achievement and allow for mistakes within reason you are creating a teamwork approach to the workplace. I have always tried to hire talent more knowledgeable than myself in areas where I was the weakest. I included the key people in the decision making process regarding time frames to complete, types of resources and budgeting. I kept the door open to discuss outstanding issues and communicated on almost all issues related to marketing, sales, funding and profitability.

If a team leader is cocky and takes all of the credit for what the team does and does not pass along the accolades to the people that made it happen, teamwork disappears. When communication ceases, employees become suspicious of each other, clicks form, destructive gossip passes through the organization and employee

Navigating Points:

Team leaders constantly explore new methodologies and techniques, encourage training, acknowledge accomplishment, understand the competition and share resources with other team leaders when required.

TEAM
TOGETHER
EVERYONE
ACHIEVES
MORE

turnover ensues. Be aware of your team and look for signs of complacency, gossip, missed deadlines and turnover. Nip it in the bud before it becomes infectious and destroys your organization.

Team leaders constantly explore new methodologies and techniques, encourage training, acknowledge accomplishment, understand the competition and share resources with other team leaders when required. Team leaders do not need to be the best at all tasks but they should be able to understand the big picture, be able to motivate others and understand the intrinsic values that motivate each employee to be the best that they can be. Team leaders should not be afraid to hire the best people in areas of expertise that will improve the skills of the team.

Be aware of your team dynamics and watch for clicks being formed, gossip, lateness and reasons for excuses. When these actions start occurring, employees become polarized and suspicious of each other, morale erodes and turnover begins. Stop these internal viruses before it becomes contagious and destroys your organization. Team leaders constantly encourage out of the box thinking. Team leaders should be good managers, communicators, know what every person in their team is doing, and be able to back anyone up. Your team leaders need to understand and constantly communicate the company vision.

I cannot stress how important understanding the intrinsic values of each member of your team is. When you aid your employees in achieving their key values, they be-

The key to a successful project is including those that are responsible for the deliverables; it is important that they have a say in creating the plan.

I include everyone in every project I take on, just as it takes a village to raise a child, it also takes a team to build a business.

come more productive.

4. **A New Product Planning Process Appropriate to the Task**

This process should work side by side with the task at hand. If the product is serial and only one part of the product can be worked on at a time a relatively simple product plan is all that is required. If there are several tasks with many departments working towards a common goal, a detail project management program can be used to track progress. The Microsoft Project application, or a similar program, is excellent for this task. MS Project tracks and schedules resources, materials and prerequisite tasks to follow the overall a plan.

The key to a successful project is including those that are responsible for the deliverables; it is important that they have a say in creating the plan. During the project, an unbiased, appointed coordinator should be given the responsibility of gathering the facts pertaining to the status of the project. The status is updated daily, meetings are scheduled to update the group as a whole and if there are milestones in jeopardy of falling behind schedule, it will be the job of the coordinator to inform the appropriate parties and discuss how to bring the schedule back on course.

I have found, after the successful completion of over 250 projects, that the number one key to success is communicating the status of the project and confronting the group immediately if there is a delay. Implement a priority change request procedure for issues that are mandatory and can't proceed if not completed, and lesser

Navigating Points:

A product plan can fall flat on its face if there is no leadership from executive management. Empowering your key managers to administer and ensuring that they adhere to the plan is critical to the success on the plan. The project lead should be empowered to coordinate resources when additional funding for personnel or equipment was not foreseen in the original plan.

priorities for minor issues down to misspellings in the documentation. Route the change orders to those that need to know; this is the foundation of the daily or weekly status meeting to update the project plan.

5. **Professionalism in Product Planning and Development**

A product plan can fall flat on its face if there is no leadership from executive management. Empowering your key managers to administer and ensuring that they adhere to the plan is critical to the success on the plan. The project lead should be empowered to coordinate resources when additional funding for personnel or equipment was not foreseen in the original plan. Executive management should be informed on a weekly or immediate basis on all milestones that are in jeopardy of being missed.

6. **Consistent Funding Support in Good Times and Bad Times**

A good manager will plan, and have a contingency plan in place, for funds in case of delays caused by insufficient resources in personnel, materials and equipment. A lot of startup companies over estimate the capability of key individuals and their ability to make things happen during the processes necessary to be successful. As an example, If you have not been through a startup before, you make assumptions and usually underestimate the time it takes to get regulatory approval from a government office, funding from your venture capitalists, possible acts of nature, personnel issues, customer acceptance, and printing as well as a myriad of other issues. If it can go wrong, it probably will and especially if

if you have not been through a startup before, you make assumptions and usually underestimate the time it takes to get regulatory approval from a government office, funding from your venture capitalists, possible acts of nature, personnel issues, customer acceptance, and printing as well as a myriad of other issues. If it can go wrong, it probably will and especially if you have not been through the process.

you have not been through the process.

If you are funded by a venture capitalist firm, they are aware of all of the possible delays that can arise in a startup venture and usually have an appointed partner from the firm to oversee the operation. This person may be appointed to the board, be an active day to day operations person or, if they feel confident in your ability, let you run with the ball and report the progress on agreed to schedules.

If you are experiencing delays that are cause for additional funding, the venture capitalist firm understands this can, and usually does, occur. Venture firms will not let a project crumble for lack of funds when perhaps hundreds of thousands or millions of their investor's dollars are invested in your project. They will scrutinize the market and give reasonable assurance to their investors that they will get a return on their investment. If they continually failed, they would not be in business. Be aware, when not meeting deadlines, it is anticipated that you will need more cash and in return, you should be ready to give up a majority position in both stock and authority.

7. **Strong Commitment to Quality Market Research**

If you are funded by outside capital from an IPO or venture capital firm, you will be forced to prepare a solid Business Plan, supported by thorough marketing that can stand the scrutiny of due diligence. Usually the due diligence will be performed by persons from the lending organization and they will call in specialized industry consultants, analyze your competitors, examine technology and pour over your contacts that support your Business Plan.

Navigating Points:

If you have a high tech product that is computer or telephony based, look to the market for new needs that can be incorporated or added to the current offerings or be compatible with another product.

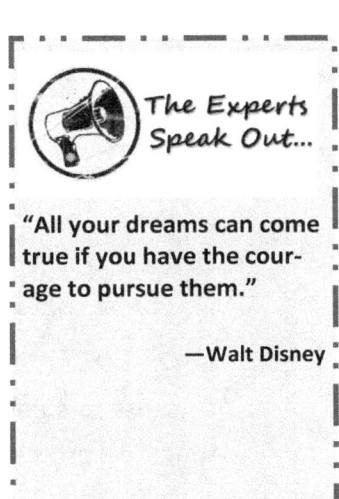

The Experts Speak Out...

"All your dreams can come true if you have the courage to pursue them."

—Walt Disney

If you are investing your own money to fully fund the project, you should hire a specialist to verify what you believe is true about the market and your Business Plan. You may end up with 100% of the pie with your own dollars but if you fail, you lose 100%. Be aware that the majority of startup companies fail for lack of market intelligence and sufficient funding.

8. Build New Products into your Business Plans

Design new products or enhancements; add mid-life kickers and razor blades to enhance the potential for success of your product. Venture capitalists channel to market partners and customers like to deal with manufacturers that have more than one product. Mid-life kickers are enhancements that offer more benefits and features that can be added to the existing product or offer supplies known as the razor blades. Razor blades are the supplies that only you can sole source to support the longevity of your product. New products can be as simple as changing the color, shape, size or material of a product such as a yo-yo, Frisbee, bicycle, Hula Hoop, computer or any other product that is in demand. Changing the color, making it larger or faster or changing the material can be simple and enhance the life and margin almost forever.

If you have a high tech product that is computer or telephony based, look to the market for new needs that can be incorporated or added to the current offerings or be compatible with another product.

Maintenance and upgrade agreements are almost a license to steal and you have a captive market. Sometimes the product can be reduced in size to open up the

Navigating Points:

If you are investing your own money to fully fund the project, you should hire a specialist to verify what you believe is true about the market and your Business Plan. You may end up with 100% of the pie with your own dollars but if you fail, you lose 100%. Be aware that the majority of startup companies fail for lack of market intelligence and sufficient funding.

market for wider distribution. On a grand scale for example, Boeing shortens or enlarges a 737 or 747 to increase market share without having to completely redesign and manufacture a complete new airplane. It's genius.

The most significant reason for adding products to your Business Plan and prospectus is twofold. Investors that review your Business Plan like to see that your company is forward thinking and keeping abreast of the ever changing demands of a market and aware of their competitors offerings. A product family gives investors' confidence that the company is not standing still and depending on the success of just one product.

Channel to market distributors and the end user like to deal with a manufacturer that has a family of products or a product that can be enhanced for a greater life expectancy and value to the end user. I always get asked by Product Managers and executives for input on bringing out new products or enhancements. If your product is well received, of good quality, supported well, priced right, distribution in place, then the and end user will be very receptive to enhancements and new product offerings. Distribution can capitalize on past success and the end user finds it easier to budget in order to acquire your product as you are an established vendor.

9.   **Realistic Budgets and Time Frames**

Experience has taught me that engineers and accountants should not be left alone to establish budgets for the formation of a startup company. A team of ex-

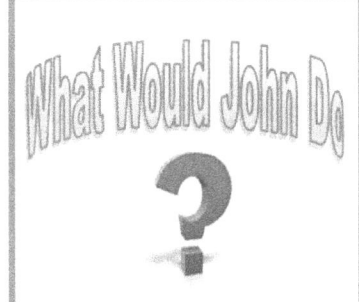

If you are building a first home as I have done, I drew out what I thought I wanted and it was a 10,000 square foot home. I could not afford what I had envisioned and eventually scaled back to a 3,000 square foot home that we were happy with. The same is true when budgeting for a new product development. When all of the team members are in a room and are asked to justify what they have budgeted in front of the other managers, funding priorities come in line and there is usually an amicable agreement on the allocation of funds.

perienced managers made up of marketing, sales, engineering, finance, product development, operations and the funding organization should submit budgets for their departments. Once received, finance and product marketing compile the budget figures to time frames on a project planner. This is a key element in being able to analyze why, when and the priority each department should have in the funding process. After the development schedule is transferred to the project plan, each manager presents their funding requirements to the group until realistic budgets and time frames can be agreed to by the group as a whole. Using this approach, you will be able to budget and manage your cash flow as different departments require funding.

As an example, if you are manufacturing a product either internally or externally, massive amounts of cash are usually allocated to build injection molds and to manufacture large quantities of the product in order to reduce the unit price. Sales on the other hand may not need funding until the later stages of the product development.

This process may take several iterations. It can be compared to buying or building your first house. If you are building a first home as I have done, I drew out what I thought I wanted and it was a 10,000 square foot home. I could not afford what I had envisioned and eventually scaled back to a 3,000 square foot home that we were happy with. The same is true when budgeting for a new product development. When all of the team members are in a room and are asked to justify what they have budgeted in front of the other managers, funding pri-

Navigating Points:

As an example, if you are manufacturing a product either internally or externally, massive amounts of cash are usually allocated to build injection molds and to manufacture large quantities of the product in order to reduce the unit price. Sales on the other hand may not need funding until the later stages of the product development.

orities come in line and there is usually an amicable agreement on the allocation of funds.

If you are developing a budget by yourself and this is your first project, you could be your own worst enemy. Any kind of funding is usually good to get you going but if your budgets are way short and you have to keep going to the well, your investors soon lose faith in your ability to budget and that may over shadow any talent you have in other areas. An example of what is usually overlooked in the budgeting process is time delays for almost every step of the project. The most common errors are made in estimating the time it takes to get your product through testing, writing quality documentation or instructions, and getting your product to market.

Depending on the technology you are using, lack of raw materials, labor turnover and parts can be cause huge time delays. What happens when you have a milestone delay that is serial, this means that all of your labor force is still drawing salary while nothing is being accomplished. Planning and having solid contingency plans is the foundation of project planning and product development.

10. **Politics**

Empowering managers to think out of the box within the parameters of their job will minimize the politics associated with designing, developing, manufacturing and delivering a product to market. Quality managers understand the empowerment process and the need to minimize the laborious meetings associated with the minor decision process.

I have pointed out on many occasions in meetings that I have attended that there needs to be a change. Where it was a requirement, not a necessity, that 10 people who had no reason to attend have had to sit for two hours and hear about promotional campaigns it is a waste especially when they were associated with manufacturing or engineering. We wasted the time of the managers who are our most costly resource and when you multiply the value of their time on unproductive meetings, you can run up a large number in a short time.

More time is wasted if the corporate culture is to have a staff meeting every time there is a decision to be made. Ground rules have to be established depending on the product and what regulatory issues are involved. Some sort of Engineering Change Order (ECR) or Change Order process has to be in place to monitor any changes but that doesn't mean that you can't give your people parameters to work within and still stay on schedule. Give each of your managers' boundaries to work in and if they require resources outside of those boundaries only then should it be brought to the table for discussion.

Minimize bureaucracy and the political process in your company and two things will happen. The first is better moral and the second is more production; both result in better cost management. The two go hand in hand. If a manager feels good about his responsibility and authority, it passes to his subordinates and less worry and gossip is passed and this leaves more time for the positives, such as being more productive and meeting deadlines.

Entrepreneurial companies tend to have fewer politics because they are driven by delivery dates and revenue in order to keep the doors open. These companies are usually driven by venture capitalists with investors that want to see the product and a return on their investment in a hurry. Governmental contacts and established companies have more politics and red tape because of the steps in the decision process. Empowerment of the manager to get the job done is not as prevalent so it has to pass from one department to the next until someone will take responsibility for the decision.

Navigating Points:

Marketing is the wisest investment decision you can make. Marketing can make or break you and the more you know about your market, the better chance for your survival and success.

The Experts Speak Out...

"Instead of one-way interruption, web marketing is about delivering useful content at precisely the right moment when a buyer needs it."

~ David Meerman Scott

Look for ways to minimize the political process and red tape in your company. I have pointed out on many occasions in meetings that I have attended that there needs to be a change. Where it was a requirement, not a necessity, that 10 people who had no reason to attend have had to sit for two hours and hear about promotional campaigns it is a waste especially when they were associated with manufacturing or engineering. We wasted the time of the managers who are our most costly resource and when you multiply the value of their time on unproductive meetings, you can run up a large number in a short time.

Empower your finance department to maintain quality financial records and monitor budgets as well as report trends that could lead to an overdrawn condition. Finance can, and should, be a vital management function to not only record and pay invoices but also to recognize conditions that are not in line with the Business Plan.

11. Investment in Marketing Programs

Marketing is the wisest investment decision you can make. Marketing can make or break you and the more you know about your market, the better chance for your survival and success. Marketing and documentation are the most overlooked and/or underfunded aspects of a startup company. So many people think that sales is marketing when it is not. Sales brings in revenue but marketing targets where you sales will come from. Marketing will make your sales peoples time much more productive. Marketing will identify where and who your competition is, where the most vulnerable markets are, who to cherry pick In order to get quick sales and target major customers or channels of distribution that will make you, in the short and long term, successful.

Quality marketing will give you a grasp on:

A. The size of the market

B.   The demographics of the buyer

C.   The Windows of Opportunity

D.   The holes in the market

E.   Who your competitors are

F.   Available technology

G.   Your ability to perform

H.   Channels to market

I.   Pricing thresholds

J.   Support and warranty

Each of these points can be broken down into multiple headings for a more detailed look at a particular segment. Ask advice from those that have experience and are successful. Don't necessarily take advice from someone who has continually failed, however pay attention to what they have to tell you because then you will understand what NOT to do. Marketing is like quicksand, you jump in with both feet and before you know you are up to your neck in information that may or may not be useful. What sometimes happens is that you spend more time with those that support you and slap you on the back for such a great idea telling you how successful you will be. You need supporters but you also need to understand the difficulties in reaching the market and the strength of your competitors. There are many unforeseen things that can cause misjudgment of the market. The more thorough you are in your marketing the better your chance for success.

12. Finance Department Support.

Empower your finance department to maintain quality financial records and monitor budgets as well as report trends that could lead to an over drawn condition. Finance can, and should, be a vital management function to not only record and pay invoices but also to recognize conditions that are not in line with the Business Plan.

Chapter 3

New Product Assessment

Assessing the viability of a new product for a startup company can make or break your company in pretty short order. If you are an existing company looking to bring on new products, develop new products or enhance existing products, the analysis of new products benefits can be as crucial as if you were a startup; it will not break the bank in most instances. In either instance, if the decision is wrong, personnel will lose jobs and, in some cases, credibility will be lost and will have to be regained through other efforts or ventures.

Critical to the success of a new product is having all of the input possible to make a comprehensive decision. Input critical to the decision process can come from a variety of sources and should be as varied as is available. The biggest mistake one can make is to have the input come from one individual and surprisingly, most companies are started this way. On the other hand, most companies that start this way usually have the greatest fall out as well.

If you are a member of a product evaluation team or the chief investor or engineer, set your pride aside and search for and ask for and pay for, if necessary, the best advice on the viability of the product that you are considering as the flagship of your new company. Also follow this pattern if your aim is to enhance your current product line.

Close to, but not necessarily in this order, are the types of people that you should ask to assess the viability of the proposed product.

- Potential Customers (end users)

- Potential Distribution Channels if not selling direct

- Professional Marketing firms, university or college marketing

Navigating Points:

If you are a member of a product evaluation team or the chief investor or engineer, set your pride aside and search for and ask for and pay for, if necessary, the best advice on the viability of the product that you are considering as the flagship of your new company. Also follow this pattern if your aim is to enhance your current product line.

departments

When discussing the viability of the proposed product, discuss the price with the end user, and factor in what markup is required if going through resellers. After you have determined the viability of the product to the consumer, you need to determine:

- Size of the marketplace

- Channel to market to gain the market share as quickly as possible

- Window of Opportunity before competition enters

- Who are my competitors and why would they enter the market?

- How quickly could my competitors enter the market?

- Is the product patentable or copyrighted?

- Should I look for partners to develop and sell the product?

- What are the costs and how much time will it take to develop the product?

- Does the product require support and what is the cost of support?

- Are there regulatory requirements or approvals that could be difficult to attain?

- Will the product support price decreases/increases?

- What is the product life cycle and can it be enhanced?

- Are there synergistic products that can be developed to continue to fill the channel?

This session will focus on the vital questions that need to be answered about your new product or service. The answers

Asking yourself continuous questions along the line is key to success in any business. I ask the experts, my mentors and even family members for their opinions on any project I take on. More importantly, I ask potential clients or customers.

you come up with will serve as a formal supporting document to your Business Plan when presenting your case for approval and funding either internal or outside.

Purpose

The purpose of completing this is to determine if a business case should be developed for the delivery of the product. The second consideration is to ask the same questions of existing customers, prospects and proposed resellers of the product. Weigh each question and subsequent answer and when all of the answers are tabulated, the higher the weight the better your chance to justify your products introduction. If the answers are not at the high end of the scale, it simply means you should look more closely at the opportunity. If the answers are at the high end of the scale, the Window of Opportunity is probably wide open and you should be aggressive in pursuing the opportunity.

1.   STRATEGIC ASSESSMENT

Strategic Fit

The answers you give here are weighed differently if you are a startup or in an established company.

Is the product or service contrary to company's Mission and Strategies?

Possible answers are:

• There is no perceived impact

• Within the core business specified in the company's Mission supports the key focus areas specified in the companies Strategies and Programs

• Advances specific company's Strategies, a major vehicle for accomplishing a strategy or Program, positions the company for long term success.

Navigating Points:

The purpose of completing this is to determine if a business case should be developed for the delivery of the product. The second consideration is to ask the same questions of existing customers, prospects and proposed resellers of the product. Weigh each question and subsequent answer and when all of the answers are tabulated, the higher the weight the better your chance to justify your products introduction. If the answers are not at the high end of the scale, it simply means you should look more closely at the opportunity.

Strategic Partners

Possible answers are:

• Partners are required but none available to enhance or support the development, introduction or ongoing marketing and sales of the product.

• Partners are available but with limited impact.

• Partners are available, significant impact or no partner required.

• Network Utilization

• Possible answers are:

• Does not utilize the network of sales channels we currently have in place.

• Uses the network, but intelligence is not in the network.

• Uses the network, intelligence is in the network.

• Uses the network, intelligence is in the network, helps reduce company costs and generates required revenue.

Having the right people on your team is a key aspect to making good, solid decisions. I often poll many people when it comes to making key decisions about business. Ensuring that you also have "strategic" partners in place as well ensures that you will have access to what you need.

2. **MARKET ASSESSMENT**

• Market Potential (Position the company for long term com

  -petitiveness and profitability)

• Possible answers are:

• No long term potential

• Limited long term in a small customer segment

• Long term-smaller customer segments

• Long term-major customer segments

• Long term-all major customer segments

Revenue Potential (Consider the profitability per unit as opposed to the gross sale)

Greater than $ _____ but less than $ _____

Greater than $ _____ but less than $ _____

Greater than $_____ but less than $_____

Greater than $_____ but less than $_____

Greater than $_____ but less than $_____

Navigating Points:

Don't necessarily take advice from someone who has continually failed, however pay attention to what they have to tell you because then you will understand what NOT to do. Marketing is like quicksand, you jump in with both feet and before you know you are up to your neck in information that may or may not be useful. What sometimes happens is that you spend more time with those that support you and slap you on the back for such a great idea telling you how successful you will be.

Customer Demand Applications

Provides solutions to major customer segments requirements, numerous applications targeted at specific customer segments.

Effect on Present Products

Possible answers are:

• Replaces with no revenue improvement

• Replaces with some revenue improvement

• No impact

• Complimentary, moderate additional revenue

• Stimulates revenue from other products

• Window of Opportunity

• Possible answers are:

• Closed, unable to capture any percent of the market

• Partially open, able to capture a profitable percent of

the market

- Open, able to capture a significant percent of the market

3. COMPETITIVE ASSESSMENT

Competitive Advantage

- Can this product be less expensive than our competitors? Is this product differentiated from our competitor's product in a way that is valued by our customers? Does the product provide a higher level of customer satisfaction to our customer?

- Possible answers are:

- Dominant competitor in the market

- Some other companies have it, but we have a marginal competitive advantage

- Some other companies have it but we have a strong competitive advantage

- No competitors, window is wide open

- Competitor Assessment

- Possible answers are:

- Dominant competitors in the market

- Multiple competitors in the market, none are dominant

- Limited competition, competition currently viable

- Limited competition, competition not currently viable

"A merchant who approaches business with the idea of serving the public well has nothing to fear from the competition." - James Cash Penney

"No matter what the competition is, I try to find a goal that day and better that goal." - Bonnie Blair, American Gold Medal Speed skater

• No competition, strong barriers to market entry

Competitive Positioning

Possible answers are:

• The product attracts customers to our company, enabling us to sell more products or services

• The product is a prerequisite to another product or service that we intend to offer in the future

• The product is necessary to a potential loss of revenue

• The product can promote the company's image

• No competitive positioning effect

• Some competitive positioning effect

• Major competitive positioning effect

Navigating Points:

Some of the costs you will have to calculate are attorney's fees for patents, web domains, facility, insurance, key man, documents and general questions. You need to also consider cost to design and prototype, documentation creation, web page design, advertising, marketing and sales.

4. Implementation Assessment

Startup costs

This is the most important question you can ask yourself if all questions are positive and indicate that this is a viable and profitable business opportunity.

Some of the costs you will have to calculate are attorney's fees for patents, web domains, facility, insurance, key man, documents and general questions. You need to also consider cost to design and prototype, documentation creation, web page design, advertising, marketing and sales. Channel to market development strategies and personnel hiring as well as facility, raw materials cost, molds for product, regulatory and end

user testing and travel expenses and benefits must all be considered.

These are a few of the costs to consider and when you have what you think are the conservative costs, multiply by 130 to give you a 30% cushion because there will be errors and possible acts of god, fluctuations in the economy and personnel changes.

After you have the costs affixed to a general ledger number, hire or train yourself to use a Project and Implementation software product like Microsoft Project to plot every activity with prerequisites and fall back strategies. Every key manager and investor should review the progress on a daily, weekly and monthly basis and update as changes occur so that there will be on surprises.

I can't stress enough the importance of everyone being on board with this activity.

Human Resources Requirement

Possible answers are:

• Significant human resources required

• Some additional human resources required

• Human resources can be met through transfers

• Human resources requirements can be met through existing staff reassignments

• No human resources required

Expertise Required

Possible answers are:

Getting The Right People On The Bus

What Would John Do

People need to give better care to human resources...without good people your business is doomed. Ask the right questions of the right people and you can build a team that is unstoppable. I always seek out like-minded people who are as goal oriented as I am/

- Employees have no skill base to support the new product

- Employees have some skill but extensive training is required to support the product

- Employee base has some of the needed skills but some additional training will be required

- Employee base has most of the skills and minimal training will be required

- Employees have the skills and no additional training will be required

Channels of Distribution Assessment.

- Possible answers are:

- No proven channel

- Available and untried

- Available and successful in marketing similar products

- In place and moderately successful

- In place and proven successful

Technical Capability (This is designed for computer/CTI products, rewrite to meet your needs.)

- Possible answers are:

- Poor network integration and not consistent with current and evolving technology

- Poor network integration and requires some network modifications

- Compatible, requires minor modifications

- Full compatibility, requires no modifications

Navigating Points:

If you are developing a budget by yourself and this is your first project, you could be your own worst enemy. Any kind of funding is usually good to get you going but if your budgets are way short and you have to keep going to the well, your investors soon lose faith in your ability to budget and that may over shadow any talent you have in other areas. An example of what is usually overlooked in the budgeting process is time delays for almost every step of the project. The most common errors are made in estimating the time it takes to get your product through testing, writing quality documentation or instructions, and getting your product to market.

Support System Assessment

- Possible answers are:

- Not available, must design and build a new support system

- Available in house, however, we must modify extensively

- Available in house, only minor changes must be made

- In place and available now

Regulatory/Legislative Assessment

- Possible answers are:

- Not available, requires extensive idea stage development

- Not available, manufacturing does not adhere

- Available, some development required

- Available no development required

Potential

- High Potential

- Aggressively pursue market introduction

- Medium Potential

Continue research and weigh the possible synergistic effects on other products. If the products extends the life on a flagship product, introduces you into another market or breaks even, you probably should continue.

- Low Potential

If you have a high end product with significant margin per unit and this product is an extension, the life extension could far outweigh the low potential. If the product is a standalone and it is determined that there is a minimal mar-

What Would John Do

There are, unquestionably, a ton of things to ask yourself before jumping into business but, if you take the time to ask the right questions, you can succeed. I always seek out the experts on whatever project I am embarking upon. Learning to ask questions is a key component to success.

ket, consideration should be given to dropping the effort.

Chapter 4
Product Survey

The Product Survey is another marketing aid to gather information about your products potential. I have used this document with modifications depending on the type of product and kind of feedback I was looking for. This survey is targeted to potential end users and resellers.

I send this survey out not only for feedback, but to get my target customers to take ownership of what I want to sell. You would be surprised at how many people want to help you and give advice and if you heed their advice, they take ownership of the product. This makes it easier for them to support your marketing and sales efforts. I would identify whether I was talking to a reseller or potential end user. On the upper right hand corner of the first page, I identify the company, contact and title, if you are mailing this form out in any media, you would probably have a promotional piece that describes the product.

Potential end users are excellent sources for feedback on benefits, uses, ease of use, where to distribute and pricing. If the product is designed for children, have the prototype product with you, approach parents and ask if the child could play with the product. Observe the interaction the child has with the product after any instructions and watch for stress signs dealing with the use, assembling and boredom. You will probably get feedback from both the child and parent. Listen and incorporate their input, if appropriate, in your product before you finalize the product for final design and production.

There are many ways to test market and there are firms that specialize in this field. I happen to like to do it myself so that nothing gets lost in the feedback. If you require heat, cold,

Navigating Points:

Potential end users are excellent sources for feedback on benefits, uses, ease of use, where to distribute and pricing. If the product is designed for children, have the prototype product with you, approach parents and ask if the child could play with the product. Observe the interaction the child has with the product after any instructions and watch for stress signs dealing with the use, assembling and boredom. Listen and incorporate their input, if appropriate, in your product before you finalize the product for final design and production.

breakage, vibration or key strokes or anything that requires regulatory approval, you should conduct the tests in house if possible before sending your product off to a regulatory body for testing and approval. If you don't conduct as many of these tests in house as possible, you will probably fail the tests at the regulatory testing agency and then you will have to get back in the queue. If you are a startup and you have major channels of distribution in place, it is possible that your distributor has access to testing for your product, so don't forget to explore those avenues.

Resellers are also excellent people to get feedback from on your idea. You should be careful in selecting who to contact about feedback as they may have the resources to develop or talk to the incumbent distributor that sells or manufacturers like kinds of products. There is a risk that someone could take your idea and manufacture it quicker than you who already has channel to market distribution in place. Make sure that you have a nondisclosure agreement signed with whomever you ask for help or feedback on your new idea.

You look to resellers or distribution because they already have the channel to market established and can reach your potential customers as fast as possible with your products. Depending on the type of product, you may never talk to the end user but only to the reseller for feedback.

The type of product, price point and whether you have established channels to market dictate whether you go to resellers or go direct. In either case the Product Survey can be a valuable document to collect and give feedback on your new product.

If you are e-mailing, snail mailing, voice surveying or using the web for your survey, write down in detail what you are looking for in terms of feedback for each of the points. The following page is a sample of a product survey.

If you are e-mailing, snail mailing, voice surveying or using the web for your survey, write down in detail what you are looking for in terms of feedback for each of the points. The only way to obtain proper feedback is to make it clear in terms of what you are seeking. Too many business owners are vague.

Product Survey

Type of feedback End User/Reseller

Company _____

Contact _____

Title _____

Tel# _____ E-Mail _____

Purpose of Survey (Brief Description)

Description of Proposed Product.

Customer Benefits of the Proposed Product.

Major Features of the Proposed Product.

Your interest in the product—10 is extremely high and 1 is no interest at all.

Why are you interested in the product? (You could add specifics such as reseller, manufacturer, support, extends the life of existing products, opens up new markets, synergistic, etc.)

Please indicate the approximate price the end user would pay for the product,

Interest scale at highest range $ _____

12345678910

Interest scale at mid-range $ _____
12345678910

Interest scale at low range $ _____
12345678910

List any additional benefits or ways the customer could use

Navigating Points:

Resellers are also excellent people to get feedback from on your idea. You should be careful in selecting who to contact about feedback as they may have the resources to develop or talk to the incumbent distributor that sells or manufacturers like kinds of products. There is a risk that someone could take your idea and manufacture it quicker than you who already has channel to market distribution in place.

the product.

_____

_____

_____

Distributor or customer awareness of existing or similar products. Please list and give approximate price or other pertinent information you feel would be valuable to us.

Surveys can be a powerful tool. Over the years I have added this to my line-up of things I use from the beginning. Obviously we can't all know everything so why not ask the people who do know what they need and expect...the customer.

_____

_____

_____

_____

Are there any improvements or suggestions that you could recommend that would make our product more beneficial or competitive to you as a distributor or to the end user?

_____

_____

_____

_____

If this product family was available in (year) _____, would you contract to distribute the product? Yes No

If your answer is yes, what type of initial stocking order would you require to launch the product?

Units _____

What would be the ramp up period for the product if the product was available in (year)?

Months ____

What number of units would you forecast for:
Years _____ _ _____ _____

_____

Would you be willing to assist in beta testing the product in the (year) quarter of year? _____

 Yes   No

Does your company approve sales spiffs from vendors to launch products?

Yes No

Does your company approve product training seminars for sales people? Yes   No

Chapter 5

Market Analysis

A *Market Analysis* test will test your theory about the need for your product or service in the segments you have targeted. Market Analysis should address those people that can assist you in determining if your product would be a worthwhile venture. There are several phases of Market Analysis and you should be prepared to evolve your market research from a discussion to a drawing/schematic and evolve to a prototype. You will develop a clear understanding and be able to describe how your product or service would benefit the market segments you are targeting. If possible, have a fair understanding of what you are building your product for and what you believe the consumer would pay for the product.

Your mix of contacts should include potential end users, industry consultants, trade journals and periodicals that report on new products in your industry. Venture Capitalists that fund new projects, college and university marketing departments and potential resellers that have major distribution in your market segments should also be considered. Armed with this information, you should be able to make a sound decision on whether to go forward and develop a Business Plan, seek funding and start your business or develop a new product for your company.

The following questions offer ideas on what to consider when conducting your market research for your product or service.

1. **Are there any significant trends in the market that could in pact the introduction of a new product?**

   Examples of significant trends that could impact your introduction are:

   • Economic downturn could discourage products that are developed for fun and relaxation. Research compa-

Navigating Points:

Your mix of contacts should include potential end users, industry consultants, trade journals and periodicals that report on new products in your industry. Venture Capitalists that fund new projects, college and university marketing departments and potential resellers that have major distribution in your market segments should also be considered. Armed with this information, you should be able to make a sound decision on whether to go forward and develop a Business Plan, seek funding and start your business or develop a new product for your company.

nies   that build products that are not vital to the well-being   of society during slow economic periods can also be a factor.

- Economic downturns can be good for new products that conserve resources speed up processes and generally save money.

- Economies on the upswing make people feel good and this prompts them to purchase products that help them relax or make them feel good.

- Technology breakthroughs that make new materials or tech nology available to a developer open up markets in all seg ments of industry. A few examples are the metals that are lightweight; stronger than steel and inexpensive enough to be used in bicycles, golf clubs, tennis rackets, cars, planes, space ships and anywhere a lighter more durable metal that would benefit or improve performance of the person or ma -chinery.

- Personal computers with universal operating systems, pro -gramming languages and LAN compatibility are opening up thousands of new opportunities for new ideas on a daily ba sis.

- The Internet is exploding with new opportunities either to sell products and services or to assist companies in using the Internet for marketing and sales. Working agreements such as NAFTA that opens up Mexico and Canada offer new op portunities for trade. Other Agreements will open up more foreign markets for American made products.

Almost any trend is good for someone and bad for an-other. If you can catch a trend on the upswing that is mam-moth in proportion, even if you are hoping for a market share of less than one percent that one percent could represent millions of dollars in potential sales. It just depends on the size and demand for your particular product. I know of downtrends where people or companies of means can ride

Almost any trend is good for someone and bad for anoth-er. If you can catch a trend on the upswing that is mammoth in proportion, even if you are hoping for a market share of less than one percent that one percent could represent mil-lions of dollars in potential sales. It just depends on the size and demand for your particular product. I know of downtrends where people or companies of means can ride the down times and can po-sition themselves for the upturn by purchasing compa-nies, products, patents, copy-rights, sales channels and when the trend reverses, the com-pany is in position to take advantage of the opportuni-ty.

the down times and can position themselves for the up-turn by purchasing companies, products, patents, copy-rights, sales channels and when the trend reverses, the company is in position to take advantage of the opportunity.

2. **What entry barriers exist in introducing a new prod-uct?**

Entry barriers can be obvious and/or hidden to the entre-preneur that is new to the ways of penetrating a new mar-ket that is run by the good old boys network of major players in a given industry.

Some of the barriers that you should explore when doing your market research are:

• Are the markets that you want access to controlled, by major Fortune 1000 firms with marketing, sales and sup-port on a national and or international basis? If yes, these companies are probably the standard in the industry and may not necessarily have the best product. As a matter of fact, in most instances they do not have the best product but they will probably end up with a solid product as time moves forward.

• The barriers that can exist for a company are not easily torn down if you are trying to penetrate a market where the product requires advertising and promotion, sales and technical support, training and inventory. The invest-ment that the distributor and retailer have to make in the current product even though it may not be state of the art usually precludes them from selecting your product be-cause of the investment in time and money it will take to get your product off of the ground. It is important that you understand the situation that your customer is in relative to the other manufacturers' products that they sell and support.

• The competition knows that they can be competing

Navigating Points:

This is never exact but you can get a good idea from trade journals that publish annual statistics on who the major product provid-ers are in specific market segments. If the compa-nies are public, you can get annual earnings' reports and make your own judg-ments. The internet and the library are good sources for information gathering or you can simp-ly call your competitors and request annual reports.

against a superior product in terms of features and benefits. They also know that their company has the resources to combat the competition by offering huge discounts on current products that may be more cumbersome and work less efficiently but are entrenched in the customer base that you are targeting.

• Price is always an entry barrier especially if you are going up against a tried and true product that is entrenched as a flagship product where everyone feels comfortable with support and reliability of the incumbent's product.

• Just because you see a price advantage with your new technology against your potential competition, don't be misled into thinking that they can't lower prices because they have not in the past. Most smart companies have built in product pricing mechanisms that allow for price erosion due to competition. They usually have lowered their cost of goods due to greater quantity purchases so that when they do lower prices, they are still profitable. Smart companies have sales strategies for introducing new products where they supplant an existing product on a customer's shelf, or an out of warranty product.

• Name recognition is a major barrier in introducing a new product. This is why many new products align themselves with other major products and piggy back through association. If you can get your product mentioned or shown alongside another product on a national ad campaign, it can do wonders in establishing instant credibility for your product.

• Channel entry without name recognition or a previous track record can postpone or even stop you from getting a meeting scheduled with a major retail or national distribution chain. This is because they are deluged with products to review from existing manufacturers. The key to getting an appointment with a Product Manager for one of the major chains is having a uniqueness that is in demand, priced right and that

Channel entry without name recognition or a previous track record can postpone or even stop you from getting a meeting scheduled with a major retail or national distribution chain. This is because they are deluged with products to review from existing manufacturers. The key to getting an appointment with a Product Manager for one of the major chains is having a uniqueness that is in demand, priced right and that will give them semi exclusivity for N period. Do not get so excited that you give the farm away because a competitor may have a similar product and may put a big move on to minimize any impact that you might have because they put a big sale on or do an inventory reduction which takes away from the impact that you might have made.

will give them semi exclusivity for N period. Do not get so excited that you give the farm away because a competitor may have a similar product and may put a big move on to minimize any impact that you might have because they put a big sale on or do an inventory reduction which takes away from the impact that you might have made.

Navigating Points:

Cost of sales in making the big impact to advertise your product in order to generate the sales is always a problem for a new company. You think that you have the greatest new thing since sliced bread and you may have, but to convince your segment, it takes dollars. Dollars for advertising and promotion, dollars for sales people, salaries, commissions, spiffs or incentives for your resellers, and support dollars when you begin the sales process.

• Most major chains do not place large orders for products. They want to trial the product in one or a few stores and measure the success before making a decision to proceed, stay status quo, or drop the product. Do not place all of your eggs in this basket and always continue to look for and secure new channels to bring your product to market.

• Cost of sales in making the big impact to advertise your product in order to generate the sales is always a problem for a new company. You think that you have the greatest new thing since sliced bread and you may have, but to convince your segment, it takes dollars. Dollars for advertising and promotion, dollars for sales people, salaries, commissions, spiffs or incentives for your resellers, and support dollars when you begin the sales process.

• Sales channels are not in place to capitalize on the Window of Opportunity - If you do not have the funds to mount a regional or national campaign to sell your product direct then align yourself with companies that will sell your product. Some companies will sell under your label, private label your product with their own name and label or OEM (Original Equipment Manufacturer), have a company combine your product with theirs or have it as a separate line item that is easy to order.

3.   **What is the market share of our competitors?**

This is never exact but you can get a good idea from trade

journals that publish annual statistics on who the major product providers are in specific market segments. If the companies are public, you can get annual earnings' reports and make your own judgments. The internet and the library are good sources for information gather-ing or you can simply call your competitors and request annual reports.

4. **What are the most significant characteristics of our compete -tion in terms of features, channels and price?**

If your competition is respected and has been around for a period of time, they probably have good peo-ple in marketing, sales, development, support and at the executive level. If their features to benefits are excep-tional and their marketing and engineering departments are very astute to the market requirements and trends, then that technology affords them to stay ahead of the com -petition.

If their channels are through national distribution and they are well established, such as they got in on the ground floor of the market opportunity, performed well and increased their visibility into a flagship product for the distribution chain then they are set. When you are a leader, other chains want to pick up your product for their visibility and to fill out their product mix to aid in becoming a one stop shop for the consumer.

Price for a high demand product can be quite inexpensive due to the advantage of potentially purchasing hundreds of thousands of components as opposed to purchasing hundreds of a specific components or parts.

Product differentiation can offset this cost and allow you to charge more for your product as long as there is a demand. Offer price discounts for volume purchases that will allow you to lower the cost to manufacture and you can

The Experts Speak Out...

"In my fifty years of experi-ence and memory, I have seen the most amazing in-crease in the standard of living of a people ever achieved anywhere in the world. This is why I am so sure that our system of free competition and industrial development is sound and must be preserved." - Charles E. Wilson, Former CEO of General Electric

potentially lower your price to the ultimate consumer and reseller.

5.   **What is our competitors positioning compared to our new product offerings?**

When you ask this question, you are trying to find out the interest level expressed in your type of product by your potential competitors. However when you ask this question, you are exposing your idea to the competition. The person you are asking will undoubtedly ask their supplier if   they are thinking of this idea and will give them their thoughts on the idea. It will then pass through the chain back to marketing and product development for review.

If you are a small company with vertical market development expertise and can react quickly to a trend, a technology breakthrough or new demand, you can react much   more quickly than a monolith that makes decisions by committee and has to go through many levels of approval. The Window of Opportunity has to be factored in as to when competition may be announcing a competitive product and you have to ask, can you be positioned early enough to gain a significant enough market share to justify being in business.

In many instances, large manufacturing companies only want to be in vertical markets that have a market value of $10,000,000 per year. They often want to search out alliances with smaller firms that have vertical market development expertise to help them compliment their current product offerings. If you are lucky enough to develop a relationship like this that works as negotiated, you will probably do quite well. In most instances, you will be expected to provide sales and support assistance in return for having them advertise and promote your product

Navigating Points:

A benchmark competitor is one with whom you will be competing on a head to head basis. If you have a new product opening up a new market, you can be a leader and your competition will be minimal. On the other hand, if you are a new company but are perceived to have a good idea and huge potential, there will be others who will capitalize on your idea and try to make it cheaper, faster and with more features than yours.

along with their name on a national basis.

6.   How will your benchmark competitors compete with us?

A benchmark competitor is one with whom you will be competing on a head to head basis. If you have a new product opening up a new market, you can be a leader and your competition will be minimal. On the other hand, if you are a new company but are perceived to have a good idea and huge potential, there will be others who will capitalize on your idea and try to make it cheaper, faster and with more features than yours. Off shore development companies that have huge manufacturing capabilities, can gear up quickly and have channels to distribute on an international basis are the ones that you should be aware of.

Will you be taking business away from or creating a new market for your potential competitors? If it is taking away from, you will be watched more closely than if you are creating a new demand. Attacks in the form of announcing to all of your potential channels to market that your competitors are in, could be one form of competing with you. They could discourage your potential channels from doing business with you because they are coming out with a new product in N months. This is a great deterrent and works in almost all cases. The incumbent manufacturer, if they have performed well in the past will   be given the opportunity to perform again and at your ex pense. What you need to do as a second alternative is to be positioned as an alternate vendor unless you are so unique that your customer has to have your product.

You will need to mount a sales campaign that will allow you to go directly to the end user while continuing to develop relationships with other channel to market distribution outlets. If the end users purchase your product,   this says a great deal about your product and may force your

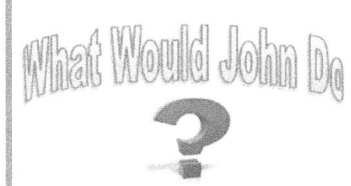

One of the most important aspects of running and growing a business is pricing. You can get it all wrong from the start and realize it too late. I have been on both sides of the coin and I'll tell you now...it's a better feeling to realize that you got it right. Take special care when it comes to pricing.

would-be channels to take a closer look at your product and develop a sales distribution relationship with you.

7.   **How does your price to value compare with the compe -tition?**

Simply look at the product the competition is offering that is similar to yours and use an Excel spread sheet or a piece of graph paper and fill in the information on the competitor, the price and list the features. Make another column with your price and features and check off where you are compatible and draw your own conclusions about how you compare with the competition. You can gain great insight about your strengths, weaknesses and position.

Sources to gather this information are from may be trade journals and periodicals, the library, trade shows or simply calling the competition for product brochures. If you are hiring personnel, target personnel working for your competitors and ask leading questions about your competitor's product offerings and their marketing, development and sales methodologies.

Navigating Points:

Market share is dependent on many factors with the greatest being the needs that your product serves. How quickly you can gain any significant market share is dependent on the sales methodology you use to promote and sell your product.

8.   **What market share can we expect to gain?**

Market share is dependent on many factors with the greatest being the needs that your product serves. How quickly you can gain any significant market share is dependent on the sales methodology you use to promote and sell your product.   Other factors to consider that may impede your market share are:

• A. Not enough capital to execute a strategy to gain market share.

• Not enough differentiation between your major competitor's products and yours.

• You are priced to high without enough product differentiation.

- New technology will make your product obsolete before you can establish any degree of credibility.

- Government regulations can cause a delay in the release of your product.

- Channels are wary of new players in your market segment because so many have gone broke trying to deliver a like product.

- The economy is taking a down turn and the need is not as great as before.

If your product requires shelf or rack space and your product falls short of the margin required for the space, you may be dropped or moved to another less desirable space.

Gaining market share takes the opposite view of prior statements and the only issue preventing you from ramping up as quickly as possible are resources to support the growth curve. Unless you are a fad item or have endorsements from major reseller channels or private label or OEM contracts, you will earn market share from trial and error with minimal learning from the error side of the equation.

Factor in all of the possible variables that can gain you market share and then play the devil's advocate and examine what could possibly deter you from gaining any significant market share. After you have completed this exercise, you will probably fall somewhere in between.

9. **How long will it take to gain market share?**

Your marketing research and Business Plan will give you a good idea on what market share you should achieve in a given number of months or years. Your Business Plan should plan for contingencies if market conditions occur that could impede your gaining market share in the projected period.

Market share is, sadly, something that many beginners don't give any thought to when beginning a business. I am awe struck at how many people just pass it by without realizing that it can make or break you. Personally it is on my top ten list of things to consider from the start-up. It should be yours as well.

You will have a better chance of achieving your goals if you have established alliances or Distribution Agreements with major players to sell your product. If you are going it alone with direct sales channels there are a great number of possible variables that could impede your market share than if you are partnering with national distribution.

Market share will be dependent on your distribution methodologies, price to benefit, reliability, support and demand. If these factors are balanced in your favor, you have an excellent chance to succeed.

10. **What needs to happen in order to gain market share?**

Not having any major economic downturns, major competitors entering the market that were unexpected, major cost over runs or part shortages, key people leaving or major disasters.

Other factors are adhering to your scheduled product development cycle, market research that is representative of the need of your product, financing to execute the development and sales of your product and personnel that have the same vision of success that you have. Pulling all of these aspects together better orients your product for the overall market.

11. **What is the cost of our product and what are margin curve effects?**

Examine the cost of goods based on volume parts ordering and the cost to manufacture based on specific volumes as well as what the cost is if volumes go up or down. Also examine what the cost for a specific quantity would be if manufactured off shore and factoring in the delivery time and impact to modify or re-run in case of a reliability issue.

Once the costs are known with contingencies,

Navigating Points:

Don't be drawn into the trap of offering a lower price when your competition is charging a higher price only to find out that you have to increase your price in order to stay in business. Customers don't like immediate price increases and become wary of a manufacturer bearing gifts of great margin when they are a new entity.

Pricing?
Good question

compare with the margin that you have forecasted in your Business Plan and see if you are still within the allowable margin for profitability.

12. **How does our price margin structure compare to our competitors?**

If your competition is priced higher with a similar product and has major market share and is using the same technology as yours, you might ask why. It could be that in order to be profitable, they need to charge a higher premium because the support costs were higher than expected, sales costs have increased due to having multiple tiers of distribution; co-op advertising has increased and so on.

Don't be drawn into the trap of offering a lower price when your competition is charging a higher price only to find out that you have to increase your price in order to stay in business. Customers don't like immediate price increases and become wary of a manufacturer bearing gifts of great margin when they are a new entity.

If you have a new technology that increases reliability, offers more benefits and can be manufactured less expensively sell the reliability and benefits and differentiate this way instead of lowering the price for a better product. You can always lower the price but once you do it is more difficult to raise the price.

If you have a new technology that increases reliability, offers more benefits and can be manufactured less expensively sell the reliability and benefits and differentiate this way instead of lowering the price for a better product. You can always lower the price but once you do it is more difficult to raise the price.

13. **Who are the potential market entrants?**

Identify your potential competitors and note their strengths and weaknesses and why they would enter your market or why they are already successful in your market segment. Being proactive is always better than being reactive when confronting competition.

By identifying your major competitors, you can

also position yourself for a takeover or merger when you decide to get out of the business, if that was your original intent.

14. **Are any competitors focused on your target market and if not, why not?**

If there are no known competitors in your target market it could be good news if you are the first with a new type of product. If you are entering an established market and your product has no competitors several questions need to be answered.

• Is the market to small?

• Is the technology to new?

• Are you simply the first to develop the product?

• Are there not enough potential customers to justify the development of a new product?

• Is there new technology emerging that will supplant the technology currently available?

• Are other manufacturers incorporating the functionality of your product into another product that will obsolete your product or reduce your target market?

• Are the government regulations to stringent to economically develop a product for the market?

Talk to consultants and potential end users of your product for input and factor their input into your product development decision process.

15. **What degree of vertical market integration could we expect?**

Market research will help dictate the degree of integration. You should research available technology, raw materials, the Window of Opportunity, potential competitors, distribution methodologies, development

The Experts Speak Out...

"When you start with what's at stake for the buyer, you earn the right to their attention."

-- Jake Sorofman

"Focus on the core problem your business solves and put out lots of content and enthusiasm, and ideas about how to solve that problem."

-- Laura Fitton

and manufacturing requirements and match the need to assist in determining the degree of vertical integration.

16.   Who has the advantage of being able to produce the least expensive product?

This is probably the simplest question to answer if you know your competitions manufacturing capabilities. If someone is able to produce an inexpensive product, they are probably a good size company and a competitor to watch out for.

17.   What advantage do we have with proprietary technolo -gy?

Proprietary means many things. It could be a patent or a copyright. It could be the material you use to manufacture your product. Examine what it is that makes you unique.

The number one advantage is the capability to open up new markets that were never before open due to a lack of technology. The new technology as an example, could make the product capable of performing more functions simultaneously, at a reduced cost. The list could be volumes so it is up to you to determine the advantage you have with proprietary technology. The technology that you are using should be stable enough and pass any regulatory scrutiny before using it to develop and/or use in the product for release to the consumer.

18.   Is state of the art technology a source of competitive ad -vantage?

State of the art technology is only a competitive ad vantage if you have a patent that gives you some degree of protection for some period of time. If the technology cannot be used in the product or to manufacture the product inexpensively, then you will not have a competitive advantage. Technology can be patented in the development of

Usually the smaller manufacturers that deal with lesser known distribution outlets are more vulnerable to competition. Startup companies usually get to the rebels or distributors that do not have a major supplier for one reason or another. They are more susceptible to adding competitive products to their portfolio.

The small company, much like you if you are a startup, can react quickly to a market trend and can get to the market in much the same manner as you,. They are the most vulnerable to lose market share but also quicker to enter and compete than the large company.

your product and when the technology becomes less expensive, you are positioned to enter the market with a competitive edge.

19. **Will state of the art technology make the products that you will compete with more attractive to potential buyers?**

Does your technology enable you to perform a procedure more efficiently such as laser surgery, higher speed transmission over telephone lines, make it lighter, stronger, faster or any other advantage that you did not have before? If technology is expensive and allows for a critical lifesaving procedure to be performed where it was impossible before, the new technology could be a competitive advantage.

20. **Which competitors can we expect to be most competitive because of our entry into the market?**

Usually the smaller manufacturers that deal with lesser known distribution outlets are more vulnerable to competition. Startup companies usually get to the rebels or distributors that do not have a major supplier for one reason or another. They are more susceptible to adding competitive products to their portfolio.

The small company, much like you if you are a startup, can react quickly to a market trend and can get to the market in much the same manner as you,. They are the most vulnerable to lose market share but also quicker to enter and compete than the large company.

Chapter 6

Differentiating and Succeeding

Keying in on differences and quickly capitalizing on them is the formula for most new companies and products to obtain success. Watching trends in technology, trends in the economy, the buying habits of different demographic market segments and where competition is positioning itself are all things to watch in determining what types of differentiation can be successful.

How can we influence the buyer to purchase our product? If there was one answer, we would all be millionaires. This segment on "Differentiating and Succeeding" will help you better understand the types of questions to ask yourself and your organization about new products and the differences that will be attractive to your market segment.

Navigating Points:

How can we influence the buyer to purchase our product? If there was one answer, we would all be millionaires. This segment on "Differentiating and Succeeding" will help you better understand the types of questions to ask yourself and your organization about new products and the differences that will be attractive to your market segment.

Identify the common characteristics of our buyers

Using Excel or pieces of graph paper write down the product and possible enhancements on the top line and down the left side list the market segments demographics such as:

- Age, income (Think in terms of international markets and the cross over possibilities)

- Industry segment

- Buying habits

- Current product that yours would replace

- Product or current name brand loyalty

- Benefits that your product offers (This could be a page by itself and if it is try to prioritize by importance the benefits)

- Seasonality

- Price threshold to gain market share

- Technology familiarity level (Will you have to launch a large

promotional and training campaign or can you piggy back on someone else's technology and education of the market place?)

1. **What are the specific benefits that this generic buyer val-ues in our product?**

Break out the benefits on a separate sheet of paper and use them for market research. Call or have a firm specializing in market research test the validity of your perceived benefits.

2. **Rank the purchasers criteria from the buyers perspective.**

At the same time as you are validating the benefits through market research, ask the potential buyers to rank your products benefits.

3. **What can our product offer that is not currently being offered?**

Using a spreadsheet, identify by product and manufacturer those competitors' products that most closely resemble yours. List the same criteria as you used for your product and summarize them by benefit and feature and see where you are strongest and weakest. You should apply some weight to the criteria to give the answer's importance.

4. **What would prevent a competitor from copying our spe-cial benefits and technology?**

If your product has technology that is patentable or can be copyrighted, then apply as soon as possible because of the wait time to process your application. It is rare that a new product comes along that does not already have some degree of previous legal protection. The patent searches will divulge if the name is currently in use, is there a patent in process or a previously accepted patent. This search could take six months if you do not have a patent attorney to speed up the process.

Keying in on differences and quickly capitalizing on them is the formula for most new companies and products to obtain success. Watching trends in technology, trends in the economy, the buying habits of different demographic market segments and where competition is positioning itself are all things to watch in determining what types of differentiation can be successful.

If you are not lucky enough to make it through the patent or copyright search and not have a conflict, you will need to have a specialist that understands how to apply for and write patents. There are people and companies that specialize and can assist you in defining the product so that it can be processed with a minimum of rewrites. This is an over looked area that should be given careful consideration before proceeding. If you are relying on venture capital or other outside investments, one of the first questions asked is about your products protection.

In order to minimize one risk of product or patent infringement, limit your advertising and promotions to those valued customers and prospects that you will rely on to give you input or distribute your final version of the product. If trade journals call you up for editorial comments and you have not completed your patent process, and your product has market appeal, competitors will appear at your every turn and your Window of Opportunity will close much more rapidly than anticipated.

5.   **What is the configuration of value activities that cre ates the most valuable product differentiation relative to its cost?**

This question can be asked in many ways but it is meant to help you understand the cost of differentiation and the value/benefit that the differentiation can give to the potential purchaser of your product. Compare the cost with the time to develop and apply these variables to the Window of Opportunity. Will you be able to deliver your product in a timely manner to take advantage of the Window of Opportunity before competition erodes the price and cuts into your share of the market?

6.   **Is your chosen strategy for differentiation sustainable?**

What is your target market for the product? Is your product a consumable such as a clothing or food item

Navigating Points:

In order to minimize one risk of product or patent infringement, limit your advertising and promotions to those valued customers and prospects that you will rely on to give you input or distribute your final version of the product. If trade journals call you up for editorial comments and you have not completed your patent process, and your product has market appeal, competitors will appear at your every turn and your Window of Opportunity will close much more rapidly than anticipated.

that the market will continue to purchase for a long period of time? If it is and you can gain market share and distribution, you can also gain brand loyalty that will min-imize the competition entering your target market. This is important in terms of long-term customer loyalty.

7. **Is your product a fad item that will have a hockey stick ramp and then drop off just as rapidly?**

If it is anticipated that this is your product niche, you should probably consider off shore manufacturing to minimize your exposure in acquiring manufacturing capability. Large quantities get the lowest cost of goods in order to come in at a high margin and be able to lower the price very quickly in order to move the inventory and still make a reasonable profit when the hockey stick curve flattens out and interest falters.

8. **Does your product have built in mid-life kickers or en-hancement capabilities to lengthen the life of the prod-uct?**

An example of this capability is a personal computer. You can add; memory, voice cards, speakers, joy sticks, different cartridges, printers and the software is almost infinite.

Sustained differentiation is only possible if you have an unlimited supply of cash or expect to put profit into re search and development to keep you state of the art and be known as a leader in your chosen target market.

If you become known for differentiation and unique solutions, other companies and competitors will approach you to OEM (Original Equipment Manufacturer) products or components for them and either pay you a royalty, a license fee or a per product cost.

9. **What major activities are required to sustain the unique**

BEST PRODUCTS

Advertising and promotions are the main ways to sustain uniqueness in the eyes of the buyer. If you are not well funded, this is the area that usually lacks the support. It is important to note that this area needs the most funding in order to succeed in the market. Depending on the size of the market and the cost of your product to the end user, you will have to decide on the channel to market best suited to deliver your product and aggressive-ly pursue the establishment of the channel.

ness in the eyes of your buyer?

Advertising and promotions are the main ways to sustain uniqueness in the eyes of the buyer. If you are not well funded, this is the area that usually lacks the support. It is important to note that this area needs the most funding in order to succeed in the market. Depending on the size of the market and the cost of your product to the end user, you will have to decide on the channel to market best suited to deliver your product and aggressively pursue the establishment of the channel.

10. **Are you imitating an existing product?**

If you are imitating an existing product, are you providing your product at a better price with greater features and benefits? Are you different enough not to infringe on existing patents and copy rights or has the statute of limitations run out on the patents?

11. **If you are copying, are you meeting or beating your competitor's benefits?**

What makes you think that you will be able to gain any degree of market share if you are copying a product? Do you have customers that request the product and prefer to have one vendor supply the products as opposed to having multiple vendors? Does the product require support that the competition does not provide and do you have support in place or will you have the same difficulty. If the product requires support and your competition is losing business for poor support ask yourself why?

Maybe the product is priced too low to afford the type of support required to sustain a profitable business. Look at why you would copy an existing product and what your long term benefits will be from entering a market with

"If you have more money than brains, you should focus on outbound marketing. If you have more brains than money, you should focus on inbound marketing."

-- *Guy Kawasaki*

"Word-of-mouth marketing has always been important. Today, it's more important than ever because of the power of the Internet."

-- *Joe Pulizzi & Newt Barrett*

another like product.

12.   What features and benefits will your product offer that is not currently offered by the competing product?

If you have decided to enter an already competitive market with another like product, you must have reason to believe that the market is large enough. You can accomplish this through your research on another competing products. If you are entering with a like product and new technology has enabled you to manufacture a product much less expensively, that could be reason enough. If you can be different enough, are less costly and have strong channel to market, you will probably have a profitable business.

13.   If you enter with a low margin cost structure, do you know that your competition cannot lower their cost and drive you out of the market?

If you are entering with a low margin regardless of the cost and you don't feel that you can take at least one hit from the competition leveled at your price, you could be in for trouble. This is especially true if your product is one that is produced in large quantities and your competition is already well established. Unless you are prepared to, or are capable of, manufacturing in great volumes to be competitive, stay out of this kind of market. If you are willing to accept a loss leader in order to gain entry into a market, this presents another set of marketing issues.

Ideally, everyone would like to set their price on value and not cost. In commodity markets where there are numerous competitors vying for the same market and in large dollar volumes, sometimes pennies can make the difference between success and failure. First of all determine if cost is the major issue and secondly, do you want to enter a market where cost is the overriding factor in determining success or failure.

14.   Can you set a price on value and not cost?

Ideally, everyone would like to set their price on value and not cost. In commodity markets where there are numerous competitors vying for the same market and in large dollar   volumes, sometimes pennies can make the difference between success and failure. First of all determine if cost is the major issue and secondly, do you want to enter a market where cost is the overriding factor in determining success or failure.

Value can be sold through reputation such as longevity with solid support, good quality and standing behind your product. Loyalty is golden and should be protected. Most established distributors would buy from a company with a long standing solid reputation and do not mind paying for value and would not entertain another like products.

Do you have a product with new technology for a new market need or have new technology for an already existing product. If your product is more reliable, easier to use, less costly, or even at more cost, you have the opportunity to enter new or existing markets because you are differentiating. The differentiation is in cost, benefits, support and reliability.

Examine the value you are bringing to the customer and then determine if you are willing to support it and that you have the resources to bring the product to market in the manner to be successful.

15.   Does your differentiation justify a premium price?

As in question 13, if you are in a new market with minimum or no competition, you can get a premium price if the customer need is there or the product represents a new fashion or trend where everyone has to have one. If you can develop a product that is trendy and not to costly where everyone says, that is neat or fun and you are in a good economy, the product can snowball through various demographic groups and into other countries.

If you can develop a technology that helps another   product become more useful, or adds life, alliances can be formed where your product is used to sell another product. If you are more into development and not into selling, become aware of the market need in various

Navigating Points:

If you can develop a technology that helps another product become more useful, or adds life, alliances can be formed where your product is used to sell another product. If you are more into development and not into selling, become aware of the market need in various segments and become known as a systems integrator. This is a company that ties products or technologies together to gain greater market penetration and make use of existing technologies.

segments and become known as a systems integrator. This is a company that ties products or technologies together to gain greater market penetration and make use of existing technologies.

The field of medicine and pharmacy can charge exorbitant prices for new cures, procedures and special care if they are new and have a breakthrough in a given area. When the cure is wide spread, as with any product, the price becomes more affordable. It is no different with new technology, fad items, fast food or any product that has a mass appeal and that can be duplicated.

16.   Does your plan to gain a competitive advantage de -pend on a broad or narrow competitive scope?

Understand your market and do not under estimate your competition. Know the strengths and weaknesses of your competition and try to mount a sales attack plan that will give you the greatest distribution for your dollar in   the shortest period of time. If you have developed a product that has synergistic markets with major distribution, try to align yourself with the major distribution or negotiate a private label or other reseller Agreement.

If you are a startup company and if you are well funded, the sales expense to take a product national with your own sales force can take a great deal of time and the ramp up period is always longer than expected. This is why I recommend that you establish channel to market partners that have national distribution in already in place and capitalize on their strengths to aid you in selling your product. You then can mount a sales campaign to major direct customers, look at off shore distribution or other target or niche markets while your distribution is selling to the mainstream.

17.   Are you relying on a particular segment to deliver

Your market research should reveal if you have a cross market potential for your product. Especially important is the volatility and vulnerability of your market segment to changes in the economy, loyalty to other like or competitive products and your ability to bring your product to this market in a timely manner to take advantage of the Window of Opportunity and meet the objectives of your Business Plan.

profitability and growth?

This question is self-explanatory. Your market research should reveal if you have a cross market potential for your product. Especially important is the volatility and vulnerability of your market segment to changes in the economy, loyalty to other like or competitive products and your ability to bring your product to this market in a timely manner to take advantage of the Window of Opportunity and meet the objectives of your Business Plan.

18.   **What are the risks associated with relying on a particular target market segment?**

The size of your market and the vulnerabilities I stated in question 16 are the major risks associated with relying on a single or target market segment. Understand your risks' and act accordingly. Know your market, your competition and the initial impact your product will make during your ramp. Estimate how long you believe that you can sustain a ramp before competition erodes the price and begins to limit the market share potential.

19.   **Are you going to extend to other market segments?**

Product cross over is always a key concern to look for when conducting your market research. Usually, you look to the market segments that will give you the quickest return on investment with your projected ramp on the product. At the same time you should be bringing along those prospects and channels that require lengthily product testing but can give you national or international distribution. As you move forward in sale of the product, look to other markets for synergistic effects. Listen to your customers and distributors for their ideas on how to modify or enhance your product for other market segments.

20. **If you expand, are there any synergistic effects that different markets would have?**

If your product is a standalone and not relying on another product for market penetration and validity, you can look to how you can modify or enhance the product to cross over to other markets. It may be as simple as changing the color, making it a different size, changing the language, getting certification to open additional markets or exploring alliances with other synergistic products.

If your product is dependent on the success of another product to open up markets, be aware of the changing environment that your product is enhancing. In most instances, if you are enhancing a products capability, the company will offer you or contract with you to provide current and ongoing compatibility by giving you release documentation on equipment or software in order to stay compatible.

A synergistic effect is one that works together or cooperates with each other. Search out and be attuned to what products or markets that your product could be synergistic with in order to broaden your market appeal.

Chapter 7

Customer Needs

Customer Needs define the demand in conjunction with the economic climate at the time. If times are good, people will purchase more fad items, take vacations, and buy that new car or other luxury items that they would not ordinarily purchase if the economic climate were poor. People and companies sometimes purchase just to be the first on their block or in their industry to have a particular product. Many people purchase only name brands even if an off brand or generic brand is every bit as good as or better than the name brand. Traditions, in families as well as companies sometimes dictate their buying habits. If people are in the lower or middle income brackets, they usually purchase more generic cars, possibly shop more at discount department stores and food chains and look for the bargain more often than the person that is in a higher income bracket.

Demographic studies on purchasing habits related to ethnic origin, economic status, age and geographic region are available to assist you in targeting a specific market for specific product. Regulatory agencies, trade journals and focus groups are sources to determine customer needs and trends. You can also hire firms to do a market study on a particular product targeted at specific demographics.

Examine what your potential competitors are doing in your targeted customer segment and find out if they are successful and if they are, why? If they are struggling, why? If you are not already a viable entity with established channels to market you better look at establishing alliances with distribution that has customers in your targeted segment. However if your product is sold on the internet, direct mail or tele marketed, it is not as important to have strong alliances and in place distribution.

Look at where the industry is heading if you are thinking

Navigating Points:

Customer Needs define the demand in conjunction with the economic climate at the time. If times are good, people will purchase more fad items, take vacations, and buy that new car or other luxury items that they would not ordinarily purchase if the economic climate were poor. People and companies sometimes purchase just to be the first on their block or in their industry to have a particular product. Many people purchase only name brands even if an off brand or generic brand is every bit as good as or better than the name brand.

of developing a product to enhance an existing technology. Take breath analyzers for instance, they are now being developed as options on new and used cars. You can look at schools and businesses, new types of cleaners, beauty aids, toys and the list goes on and can be as great as your imagination.

You could spend millions on development and the market still passes you by because you did not listen to your customers needs and/or understand what would sell or where technology is heading. For instance golf club manufacturers are using space age metals such as titanium and graphite to make the club lighter and to generate more club head speed so the average golfer can hit the ball farther into the woods. If you are considering building a club with steel shafts, there will only be a handful of players that will want to purchase your clubs but you will still need to understand the needs of the customer willing to stay with steel shafts.

When you examine the needs of your customer, take into consideration:

- The size of your market.

- Who are your competitors and who could enter the market if you become successful?

- Where is the technology of your market segment heading?

- Do I have to worry about patents, copyrights, government regulations?.

- Does my product require a direct sales force?

- Will my product sell by itself or does it have to be endorsed or sold in tandem with another product?

- Can I sell my product via direct mail, home shopping, catalog or tele market?

- Are the channels of distribution so difficult to enter that I have to form an alliance with a competitor or other company that has credentials in the market that I am trying to en

You could spend millions on development and the market still passes you by because you did not listen to your customers needs and/or understand what would sell or where technology is heading. Don't do that. Simply do the research and you will be more successful than you ever thought you could be.

ter?

- Will my product have a life cycle of greater that one year?

- Can enhancements be made to my product that will lengthen the life cycle and prolong profitability?

Answering the following thirteen questions, will assist you in focusing in on the needs of your customer.

1.   Who is the ideal customer for our new product?

This is a brainstorming question and is meant to get everyone's ideas out on the table. Remember no idea is a dumb idea; some are just better than others. I still recommend the old fashioned brain storming session where cell phones and hand held devices are turned off and the group is secluded in a room with white boards and easel pads. As ideas are brought up and discussed, you write them down and tape them to the wall so everyone can see what is and has been discussed. It stimulates the thought processes for creativity.

Each idea could possibly generate food for thought that could broaden the spectrum of possible ideal customers. Remember that a customer is   ultimately the end user but you may not be selling direct to   the end user but possibly through a distribution partner that has access to your customer demographic with existing products. Use Microsoft Word or other like software to compile the notes for further dissemination.

2.   What are the demographics of the selected ideal customers?

This is a follow up question that may not be answered at the time of this meeting because you are trying to assess who the ideal customers for your product could possibly be. Once you determine who your ideal customers are, you need to determine the need of this customer for your product or service.

Navigating Points:

Examine what your potential competitors are doing in your targeted customer segment and find out if they are successful and if they are, why? If they are struggling, why? If you are not already a viable entity with established channels to market you better look at establishing alliances with distribution that has customers in your targeted segment. However if your product is sold on the internet, direct mail or tele marketed, it is not as important to have strong alliances and in place distribution.

Three parallel activities should take place to determine the size and demographics of proposed market. A third parallel activity is one of determining the channel to market to optimize the dollars to take the product to the market place. By determining the demographics of the potential end user, you can identify which distribution methodology can best take your product to market. Demographic information is available at various government regulatory agencies, trade associations your product demographics closely resemble, consultants that specialize in demographics, university and college marketing departments. Survey companies, trade journals and firms currently selling into your demographic mix.

3. **What order of importance are our target customer's primary needs for our product?**

Break this question down to the elements that pertain to your demographic customer needs. A few examples are:

• A fad item might have a short life cycle but immense volume. The demographics might be teenagers that purchase the latest new fad such as sun glasses, a special hat, funky shoes with psychedelic colors, the latest internet application or video game, or the pro sports logo on any piece of clothing. If you do not have an item that is in, you are on the out with your peer group. If you are lucky enough to come up with an idea that can turn into a national fad overnight, you can become a millionaire very quickly.

• Microsoft and Apple have fostered a cottage industry of application developers that generate billions of dollars. Facebook, E-Bay, Google, Craig's List, the list goes on and on where entrepreneurs take advantage of developing tag or add on applications. The big guys love it since it locks new customers into their application and they, in turn, can sell more advertising, hardware and most of all the razor blades. Razor blades are the software, applications and hardware enhancements that make your product relevant and state of the art. A programmer or analyst thinks of a faster and easier way to paint a screen, download a new application or integrate multiple applications on a single device.

• Excellent examples are the Madden games that come out every year, Xbox add-on's and there are a million other like kinds of products that sustain themselves through building a family of products that have addictive qualities. Other products are the designer cases for all of the hand held devices.

Decentralization of major retailers from shopping malls is becoming more prevalent. Major retailers are building facilities by themselves because the demographics of the buyer are telling them that they do not like going to malls because of the crowds.

More and more companies are using telemarketing/call centers and the internet to sell products. They purchase demographic lists from the government and other like businesses and sell everything from credit cards to vacations and insurance. They do this because it works. Technology has allowed them the luxury of using a predictive dialer that loads in millions of numbers and dials 24 hours a day seven days a week if required. When a connection is made, the call is routed to an agent and the spiel is given for the product. One telemarketing agency may sell many products.

Navigating Points:

By determining the demographics of the potential end user, you can identify which distribution methodology can best take your product to market. Demographic information is available at various government regulatory agencies, trade associations your product demographics closely resemble, consultants that specialize in demographics, university and college marketing departments. Survey companies, trade journals and firms currently selling into your demographic mix.

The order of importance is dependent on the target audience. Are they purchasing the product to be accepted, offer more services, be the first on the block, expand their business offerings, increase margin, penetrate new markets or project a new image just to name a few reasons.

4.   **Do you have more than one group of ideal customers?**

This question is more of a reminder to place into perspective that there may be more than one group of ideal customers for your product but that you can't reach with your current resources. Why can't I reach this other customer base if they need my product? This question can be the most frustrating for you as a marketing or sales manager will ever be confronted with. Your peers, investors, and developers keep saying that this is your job to bring this product to the customer. In order to satisfy your critiques, put a plan together that encompasses all of the ideal customers and a methodology, if executed, will bring your product to the ideal customers.

Let us examine some of the obstacles that you will be confronted with if you are not using telemarketing, the Internet, fax broadcasting, home shopping networks, newspaper ads or catalog sales to bring you product to the market.

5.   **Your customers do not want to deal with another ven dor. How do you deal with this objection?**

First and foremost you educate your potential customer which, in this case is a distribution or channel partner, on the benefits that your product will bring to the end user of your product.

Use grass roots sales. This means that you create the demand by going directly to their customers through the internet, direct calls, direct mail or other media advertisement. If you can show that there is demand for your product and have their customers call for your product you have a win. The distribution partner will be more receptive to carrying your product if this is the case. If you do not have unlimited funding and direct sales people, you will need other sales and distribution channels to market and sell your product to reach all of your targeted customers. The benefit to this technique is that you become established as a viable vendor/ manufacturer very fast and as you develop new products, this channel will, with little difficulty absorb new products into their catalog and make them available to your target audience.

You now have an asset that another company could use and if you ever want to sell your company, the buyer will look at what channel to markets you have that are different than theirs to determine if they can move their products through your channel.

Your competitor will bad mouth your product. They will say that you have not been in business long enough, you are not funded adequately, you will be the first to sell the product, you don't have adequate support, you are looking for buyers, etc.

You address these questions as soon as they come up. Offer quality documentation, always follow up, and show your product approvals and/or certifications. If test drives are possible from Consumer Reports, trade associations, industry rags, other like customers, consultant reviews or customer testimonials, have them written up and give them to support your claims that you are in the business for the long haul.

Additional funding may be in order in order to get at other ideal customers for more direct sales people, additional advertising, supplies and equipment. Partnering through alliances, OEM or private labeling may be in order to reach other ideal customers. Time permitting, and we all know that there is never enough, establish your product with solid references and bullet proof your infrastructure before you tackle the world. The hockey stick curve for growth is usually unattainable and if you do reach this growth curve, the logistics of management and distribution, if you have not planned properly, can bring your company to its knees.

6. **Assuming there is no comparable product, what are your target customers buying or doing currently to meet their needs?**

Examining different customer segments, one being the direct sale to the end user and the other selling to a channel that will sell your product offer entirely different opportunities. We also have to look at the product, is the product a consumable, a fad, electronic or computer related? Does the product require sales and post-sales support or is it purchased off of the shelf? Let's look at examples where your product is new and there is not a perceptible need but you feel that there is enough market to support your entry into the industry.

7. **Consumable or fad product?**

Look at sun glasses as an example. Sun glasses are sold everywhere including street corners for as little as a dollar a pair. You have a Ray Blocker sun glass that repels the entire glare, is adjustable to the forehead and ear, and comes with a chrome carrying case and exchangeable lenses and frames. It is proven time and again that most of the inexpensive sun glasses that you purchase off of the street corner block out the glare so how do you begin to sell your product? Many hi-tech or fad products align themselves with a product like Porsche or Harley Davidson or a high fashion clothes firm that caters to the market that would purchase your product. Sometimes these types of products are sold in the middle of malls where the teenage or demographic group you are trying to reach frequent. Major ads in national newspapers, magazines and on the home shopping channels are also good avenues to introduce new consumer and/or fad types of products.

You need to create the need if there is not one read-

What Would John Do?

Your competitor will bad mouth your product. They will say that you have not been in business long enough, you are not funded adequately, you will be the first to sell the product, you don't have adequate support, you are looking for buyers, etc.

You address these questions as soon as they come up. Offer quality documentation, always follow up, and show your product approvals and/or certifications. If test drives are possible from Consumer Reports, trade associations, industry rags, other like customers, consultant reviews or customer testimonials, have them written up and give them to support your claims that you are in the business for the long haul.

ily apparent. You do this through marketing, advertising and executing a sales strategy very quickly and concisely. This takes money and access to distribution channels that have access to a customer that already buys your type of product.

8. **Distribution or channel selling?**

If you believe that your product would be best sold through Office Depot, Costco, Target, Radio Shack or any regional or national chain, you have another set of opportunities.

I have approached and sold to some of the major chains and to just get an appointment with a Product Manager is a major accomplishment. Each Product Manager manages a line of like products and deals with a great number of vendors. To get an appointment, you have to have something very unique to sell and it better be priced right because of the margins they require. Be prepared to leave   samples and you will be put in the queue. Don't expect   overnight success and don't put all of your effort into this one channel because you might go broke or lose your job due to the long sales cycle and low probability of closing the deal.

There are ways to speed this process up if your product has a track record, or is in high demand. If you know someone at the office it helps and if you know other   persons like yourself at companies that sell through this company, ask for their advice. Networking can pay high dividends and reduce the queue time enormously.

9. **Synergistic products?**

Most companies startup through discovering a product that makes another product more salable, easier to use, reduces cost or time or minimizes erosion of a customer base by a competitor. Let us look at a few exam-

Navigating Points:

First and foremost you educate your potential customer which, in this case is a distribution or channel partner, on the benefits that your product will bring to the end user of your product.. Use grass roots sales. This means that you create the demand by going directly to their customers through the internet, direct calls, direct mail or other media advertisement. If you can show that there is demand for your product and have their customers call for your product you have a win. The distribution partner will be more receptive to carrying your product if this is the case. If you do not have unlimited funding and direct sales people, you will need other sales and distribution channels to market and sell your product to reach all of your targeted customers.

ples of what a customer is or was doing and why they would have considered purchasing a product.

Radios are a good example of the changing "need" that people weren't aware of at first. They were usually table mounted or installed in an automobiles dash for convenience. The radio played music, news and you could hear your favorite mystery or comedy program over the air waves. As new technology emerged, clearer sound was available to the astute ear through stronger signals and AM, FM, Cable and now Cirrus came into being.

For a certain demographic group, this capability was a necessity and a new need was created. Next thing that occurred was Hi Fi, and then stereo, surround sound for your car and home and then technology created tape players. Movie theatres advertise the latest in sound to draw in more customers. Soon eight track tape players were the rage and they were available in the car and at home and even with batteries so that you could listen as you walked or ran. Tape passed and the new wave is CD players, HD/TV, One to 10 G, I phones and Blue Ray players. All offer clearer viewing and sound than ever before and again, it is available in cars, home and for your PDA.

I point out this evolution of sound technology as an industry creating a need and turning it into a multibillion dollar industry. The bottom line is margin. If margin had been great enough with the old technology, new technology would not emerge as rapidly. What happens is a copycat mentality. Countries with cheap labor, large manufacturing capabilities and strong channel to market organizations are notorious for lowering margins, buying markets and forcing competitors out of business because they can't compete on a cost basis and maintain profitability.

Telephony technology has created new industries almost overnight. What was once a simple pad of paper to leave a message from a caller has now snow balled into the voice mail, Facebook, dating services and e-mail providers industry. Not wanting to lose a message or lose the voice where, if you couldn't hear the person, you might miss the intent of the message became a necessity.

Voice recording machines were invented to work off of the telephone line. Hundreds of providers now offer all sizes of voice mail for the home and office and every type of computer and PDA and billions of dollars are being made. The large telecommunications manufacturing giants and Regional Bell operating companies realized that a great revenue source was at their fingertips and they should capitalize. The central offices that routed your call had to be capable of storing and forwarding messages from an assigned mail box. The equipment manufacturers discovered capabilities to store the messages and have them retrieved by the customer.

Alas, a new means of minimizing customer erosion by offering voice mail through your local telephone company. Cellular telephones, pagers, fax, video phones and the list goes on and on where a new technology could replace a methodology that a potential customer could use. When examining the market, look at the overall market and determine the niche you would like to get into that gives you the widest Window of Opportunity with minimal competition. Most products are brought into being through looking at how something is being done now and how new technology could improve the time to complete a task, reduce the cost, make it more fun or enhance the service.

10. **Are your target customers buying more than one product to meet their needs? If so, will your product eliminate or reduce the need for multiple purchases?**

If you are a startup customer with a single or

limited product line, and you require distribution to sell your product, one strategy is to come in as a secondary product to the flag ship product. If you are accepted it will be because you offer a product that is complimentary or offers capability that the flag ship does not offer.

The incumbent will fight you tooth and nail since they are established with the sales force you are trying to penetrate. You will have an uphill fight to penetrate the good old boy network even though corporate has given you the opportunity to schedule appointments with the various regional offices. If you are lucky, you will be asked to make presentations at national sales meeting or participate in national and regional trade shows.

Co-op advertising is another way to advertise your product. Chances are that your channel has a newsletter, uses the internet, sends bingo cards, and sends precut literature or any number of co-op advertisements. Be prepared to offer Spiffs or special incentives to corporate, the region, the branch or direct to the sales person depending on the policy set by home office.

If you know that you have a better product that will fulfill more needs for the customer that the competition or incumbent can't, the only way to get your product in front of the target customer if you are going through distribution is to offer exceptional pre and post-sales support to home office, regional and branch offices.

Just because you have a contract with a distribution channel to sell your product and you know that your product will fulfill more needs than your competition, doesn't mean that the channel will drop the current product and sell yours. You can ask why if your product does more, is supported better than the competition, is priced better and so on?

One of the biggest obstacles to overcome is the

The Experts Speak Out...

"The media wants overnight successes (so they have someone to tear down). Ignore them. Ignore the early adopter critics who never have enough to play with. Ignore your investors who want proven tactics and predictable instant results. Listen instead to your real customers, to your vision, and make something for the long haul. Because that's how long it's going to take."

-- Seth Godin

one of loyalty and friendships. If the incumbent's product is totally behind the times, is lacking quality support, advertising and is priced wrong, you have a much better opportunity. If on the other hand, the competitions product is well supported and will do the job but not as well as yours and is entrenched in the customer environment, you are going to have a great deal of difficulty penetrating the sales distribution chain.

Another major reason, and again if your product is technical in nature this applies, is the one of training. If your product takes training and support and the other product is doing well even though it is not as sophisticated as yours, managers do not want to take support and sales people out of the field to train on your new product unless it is entirely new and will help them substantially increase sales and help towards their quota.

How do you overcome these obstacles? The answer is simple but expensive. You have to either go direct and sell to the customers developing name recognition, loyalty and/or get testimonials from key customers and bring them to your newly acquired distribution channel. This is called pull through. Your boss will ask why would we want to do this if we sell the account, why not keep the account direct and make more money and save the margin. You are ultimately trying to win the support of a major distribution channel with possibly hundreds of salespeople that are in touch with thousands of customers that could have a need for your product. This is the reason for selling a customer and pulling it through distribution.

Chances are the reason that you are in business or thinking about going into business is because you believe that you have a product that will either:

A. Save people money.

Navigating Points:

Just because you have a contract with a distribution channel to sell your product and you know that your product will fulfill more needs than your competition, doesn't mean that the channel will drop the current product and sell yours. You can ask why if your product does more, is supported better than the competition, is priced better and so on? One of the biggest obstacles to overcome is the one of loyalty and friendships. If the incumbent's product is totally behind the times, is lacking quality support, advertising and is priced wrong, you have a much better opportunity.

B. Help people do their job more efficiently

C. Give access to new markets

D. Relieve pain and suffering

E. Fad or fun to have

F. Takes advantage of new technologies

G. Combines large into small and or many functions into a single function

These are a few of the ideas that should give you food for thought on how your product could reduce the need for multiple purchases by a potential customer.

11.   How important is low price to your target customer?

Price is always important to the product sales equation. You have probably heard it said many times; if we can sell enough we can manufacture the product cheaper and offer it for less. If you are selling a commodity product like an office supply, a computer or peripheral, pharmaceutical, generic toy, automobile, food item, espresso or the like, pricing is most important. If you are going to enter a commodity market and you are not unique, you better be able to build it cheap and have channels of distribution to sell a lot in order to make any money.

The pitfalls of having price be your number one market strategy are:

• Can you build the product inexpensive enough to support your Business Plan?

• Did you build in sufficient profit margin to support your sales methodology? In most cases you will have established a published CLP (Customer List Price) that for whom ever buys your product for resale will not sell higher than the CLP. An example is a product with a CLP of $1.60.

If you are a startup customer with a single or limited product line, and you require distribution to sell your product, one strategy is to come in as a secondary product to the flag ship product. If you are accepted it will be because you offer a product that is complimentary or offers capability that the flag ship does not offer.

The incumbent will fight you tooth and nail since they are established with the sales force you are trying to penetrate. You will have an uphill fight to penetrate the good old boy network even though corporate has given you the opportunity to schedule appointments with the various regional offices. If you are lucky, you will be asked to make presentations at national sales meeting or participate in national and regional trade shows.

• You sell direct at a 60% mark up from the cost. You make it for $1.00 and sell it for $1.60 plus taxes.

• You sell to a second tier sales distribution channel and they mark up the product 60%. If you held to your markup, the product now sells to the end user for $1.60 (your sales cost), add 60% more for the second tier markup and the product sells to the end user for $2.56.

Not uncommon are three tiered sales structures where you manufacture the product, sell it to a distributor and they in turn sell it to local stores or chains. If the formula in one and two were held, the third tier would sell your product for $4.10 to the end user. Your product is now almost three times higher than your published CLP. Your product will probably not support the additional markups.

If your product is hard goods and requires materials to manufacture, is not a fad, does not use new technology and has does not replace or considerably reduce the time or cost to the end user, you better think hard about developing a product and entering the business.

If your product is high tech and/or is software as an example, your cost to manufacture is your overhead and a few supplies. Your risk is limited and if your market is large enough you could reduce your markup or margin to support multiple tiers of distribution and still be profitable.

Price is always important and especially so if you are producing a product similar to one already in the market with an established track record and industry standard price.

12. **Is your ideal customer willing to pay more if they re -ceive a higher quality product or better solution to meet their needs?**

Higher price is dictated by perceived value of the end user. The channel purchasing the product is also a

Navigating Points:

You have to either go direct and sell to the customers developing name recognition, loyalty and/ or get testimonials from key customers and bring them to your newly acquired distribution channel. This is called pull through. Your boss will ask why would we want to do this if we sell the account, why not keep the account direct and make more money and save the margin. You are ultimately trying to win the support of a major distribution channel with possibly hundreds of salespeople that are in touch with thousands of customers that could have a need for your product. This is the reason for selling a customer and pulling it through distribution.

consideration and, to a great extent, your competition. Best case scenario is a new product that is fun and exciting for the general public, easy to make, great profit margins, few government regulations and you can't make enough to meet the market demand. If the product enhances, reduces time or cost, opens up new markets, is new technology that can be used for other projects or prolongs the life of something, you can usually command a higher price for your product.

As I have so often stated, solid market research is the foundation for your success. You need to understand the demographics of the customer mix that you are targeting your product towards.

13. **If you group your customers based on how they would use your product, what would these groups be?**

Grouping can be done by demographics such as age, income, geography, race, education, political party, weight, height and past buying history or if your customer participated in another survey or gave money to a charity. Companies can be grouped by SIC (Standard Industrial Code) which is a five digit code that breaks industry down into metals as an example and type of metal is represented by another digit in the SIC code. Further breakdown is available by number of employees, gross sales, key people, headquarters location, branch offices and zip code location.

By establishing groups of potential customers for your product or service, you are on your way to determining the size of the potential market.

14. **If you add value to your product will your customers pay more?**

When you add value to your product it can be very instrumental to the long term profitability of your product. If you are developing a unique product with no competition and a perceived wide Window of Opportunity of two years before competition enters the picture, do not add value just to be adding value. One of the biggest mistakes a new company can make is to develop a product and never freeze the product specifications. If you don't freeze the specifications, the product will never get finished, your employees will get frustrated, the Window of Opportunity closes and your prospects and customers may look to a lesser product but one that is ready to go to the market.

Your market study will determine if the feature and benefit should be offered at a cost that will attract the largest share of the prospect base for your type of product.

When you are successful and competition offers a similar type of product, you will have the benefit of working with your customers and distributors and determining what new enhancements can be made to the product to lengthen its life cycle. You should have developed cost saving steps to manufacture the product by now and new releases can reflect what the customers and new prospects need to keep and expand on your market share.

You need to keep your competition guessing and in a catch up mode. By working with your customers and distributors and listening to their input, they will take ownership of the product and when they take ownership of the product, they will pay for value that your product or service will give them.

15. **What are the needs of the top three or four segments of the market that you feel that you should target?**

Again, what is the product and who is the market for your product? Are you developing a new technology, enhancing a technology, developing a fad or fashion product or something else? Examine the demographics and purchasing patterns of the major segments you are targeting. When you have identified the market segments, do some live surveys and get real feedback on the needs and ask leading questions. A leading question   is one that asks for input that can be fed back to respondent for further clarification.

For Example:

I am developing a new shoe similar to a tennis shoe but with replaceable soles. One sole can be used to grip a floor for basketball or handball, another for running cross country and another for walking. Would you be willing to pay $30.00 for the walking shoe and another $10.00 per sole? Wait for an answer and then ask what activities they participate in and discuss the type of sole required for their activity.

This dialog could be interesting if the person is active at all and the fact that you are asking for their Input can give them ownership of the product. Follow up with a letter and if you develop the product, contact them and let them know where the nearest outlet will be.

16.   What are the buying processes of the identified buying segments?

Identify if your product or service is an impulse, a try it you will like, free trial, why not it isn't expensive, a comparative purchase, the Jones have one we better get one or just a must have product, purchase. Is your product purchased by an age group, does the product go out for bid or on an RFQ (Request For Quotation), leased or lease purchase. If you are expecting quick revenue and the buying process is a long sales cycle of three to eighteen months, you better have planned for the drain on cash until your first sale comes in.

It is vitally important to understand who and how the

Co-op advertising is another way to advertise your product. Chances are that your channel has a newsletter, uses the internet, sends bingo cards, and sends precut literature or any number of co-op advertisements. Be prepared to offer Spiffs or special incentives to corporate, the region, the branch or direct to the sales person depending on the policy set by home office.

The Experts Speak Out...

"Don't be afraid to get creative and experiment with your

marketing."

-- Mike Volpe

purchase of your product will be done for Business Planning purposes. I have stated many times that the most over looked expense item is the marketing and subsequent selling expense. Look at others that are in your same or similar types of business and talk to their customers and to them trying to understand the sales cycle so that you will not fall into the trap of being strapped for cash until your first sale comes in.

17. **Are there similarities in the way the product is used in the top three or four segments of the market?**

This question is meant to stimulate your thought process on how your product is perceived and purchased for use in your identified market segments.

An example might be a liquid detergent or wax AND when packaged differently, they are Identified with different markets but with the exact same contents, A strong detergent might have the properties to take away bath tub and shower stains and your logo has a tub stain with a sponge going through it showing how white your detergent makes the stain with one swipe of the sponge. Repackaging could be in a gallon container with the picture of a house with mildew and a hose spraying from the container with the mildew fading away.

Adding new functionality and emphasizing the benefits can change the marketability of the product significantly. The rubber hose that is used in hospitals and clinics is advertised as a sling shot propulsion mechanism and is also used for rehabilitation by creating force that a body part pushes or pulls against for resistance.

A voice mail system offered by your telephone company has been brought down to a single residence with any number of features and benefits. What was originally a business device has now developed into a market for anyone with a telephone. Both of these examples offer a look at how functionality and emphasizing the benefits works for some products. Don't be afraid to think outside the box.

Chapter 8

Marketplace Changes

As the marketplace changes we must change also in order to remain competitive and meet the needs of current and new customer. Can you afford to be proactive and do you have the resources to determine or track movement in the marketplace? If you are a large company with a dedicated marketing department, one of their tasks is to track marketplace changes. Tracking the changes in the marketplace will assist you in being proactive.

Ways to track the movement in the market can be as close as your sales order function. Are orders increasing, flat or decreasing? In any of these situations, your customers are your most important resource and your salespeople and support department usually have a good understanding for any of the three sales figures.

If sales are increasing, you probably have a cutting edge product that has leading edge benefits with minimal competition or a huge market that will take a period of time to saturate; this is the best case if costs are in line with margin. What could hurt you dramatically is the building of an infrastructure that encompasses a large development, manufacturing, administrative and sales staff for a single product. If the window suddenly slams, what do you do with all of the personnel and equipment?

Many times entrepreneurs seeing margin slipping away to the manufacturers and resellers will want to keep the short term profit, believe that by employing a large direct sales force and bringing in-house manufacturing capability they can reap huge margins. This is true depending on the size of the market, the cost to develop your product and the method of reaching your customers. The key to marketing is to understand the possible variables and be proactive in the scenarios to deal with the marketplace changes

Navigating Points:

Ways to track the movement in the market can be as close as your sales order function. Are orders increasing, flat or decreasing? In any of these situations, your customers are your most important resource and your salespeople and support department usually have a good understanding for any of the three sales figures.

A startup company would be wise to consider contracting as much of the manufacturing and development as possible with clauses to decrease cost to manufacturer as volume increases. You should consider developing channel marketing partners that have ready access to your defined markets. Gaining entrance to a market by yourself can be next to impossible and very time consuming at best. All of this time closes the Window of Opportunity and allows for competition to dose the gap on developing a better product and moving it through established channels to market.

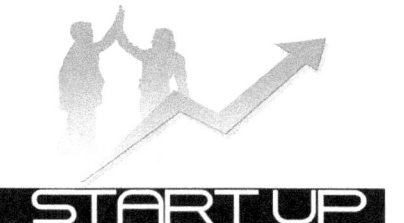

Be aware that there are exceptions to every rule, but the exceptions are few and far in-between. Be cognizant of the market, your competition, your costs to develop your channel to market and do a test of reasonableness on every decision.

The test of reasonableness is one that objectively views an opportunity or obstacle and says, which is the best way to deal with the issue? Subjectively, you might look at every opportunity or obstacle and say, we can do that if I allocate or raise X dollars. In other words, you are throwing dollars and resources at every issue and not examining or taking into consideration the ramifications of the Window of Opportunity. These ramifications are how long it takes to get to the market if you go direct or in-house manufacturing and development as opposed to going outside for manufacturing assistance.

The greed factor enters into most decisions because we want as big a piece of the pie as we can bite off. Our mouths are usually smaller than we think and we choke on the big bite. Your business plan should have contingency plans built in for success at various target sales levels taking into consideration different scenarios for channel to market.

In this segment we will consider "Marketplace Changes" and if you answer them all, you will have a better understanding of how to be proactive and recognize the changes before they force you into a reactive mode. The following 11 questions will give you on market place.

1.   What are the most significant assumptions that we

have made about your new products' performance in the market?

Performance is the key word here. As you consider perfor-mance go back in time and think about why you got into your business in the first place.

• Did you have a Mission Statement from which all products have to adhere?

• Are you developing new technology beyond the scope of your current capabilities?

• What facts indicate that you have a significant opportunity and Window of Opportunity?

• Are there competitors that have the resources to develop and enter the market faster than you?

• What impact will you have if you are second or third in the market?

• Are you entering a market where performance is measured in high reliability with exceptional support?

• Are you a stand-alone or added value product? A standalone product can sell based on inherent benefits where an added value product enhances the value of an-other product. If you are an added value product, there are contractual issues to deal with in order to protect yourself if your partner does not have a competitive product and sales flatten.

• Does your product lend itself to being upgraded or ex-changed as new technology evolves or is it a throw away and you replace it with a new one?

• Is your product patentable or copyrighted?

• What about price to performance? Do you have enough margin/profit to sell through channel and discount as the life of the product decreases?

Navigating Points:

Questions to Ask...

Are you a stand-alone or add-ed value product? A standalone product can sell based on inherent benefits where an added value product enhances the value of another product. If you are an added value product, there are con-tractual issues to deal with in order to protect yourself if your partner does not have a competitive product and sales flatten.

- Can you meet the regulatory requirements that this product requires before entering the market?

- Is seasonality an issue relative to when your product will be ready to hit the shelves?

Make a check list of the most important assumptions about your new products' performance in the market-place and review them internally. Gather input from as many resources as possible. Look internally, at end users, at your resellers, consultants, and have marketing firms examine your plan. If you have a focus group of customers this is an excellent method to determine need and get feedback on the competitive environment.

If you are still positive and there are no red flags or major objections and you have the funding and resources to make it happen, success is waiting.

2. **What actions will you take if your assumptions are not ac curate?**

This is the $64 dollar question and the reason more companies fail or miss their projections; their assumptions were not accurate. Having been in this position of making as-sumptions on the market demand and having to step up and take responsibility for sales forecasts, I know the variables that can affect your assumptions. I have firsthand experi-ence in making assumptions and through factors out of my control, my assumptions on one project were not even within 80% accurate. This is an after the fact statistic be cause the product was 36 months late and competition came out with a similar product that worked as advertised.

My product was a high tech telephone, first to use DSP with state of the art capabilities to connect fax, display incoming caller ID information, have multiple lines, speaker phone, a directory of numbers, conference calling, a message waiting light and software that would allow for mo-

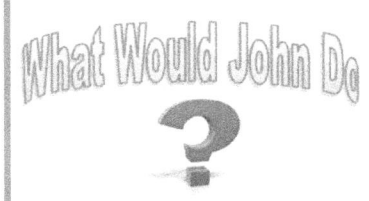

There is a saying...assuming makes an ass out of you and me. It's a play on words of course but it is also very true. Making assumptions based on false information is one of the biggest issues businesses today have. It is best to ensure that your facts are correct before putting the pieces together and if you can't make sure that they are correct...don't make as-sumptions.

dem connection. It also allowed for upgrading the telephone as enhancements were made by the manufacturer or the telephone company. The telephone was the first of a kind universal telephone family and designed to replace 30 plus telephones currently on the market.

I had the design in hand, a pitch for all of the benefits and how we would meet the regulatory requirements. I also had the cost to margin which was excellent so that everyone could make money and it looked like that we had a real winner. I was pumped and would go on the road for weeks at a time calling on telephone companies, interconnects, supply houses and any channel that could bring my product to market.

Everyone was excited and since I did not have a working model, I pitched ownership of the product and solicited ideas for enhancement and used many of their ideas in the ultimate development. I, in turn, conveyed back to the prospective resellers of the product that we had used their ideas and it broadened their market and gave them ownership of the product. In the phone business, the big manufacturers very seldom ask for input and just shove new products out the door and soon they are obsolete. Our telephone would last for the ages and cross over many markets and could be upgraded as technology improved. This was exciting to the resellers because they could minimize inventory, incur less training, have less support costs and it was a win for everyone.

Jumping forward about six months, I had working models and made the same trip and this time I was able to get real forecasts from decision makers with expected delivery times. Channel partners advertised our product in their catalog and at trade shows and I was invited to trade shows to demonstrate the product. We received great write ups in significant and influential trade journals. We were having to raise money to further develop and

Navigating Points:

Make a check list of the most important assumptions about your new products' performance in the marketplace and review them internally. Gather input from as many resources as possible. Look internally, at end users, at your resellers, consultants, and have marketing firms examine your plan. If you have a focus group of customers this is an excellent method to determine need and get feedback on the competitive environment.

manufacture and the only way to raise money was to have customers that would commit to purchase orders to justify the development. I proceeded to get commitments for 150,000 phones for the first year with projections for upwards of 200,000 annually thereafter.

Investors called my customers and they verified what I had said was correct and they were very encouraging. The investors invested and we raised approximately $30,000,000.

All of a sudden red flags were going up everywhere. We had never built telephones before and the regulatory requirements were horrendous. We could not meet them and we had to retrench and search and hire new personnel that had built telephones, we also had to purchase additional test equipment and then we discovered that the plastics were not conforming to specifications. I had to go to the customers that were expecting delivery and hold them off. They were understanding because no one ever met their delivery schedules in the telephone business. I still felt terrible but the worst was yet to come.

Our original Window of Opportunity was approximately 36 months before competition would rear its ugly head. We had one delay after the other and when we finally released the first version of the telephone it was almost three years late and we had all kinds of problems in the field. It is not rocket science as to what happened to my assumptions on sales.

Competition entered the picture with a telephone without all of the bells and whistles that ours had but it had enough that they were able to take all of our thunder away and they had a name and established channels. We ended up selling about 10% of the projections, had to lay off most of our personnel and struggled to stay alive.

Because we could not meet the regulatory requirements as previously thought, our costs to develop the telephone were more than we sold it for. Investors were upset and heads rolled. I am not an engineer, I am a marketing and sales person so I took for granted that what the engineering department said about the development early on was accurate. To me, a telephone seemed like a relatively simple apparatus to make. The set was software based and I did know software and it seemed to me that it was not that difficult. But anything that could go wrong, did.

The lesson to be learned here was learned the hard way. If you are developing technology products for markets of which you are not familiar, make sure that you have the technology to develop and the resources to perform. You may be like me and just have to have trust in your engineers if not. Be aware of the red flags that jump out and ask questions. There is no real answer to this question but up front planning and making sure that you have the resources to perform the task at hand are crucial to your success.

3. **Can we develop a contingency plan if our assumptions are not accurate?**

A contingency plan should be in place for:

- Loss of key personnel

- Multiple sources for parts

- Outsource for unexpected demand

- Test equipment for meeting regulatory requirements

- Technical resources for unexpected problems

- Cash sources to meet unexpected delays

- Cash sources to meet unexpected product demands
New channels of distribution if some go sideways

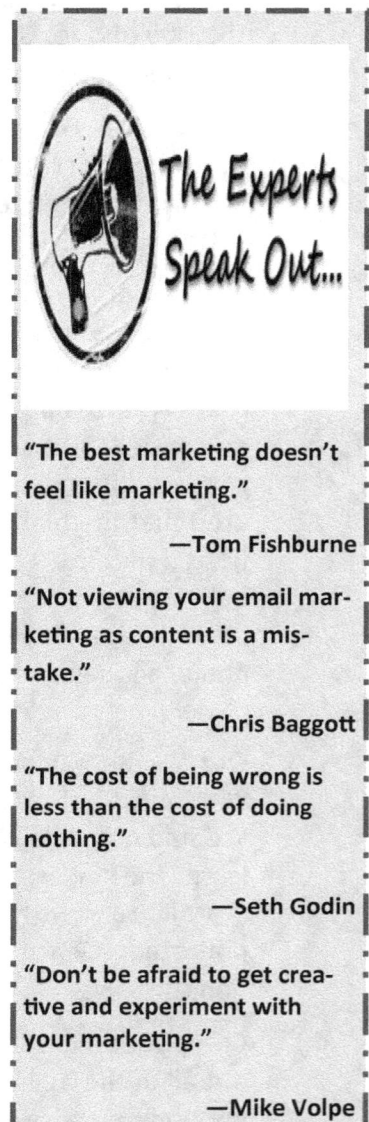

The Experts Speak Out....

"The best marketing doesn't feel like marketing."

—Tom Fishburne

"Not viewing your email marketing as content is a mistake."

—Chris Baggott

"The cost of being wrong is less than the cost of doing nothing."

—Seth Godin

"Don't be afraid to get creative and experiment with your marketing."

—Mike Volpe

• Ways to fire sale what is left if all else fails

4. **What about changes in performance or new technolo -gy from a competitor?**

This happens more frequently than not and especially if you are in the high tech or consumer electronics arena. You may have the fastest, most feature rich whiz bang product to reach mankind and zap, here comes the compe -tition with a technology breakthrough that practically makes your product obsolete before you get it out the door.

China does not have the copyright and patent laws that the US has in place so if they get wind of an idea, they can come in and copy or manufacture your idea almost overnight and your market projections will be shattered; be careful who you talk to until you are ready.

If you planned out your product life cycle, and I am as-suming it is not a fad or consumable product for this dis-cussion, you should have only a minor blip in your pro-gress. Most fad, fashion and high tech products are de-signed to meet a target or global market. You should have a good handle on who your competition is and you should have commitments from channel to market part-ners for your product.

Look for areas to personalize your product for a specific in-dustry or demographic market. This could be as easy as giving it a different name or color that is associated with your target market. If an industry perceives that you have dedicated the time to identify with them and taken that extra step, your product has a better chance of an-ticipated acceptance even with competition.

I have seen products that were far better designed for a given market than the competitors but because one identified with the market and the other did not, the one that identified got the lion's share of the market.

Navigating Points:

If you planned out your product life cycle, and I am assuming it is not a fad or consumable product for this discussion, you should have only a minor blip in your progress. Most fad, fashion and high tech products are designed to meet a target or global market. You should have a good handle on who your competition is and you should have commitments from channel to market partners for your product.

If your product success relies on speed of processing, density or storage, flexibility or features, concentrate on selling the benefits and don't get into a feature war. If you do, the buyer will simply stack your product up against the others and the one with the best features will usually win. If you are not the fastest, cheapest or have the most whiz bang technology, sell benefits and target them to industry or demographic needs.

If your product has a planned release cycle for enhancements look to add additional enhancements to the product as an incentive for the buyer. If this is not possible, maybe you discount the product to keep your channels interest and customer demand.

In many instances and I found this out the hard way- you don't always have to have the latest state of the art product to be successful. The pitfalls and chances for failure with new technology are greatest with the first company that releases the product to the market. If you release a new product with state of the art technology and you fail, it is difficult to regain your momentum. A competitor can come in with a lesser product that is solid in workmanship and technology and gain a strong foot hold. A segment of the market is captured, reliability is established and as new products are released, the buyer is ready to accept the next product or enhancement readily because of their previous experiences.

I was once told that I had some of the greatest ideas and was an excellent missionary and visionary but if I couldn't deliver, the big boys would take my ideas and beat me to the punch; I've heard that more than once. And they sure did,this is one ploy that you have to look out for when you are trying to take market share away from a global competitor with unlimited resources. Many times large conglomerates look at startup companies and follow their progress with new technology and

I was once told that I had some of the greatest ideas and was an excellent missionary and visionary but if I couldn't deliver, the big boys would take my ideas and beat me to the punch; I've heard that more than once. And they sure did,this is one ploy that you have to look out for when you are trying to take market share away from a global competitor with unlimited resources. Many times large conglomerates look at startup companies and follow their progress with new technology and when the time is right, they purchase you or develop a product that is similar and they quickly take market share. This is not all bad and many startups begin with that as a target strategy to get purchased and turn a quick profit.

when the time is right, they purchase you or develop a product that is similar and they quickly take market share. This is not all bad and many startups begin with that as a target strategy to get purchased and turn a quick profit.

Remember that they have the channels established and you are trying to make inroads into their market. If the market is limited, you may be left alone but if it is perceived to be a threat to their keeping market share, you will be quickly minimized in the target market. Major channels to market that rely on major manufacturers with name recognition will sell your product but will quickly jump to the incumbent when they have a similar product to meet the customer demand.

Product positioning is critical to your entry into a market. Understanding the relationship of your major competitors in your channel is especially acute to your success. Don't for a minute think that because you have a channel locked up that you're solid as granite. Remember your channel was there before you and they are there because people like you did the same you're doing. There will always be someone over your shoulder trying to knock you off of your pedestal.

5.   **Identify areas where problems are most likely to occur?**

The best way that I have found to do this is solicit input from your key managers, industry consultants, investment firms and from other managers of companies that develop like products. Break out the key areas and identify the critical areas by time, dollars, resources, competition, eco-nomic climate and a disaster recovery plan.

After you have identified all of the potential areas where there could be a potential problem, using a popular project management program, plot the tasks by time, activity, resource and pay particular attention to the pre-requisite activities required. So many times events are timed and

dependent on each other before each can be completed or begin. A critical path or project plan needs to be monitored daily to anticipate possible problem areas. If monitored, your surprises will be minimal and you should be able to deal with them without each being a crisis.

6. **Can you build more flexibility into your product so that you have the capability to respond to changes in the marketplace or competition?**

This question can be asked of anyone associated with your product. Any internal personnel, outside consult-ant, reseller, customer or prospect. Many times the developer can't see the forest because of the trees. The developers get trapped in a form of tunnel vision and it is the job of marketing to relay possible enhancements that could add new benefits and features. It is also wise to take product developers on visits to prospects and customers allowing them to hear firsthand what you are hearing about the product.

I have been asked a hundred times by a Product Manager as to why a product is not good enough to sell in the market. If continual feedback says it does not have the benefits to be competitive, then new features have to be added in order to make it competitive. If a Product Manager can hear this from a customer or reseller, it makes your job of internal selling much easier.

Especially look to simple changes such as name, color, packaging, language and build the product with the capability to be upgraded. By doing this, you enhance the life of the product, and open up new markets with minimal effort and expense.

Products such as cosmetics, fashion, consumer electronics, LEGOS, Barbie Dolls, train sets, Hot Wheels and high brand name visibility products just keep going by bringing out new versions with different features. Probably the hottest in

The critical ingredient is getting off your butt and doing something. It's as simple as that. A lot of people have ideas, but there are few who decide to do something about them now. Not tomorrow. Not next week. But today. The true entrepreneur is a doer, not a dreamer.

—*Nolan Bushnell*

The golden rule for every business man is this: "Put yourself in your customer's place."

– *Orison Swett Marden*

the late nineties was the Beanie Baby; there must have been a 100 different Beanie Babies. Food chains build demand to collect every version and this attracted millions of customers into the restaurants. These customers than bought the food which was profitable for the restaurant and the Beanie Babies company. It was a real hook and they just keep coming, so develop a hook type of a product to generate demand.

Most computer and telecommunications products are memory based and have specialized ports to attach new devices and have the capability to upgrade their memory. These benefits keep the customer coming back. Another product to consider is the Frisbee. The product is the same shape as it has always been, however now they come in different sizes and colors. Some even have lights, are florescent, some are made for target competition, some are built for length of flight and some for dog competition; they have covered many bases with one seemingly simple product.

Being proactive is key to survival in any business or you will get passed over. Once you set back on your laurels and get complacent, competition will swallow you up and pass you by like you were standing still. The best example of not being proactive and listening to the market is IBM. IBM was the leader in almost every phase of data processing technology but they did not listen nor did they react to the market.

Windows based technology monopolizes the industry and IBM's OS/2 and their computers have hardly made any significant impact ever since. IBM did not recognize the trend in technology and the booming requirement for home and business based personal computers to their determent.

I have been asked a hundred times by a Product Manager as to why a product is not good enough to sell in the market. If continual feedback says it does not have the benefits to be competitive, then new features have to be added in order to make it competitive. If a Product Manager can hear this from a customer or reseller, it makes your job of internal selling much easier.

Especially look to simple changes such as name, color, packaging, language and build the product with the capability to be upgraded. By doing this, you enhance the life of the product, and open up new markets with minimal effort and expense.

7. **Can you relate your contingency plan about your cus-tomer's response to your introduction or to actions that your competitor might take?**

Contingency plans should take into consideration:

The loss of key personnel due to any reason. Look to purchase key man insurance. Insurance will not help if the ideas and plans of the individual are not written down but it can ease the burden of lost cash flow until you find someone else to replace them.

Identify potential resources both internally and externally that can fill the shoes of a key person. Are there people at your competitors that are unhappy and would consider a move? Place ads in the paper and interview prospective candidates, keep the resumes for future reference. As you grow, you may need an Operations Manager of CFO. Plan for when you will need those types pf personnel and begin the search months in advance.

Your customer may not be your end user but a channel to market partner that has established channels to take your product to market. How you get to the end user is primary to unlocking the door to your success. Do you go directly with person to person contact, tele market, use bingo cards, sell through home shopping, national chains, manufacturer's representatives, MLM or are you going to OEM, private label or license?

The launch of your product will take different forms depending on the channel to market you use. Three things can happen when you launch your product. No sales, slow sales or widely successful. Some products will ramp up slowly, level off and then drop off completely. Others ramp up like a hockey stick and can trail off just as fast. Still others ramp up like a bell curve and the top of the curve could be weeks, months or years away. The product ramp can't always be forecasted and contingency plans should be in place to manage the ramp. Your Business Plan should reflect the high and the low with marketing supplying the input to support the numbers.

Navigating Points:

Identify potential resources both internally and externally that can fill the shoes of a key person. Are there people at your competitors that are unhappy and would consider a move? Place ads in the paper and interview prospective candidates, keep the resumes for future reference. As you grow, you may need an Operations Manager of CFO. Plan for when you will need those types pf personnel and begin the search months in advance.

8. What are the most important trade-offs that you have had to make in bringing your product this far towards commercialization?

Tradeoffs are made when technology, personnel, parts or raw materials, channels of distribution or an act of God create an unexpected circumstance that causes a delay in a process. This question is asked to remind you that you may not always be able to build the perfect mouse trap. If you cannot release the product as designed, what impacts will various tradeoffs have on the acceptance of the product in the market?

The major item that causes most tradeoffs is not always the lack of funding but over running your budget for product development. What usually happens is what you read about in the papers and internet articles - cost over runs. Cost over runs do not occur just in government or sports projects. They occur every day in every business and thus you have to make tradeoffs. Can I substitute this for that, can this person do this instead of that, can I cross train personnel to eliminate hiring additional staff? These are tradeoffs that you will have to deal with when you begin the development process.

The impact of not having sufficient funding to continually change your product before release is what the entrepreneurial spirit is all about. You need to adhere to a plan of development in order to create a level of continuity and saneness in your personnel. Nothing is worse on a staff than continually changing the specifications on a product. The ripple effect goes through every department and everyone is delayed; this is the root of most cost over runs. You need to be resourceful. Sometimes you have to juggle payables, time the truth, use smoke and mirrors, use show and tell designs instead of the real product but remember that you must never lie.

The Experts Speak Out...

Business opportunities are like buses: there's always another one coming.

– Richard Branson

Leadership is doing what is right when no one is watching.

– George Van Valkenburg

There is no royal, flower-strewn path to success. And if there is, I have not found it. For if I have accomplished anything in life, it is because I have been willing to work hard.

—C.J. Walker

Business is more exciting than any game.

– Lord Beaverbrook

9. **What major problems will you have to overcome in order to get your product successfully commercialized?**

There are eight areas that I have determined that are required to commercialize your product:

• Adequate funding - Without it, your idea will always be an idea and unless you take your idea to another company or sell the rights, you will be just another employee.

• Personnel that have the expertise in the areas necessary to bring your product to market and that can work as a team.

• Mature technology -There are exceptions but without it, you have to make educated guesses on what the technology is supposed to accomplish. It is very time consuming to test and validate technology claims not including the stringent regulatory issues the government establishes.

• Competition can close the Window of Opportunity faster than anything so be aware of the Window of Opportunity and be ready to counter if competition rears its ugly head.

• Market awareness - What methodologies will you use to promote your product?

• What channel to market makes the most sense to deliver your product to the customer? This is a parallel activity with development and if not in place can impact your Business Plan and cause you to lose confidence with your investors and employees.

• Do you have manufacturing capability? If you do not have it internally, will your external sources reduce your cost as your volume decreases? If you go off shore, does the manufacturer meet the quality required for your product and market?

• Can you provide the support and warranty requirements for your product?

Navigating Points:

The impact of not having sufficient funding to continually change your product before release is what the entrepreneurial spirit is all about. You need to adhere to a plan of development in order to create a level of continuity and saneness in your personnel. Nothing is worse on a staff than continually changing the specifications on a product. The ripple effect goes through every department and everyone is delayed; this is the root of most cost over runs. You need to be resourceful. Sometimes you have to juggle payables, time the truth, use smoke and mirrors, use show and tell designs instead of the real product but remember that you must never lie.

10. **Are the organizations that would have to act quickly to im -plement one of your contingency plans bought into your program?**

A difference has to be made between a startup compa -ny and an established company that has experience bringing new products to the market. The startup makes more decisions based on theory than an established compa -ny because it may be the first experience performing a spe -cific task. The established company usually has policies and procedures for most tasks and has experience to base development decisions on. If a contingency plan has to be implemented, the marketing and sales organizations should not be blindsided but instead be made aware of a change or delay so that they can inform their pro - spects or channel to market resellers assuredly.

Some thoughts on what should be in place if the unexpected should occur.

A. Access to outside technology and personnel if your in house capability suddenly went away

B. Access to additional capital

C. Alternate channel to market methodologies

D. Internal resources that are cross trained in the event of an emergency

E. Alternate sources to parts

F. Additional capability for manufacturing

G. A human resources function that is proactive

H. Options for additional space

11. **Will there be resources available to act on the contingency plan?**

Your contingency plan might be to have outside manufacturers available to handle the unex-pected demand. Try to find like manufacturers that are famil-iar with your manufacturing process for this. This will ena-ble you to maintain the same high quality standards. You may want to farm out pieces of the manufacturing process such as assembly, painting, testing or packaging. Usually you require testing standards be in place that will surpass your standards as demanded by your customers or you could be liable.

Why ask the question if you do not expect to have the resources to act on the contingency plan? A contingency plan could be positive if growth exceeds forecasts. Possible scenarios are:

Your contingency plan might be to have outside manufacturers available to handle the unexpected demand. Try to find like manufacturers that are familiar with your manufacturing process for this. This will enable you to maintain the same high quality standards. You may want to farm out pieces of the manufacturing process such as assembly, painting, testing or packaging. Usually you require testing standards be in place that will surpass your standards as demanded by your customers or you could be liable.

Parts availability is key in order to meet increased demands. Try to use industry standard parts that are available from multiple sources. Locking yourself into a sole source could be dangerous if you are a customer that they deem expendable. This means that your product is expendable from the viewpoint that if a customer orders 10 times your order and you do not have stipulated in your contract that you will receive your parts when ordered, you may get pushed to the back of the line and delays could force you to lay off personnel and greatly distress your sales people, your channels and the end user that was promised the product from their supplier.

Lines of credit or ready cash is important to meet the need of unexpected demands. Many times your receivables are 30-90 days out depending on how you structure your receivables. In any case, you need to make sure that you have resources of
cash to meet unexpected demand for parts and labor.

Delays are encountered due to re-engineering. Your business plan only allocates so many dollars for engineering and development, so you must ask yourself, where do I go to get additional dollars? First, think about delaying the outlay of moneys for parts to manufacture. You usually have to commit to large quantities in order to get the best price. Hold back for as long as possible or negotiate new terms. Don't bring in the equipment; look to outsource what you can. Outside resources may cost more

initially, but you don't have to pay benefits and you don't get emotionally attached when you have to release them or their contract runs out.

If you are a private company with outside investors, most have invested knowing that there might be this possibility. You can usually get more cash at a higher premium which will dilute your equity position, but you be the judge. If delays are minor and orders are in hand, it makes it easier to get the required cash to complete the project.

Your delay allowed for the competition to enter the market and you have no competitive advantage for entering the market. What alternatives do I have?

Lowering your price is the easiest thing to do but this may be perceived as a weakness in your company. Have a campaign to offset the delay such as:

• Initial discount of X percent for all orders greater than X for X time.

• Press releases announcing the product with availability and benefits.

• Personal visits to key channels as an added launch idea.

Your delay used all of your cash and your credit is nil and your product is ready. You have identified potential competitors or distributors that showed an interest in your product that could possible pick up on the operation to minimize your loss. Your equity position is greatly minimized but you may have a job and most of your key people will stay employed.

Chapter 9
Products Sensitivity to Change

Will your product survive the rigors of strong competition, a downturn in the economy, new technology or increased costs to manufacture? If you can grasp where your product or company is the most sensitive, you can minimize the change and capitalize on your strength in the market. The next series of questions are designed to help you be proactive in being prepared for the unexpected.

1. **What are the major factors that would make you most vulnerable, such as technology, component parts, competition and economy?**
   Not necessarily in this order but these are some of the things I would consider when examining my "Product's Sensitivity To Change".
   Some of the types of questions I would ask myself are:
   - What is my product?
   - Is it labor intensive and what type of labor is required?
   - Is it less expensive blue collar or high tech white collar labor that is required or a combination of both?
   - Can I afford to decentralize my operation and relocate manufacturing to less expensive labor or off shore and keep my development, sales and marketing in a high tech labor corridor?
   - Are component parts available from multiple sources or do I have to depend on a single source for my component parts?
   - Is technology emerging that will make my product obsolete or at the least, dilute my market share?
   - Is my Window of Opportunity closing due to competitors entering the market with like products?
   - Does my competition offer a like product less expensively?
   - Can my product be copied overseas and, if so, what would

Navigating Points:

Delays are encountered due to re-engineering. Your business plan only allocates so many dollars for engineering and development, so you must ask yourself, where do I go to get additional dollars? First, think about delaying the outlay of moneys for parts to manufacture. You usually have to commit to large quantities in order to get the best price. Hold back for as long as possible or negotiate new terms.

be the ramifications?

- Are my customers loyal to the product or to the company?
- If the economy takes a down turn can I survive?
- What happens if my volume increases beyond my expectations? Am I prepared to meet the demand?
- What dictates the needs of my target market relative to the use of my product?
- Is my product a stand-alone, or does it work in conjunction with another piece of equipment?
- If it works with another piece of equipment, what is my plan to stay compatible?
- What affects will patents and copyrights not being approved in a timely manner, infringement and lawyers debating over who has what rights have?

2. **What happens to your sources of competitive advantage if you vary your assumptions about component parts?**
    This question is only pertinent if your product is manu-factured. Most companies play what-if games based on projected sales and then project the sales into end items made up of component parts or assemblies which ultimately make the end item.

    Your market research will give you various scenarios of sales projections. Based on these projections, engineering and purchasing will configure the bill of material and through talking with various parts suppliers, get estimates on various quantities. The higher the quantity the less the cost of the part and ultimately by ordering in quantity, you can lower your cost of goods. If you purchase in large quantities, you could conceivably offer the product to distribution and the end user at a lesser price. A lower price could mean greater volume, and the greater volume could give you faster name recognition and positioning in the market and with your parts suppliers.

A difference has to be made between a startup company and an established company that has experience bringing new products to the market. The startup makes more decisions based on theory than an established company because it may be the first experience performing a specific task. The established company usually has policies and procedures for most tasks and has experience to base development decisions on. If a contingency plan has to be implemented, the marketing and sales organizations should not be blindsided but instead be made aware of a change or delay so that they can inform their prospects or channel to market resellers assuredly.

**3.	What factors have the greatest potential financial im pact on the new product?**

Slow development using up available cash and having to dilute the company in order to raise additional funds is probably the area where you would be most vulnerable. You wouldn't have raised the financing if you didn't have a need with sales channels and end us-ers com   mitted to delivery in a timely manner. When you delay   the delivery and you are new in the market, the distributors tend to back off and not want to be the first to sell your product. This can change if you are so totally revolutionary or have a fad product that is in high demand.

A downturn in the economy can affect the demand of luxury items but, conversely, can help some markets by allowing them to retool or reposition themselves with new technology. If your product can save money by reducing overhead or optimizing some function, your product could remain in demand in a down economy.

An act of God such an earthquake, flood or other disaster can create a tremendous financial impact and you should be prepared with sufficient insurance. Key individuals leaving can also greatly impact the financial success of your product and you can be covered to some extent with Key Man insurance.

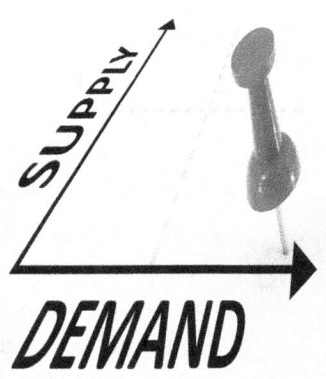

Sole sourcing parts can be a disaster. An example of this was memory chips a few years ago. A few of the major manufacturers purchased all of the chips that manu-facturing could make and only a few were available to the smaller manufacturer that use the chips in their equip-ment. They experienced delays, many went out of busi-ness and others had to find new methods to replace the chips.

The chips also increased in price which increased the cost of goods since supply couldn't keep up with the demand. Since many companies had already committed pricing to their distributors, many tried to live up to their commitment and lost money hoping that the price would go down so that a profit could be made when the chip shortage subsided. Have multiple sources for parts and try to stay away from sole source parts.

Competition blindsiding you with a like product that is established nationally and that can afford to buy the market can minimize all of your effort in advertising. This is something that has happened and you have little recourse but to be reactive and salvage what you can.

4.   **How will you monitor these factors so that you will have enough time to manage them if they signal trouble?**
There are a number of factors to consider such as:
- Careful planning is important so as not to have sole source parts; this eliminates one factor.
- Positioning yourself with back up or cross over talent in case of a key individual leaving for some reason.
- Have sources of cash so that if you are late in development you can make up for the shortfall by not having sales.
- Plan for back up manufacturing with a contract house in case your facility is destroyed for some reason.
- Try to build your product to allow for a drastic margin drop and still be profitable in case of a major competitor trying to buy the market.
- Identify potential competitors that would be in a position to purchase your company if all else fails.

5.   **What data will you need on the new products' performance in order to make good decisions when the time comes?**
Reliability figures in to show the meantime be-

The Experts Speak Out...

Nobody talks about entrepreneurship as survival, but that's exactly what it is and what nurtures creative thinking. Running that first shop taught me business is not financial science; it's about trading: buying and selling.

—*Anita Roddick*

Your most unhappy customers are your greatest source of learning.

— *Bill Gates*

Success is often achieved by those who don't know that failure is inevitable.

— *Coco Chanel*

tween failures. Times are calculated in a number of methods depending on the product. If you have a product that is composed of component parts that are assembled and fastened in your housing, you need to find out from your component suppliers what the meantime between failures is in your type of environment. If you are manufacturing a box that will have human interaction using keys or buttons, you need to build jigs to press the keys or buttons to simulate human interaction over a period of years.

You also need to devise drop tests, heat and cold operating environmental tests, vibration tests, breakage and packaging. If your product has electronics, you will need to have government regulatory tests to comply with and if you are shipping internationally, you will need stamps of approval from the countries that you are selling into.

If you are developing a food product, you will need FDA approval and to meet packaging requirements as well as the contents and directions for use.

If the product is a toy, there are numerous tests that have be done relative to danger from use, breakage, materials used and what age group the product is targeted towards. You will need the patents, engineering drawings, documentation and other documentation that was used to engineer and manufacture the product.

If you have sales channels in place and end users, you will need to have contracts available, end user testimonials, plans on how you will advertise, documentation as to what your mission statement is as well as your product theme.

Navigating Points:

Reliability figures in to show the meantime between failures. Times are calculated in a number of methods depending on the product. If you have a product that is composed of component parts that are assembled and fastened in your housing, you need to find out from your component suppliers what the meantime between failures is in your type of environment. If you are manufacturing a box that will have human interaction using keys or buttons, you need to build jigs to press the keys or buttons to simulate human interaction over a period of years.

You will need to have pricing documents for the development time and dollars as well as the Business Plan and P & L to show where the expenditures are going.

If the unexpected happens, you will need to be prepared to take the next step if you have the documentation that supports the investment, development and sale of the product.

6. **What is the economic structure of the industry in which you are planning to compete such as level of profitabil -ity, rate of new technology introduction, rate of growth, and typical amount of investment in new products?**
A few probing questions to ask yourself about the economic structure on the industry are:
- Is the industry segment enamored with new technology requiring highly educated and skilled personnel with sophisticated manufacturing capabilities?
- Is the market saturated with competition that would make it difficult to gain any degree of market share?
- What is the cost to gear up your operation with the resources necessary to compete in this segment?
- Is your product dependent on other technologies success in order for you to be successful?
- Is the industry so new and technology so expensive that companies are reluctant to purchase for fear of placing their company in jeopardy due to an unforeseen problem?
- Is the rate of growth so great that everyone will be there and reduce margins to the break-even point or can you be different enough to carve out a special niche that will be margin protected?
- Does the industry segment require inexpensive labor and manufacturing capability of immense capacity in order to produce a product that would be competitive?
- Does the industry require great amounts of continued re-

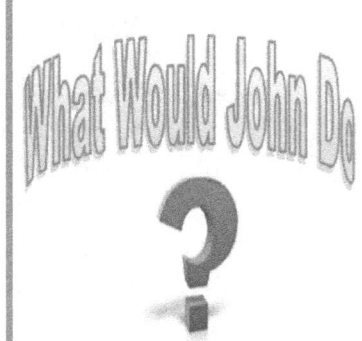

Write down the top 10-15 economic indicators that could impact the structure of your industry. Use a piece of graph paper or an Excel spreadsheet. Apply a weight to your responses from 1-10 with 10 being the best and see how you stack up against where you want to or should be relative to your growth. If your response is from 1 -6 take a closer look and try to determine if the impact is company threatening and what you can do to ward off any negative impact.

Conversely, if the impact is for continued or exploding growth, what can you do to be proactive and take advantage or reposition your company to take advantage of its growth curve? If the economy is booming, fashion, hospitality and luxury items will sell well. As soon as the economy takes a turn down, these industries usually drop off.

search and development (R& D) to stay competitive?
- Should we look to be a development arm and search out alliances or partners to sell the products because of volume sales to be successful?

7. **How do you expect the economic structure of the indus try to evolve?**

Write down the top 10-15 economic indicators that could impact the structure of your industry. Use a piece of graph paper or an Excel spreadsheet. Apply a weight to your responses from 1-10 with 10 being the best and see how you stack up against where you want to or should be relative to your growth. If your response is   from 1 -6 take a closer look and try to determine if the impact is company threatening and what you can do to   ward off any negative impact.

Conversely, if the impact is for continued or exploding growth, what can you do to be proactive and take advantage or reposition your company to take advantage of its growth curve? If the economy is booming, fashion, hospitality and luxury items will sell well. As soon as the economy takes a turn down, these industries usually drop off.

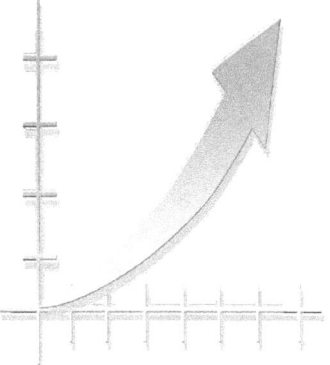

Items that compliment life or are fun and make life better do well in a booming economy. Products that expand on an industries' strengths such as a Microsoft or Macintosh with new applications also do well. Technology that the phone companies offer through their network using ISDN type products, cellular, or other voice, video and fax capabilities also do well.

Products that care for the elderly or baby boomers or watch out for the environment do well in almost any economy. New products that reduce the drain on natural resources also do well in any economy. Look at your industry, check the economic indicators and position yourself to take advantage of the trend that is developing for your market segment.

8. **Are there any potential for significant shifts in the eco-nomic structure of current factors?**

You do not bet the farm on potential as one in the hand is as good as two in the bush, but you do need to be ready to capitalize on a significant change in the economic structure and act accordingly.

Factors that have potential to cause a major shift in the economic structure are:
- Inflation
- Interest fluctuations
- Stock Market
- Cold War
- War
- Natural Disaster
- Change in political structure
- Booming economy
- New technology/cures
- NAFTA type agreements
- Recession

9. **If you see shifts, what will cause the shift and what oppor-tunities or threats will be created?**

Some shifts are more visible than others and proactive event scan occur within your company to limit your exposure or allow you to take advantage of the opportunity. Some of the shifts that are more predictable and that can be acted on pro-actively are:

The competitor to be feared is one who never bothers about you at all, but goes on making his own business better all the time.

– Henry Ford

I have known not a few men who, after reaching the summits of business success, found themselves miserable on attaining retirement age. They were so exclusively engrossed in their day to day affairs that they had no time for friend making.

– B.C. Forbes

National Elections

Whenever a new political party assumes power, government funded agencies either flourish, continue status quo or get less or no continued funding. If you are a company that exists on government funding, I would position myself with outside funding so as to continue if the political process discontinues my funding.

NAFTA

NAFTA is a good example of how a trade agreement affects some industries positively and negatively on others. Jobs that are marginal in the United States with minimum, or a bit above minimum wage, were once moved to Mexico and caused many persons to go on welfare, unemployment or go jobless because the labor pool in Mexico was greater. The impact to these workers at minimum wage was lost jobs and without transferable skills or the ability to relocate to an area with new similar jobs they increased the poverty rolls.

In Mexico, the minimum wage law is not in effect and the labor is cut in half making the transfer to Mexican workers much more lucrative. NAFTA in many instances proved worthwhile where there were companies that were going to close if they could not get labor relief. Mexico provided both unskilled and skilled labor to aid in the production of goods that helped keep many United States companies from closing their doors and kept people employed instead of losing all the jobs.

Technology/Cures

Technology brings new jobs and disposes of current jobs. If you are a company that is transferring to new technology in order to stay competitive, you have the threat of not keeping up with your competitors and of keeping your work force trained to meet the new demands that technology has created.

Navigating Points:

NAFTA is a good example of how a trade agreement affects some industries positively and negatively on others. Jobs that are marginal in the United States with minimum, or a bit above minimum wage, were once moved to Mexico and caused many persons to go on welfare, unemployment or go jobless because the labor pool in Mexico was greater. The impact to these workers at minimum wage was lost jobs and without transferable skills or the ability to relocate to an area with new similar jobs they increased the poverty rolls.

Cures for diseases and for prolonging life create new demands for health care and impose burdens on social security and Medicare. The opportunities are to provide services for its growing demographic group of society. The burden is created and needs to be shouldered by the government to reduce spending and keep the moneys that go in to Social Security there to provide for the longer life that new cures provide.

Inflation

Inflation reduces the value of the dollar and people tend not to buy luxury items or any expensive items such as houses or automobiles. The impact is huge on jobs and spending. It is during these times that the smart companies reposition themselves for the change in inflation and take advantage when the economy changes for the positive. Companies tend to down size, bring in new equipment, lower inventory, look to new markets and generally try to streamline the operation to minimize overhead and maximize what they do best.

Natural disasters and war

This is not very pleasant to contemplate but is a very real possibility. Economies usually boom because of the demand on specific products during these incidences. The natural disasters in the United States are great for the building trades. War is great for defense contractors and companies that equip the armed forces with clothes and food. Disasters and war force companies into new technologies which translate into new industries and help the peacetime process when these acts are over.

10.   **Are there any defensive or proactive responses**

that you could make to protect yourself?

There are considerable responses that one can make in response to a shift in the economic position of the United States or of specific countries. Take advantage of new technology, down size, realign yourself with new channel to market partners, merge or position to be taken over. The type of response is dependent on your industry and the economic position of the market.

11.   **What is the projected impact on your ability to differentiate and sustain your competitive advantage?**

If, is the biggest little word in the English dictionary. The number of fortunes that are won or lost because of this little word are beyond count. I personally have been involved in so many situations throughout my life, and not just in business, where if this would have occurred or not occurred such as life and death, friendships, sports accomplishments and other acts things could have been better or worse. All that we can do is to be aware of the conditions that could impact our business or personal life and have a proactive plan and hope the reactive plan will be good enough to pull you through the situation that you have been placed in.

In business, it has been my experience that controls on the finances are most important to your startup or continued success. You may not like the controls but each department head should be cognizance of how budgets are prepared, why they need to be justified and what steps you have to go through in order to track them. You need to be a person with an overall vision of the industry. Where is it heading through technology, what the growth potential is, how do we differentiate, how big a piece of the pie can we expect to have, should we consider alliances and you need the partners to achieve your goals.

In order to maintain your competitive advantage, you need to understand your position in the industry and have visionaries' that are realists but have enough of an entrepreneurial spirit to take a calculated risk when the opportunity affords itself.

Chapter 10
Product Scenarios

"What if" scenarios measure the impact of economic and competitive condition, product delays and sales ramp on your entry into the market. You should examine the more and less factors as they relate to your bottom line profitability and ascertain how soon to expect revenue contribution from the development of your product. Using Excel or a manual spreadsheet, estimate the one time and the monthly recurring expenses as well as the capital expenses for specific time periods. Time periods are usually in one quarter increments and cover one to three year time spans. Against the projected expenses, you will estimate the sales from letters of intent, current contracts and fudge factors both positive and negative. Having a combination of "what if" scenarios will help you plan for the best and worst case scenarios.

The best case "what if" scenarios are impact to sales. If sales beyond your wildest dreams occur and you can't meet the demand this can cause major problems. A note of warning - if you project maximum sales and your investors see the forecasts, they will only gauge your performance from the highest projections and nothing less will be acceptable. Be careful who you show the "what if "scenarios to. Your worst case scenario should be profitable and your sales could be one of four scenarios, flat, bell curve, hockey stick or in a downward spiral. You need to be able to plan for all four scenarios.

Let's examine a few of the possibilities and make some assumptions. A best case scenario would be to increase pro-

The best case "what if" scenarios are impact to sales. If sales beyond your wildest dreams occur and you can't meet the demand this can cause major problems. A note of warning - if you project maximum sales and your investors see the forecasts, they will only gauge your performance from the highest projections and nothing less will be acceptable. Be careful who you show the "what if "scenarios to. Your worst case scenario should be profitable and your sales could be one of four scenarios, flat, bell curve, hockey stick or in a downward spiral. You need to be able to plan for all four scenarios.

duction and to have planned for outside manufacturing to take the overload, add other shifts if you manufacture in-house or have a plan in place with your outside manufacturer to increase the ramp if sales exceed the expectations. The downside to unexpected success is where you did not plan and have to be reactive instead of proactive.

In many instances, your supplier may not have the parts or raw materials to ship you, they may have to manufacturer them and to get the product to you faster there could, and probably will, be a premium. The lead time could cause you a delay. Success is the kind of opportunity you want to deal with but, have a plan in place otherwise you will have immense frustration. With frustration comes poor logic and decision making so plan, plan and plan some more.

The downside scenarios are related to delays caused by every imaginable condition that could affect the release of the product to sales; here are a few:

- Plan for regulatory approval delays where you have to reschedule testing due to a condition not being met under the guidelines for approval.
- Engineering delays caused by technology not working as specified or engineers leaving or not available for hire to complete the task.
- Sales forecasts not reliable due to delays, competition, economic conditions changing or channels taking too long to test and get trained on your product.
- Parts shortages on your sole sourced parts and your supplier sold your demand to another because you were over the deadline to order or pay for the parts.

There are literally hundreds of reasons why you can be late delivering your product to the market and you should have a plan for the worst and best case scenarios and be able to be proactive for something in between.

The following questions are designed to help you be proactive in your thought processes related to various product scenarios that could have a potential impact on your entry into the market.

1.   **What is your most likely case scenario in terms of how you expect your product to perform in terms of revenue, market penetration, customer satisfaction, units by distribution channel and repeat business?**

This scenario should be your business plan with best and worst case scenarios. When you finalize your business plan, you will probably have a good handle on engineering and manufacturing with associated costs for personnel, facility, parts, raw materials, consulting, marketing, capital equipment, support and miscellaneous overhead. You should have a good idea from your marketing efforts on where the competition is positioned relative to your product and you should have made a choice of how you are going to sell your product. Forecasting sales ramps is a delicate science with much room for error especially if you are offering a new product.

If you are telemarketing your product through a call center, there are formulas that can tell you that if you make 1,000 calls to a specific target market with specific demographics, you will have 50 inquiries and 18 sales. (on average) If your cost of sales can justify a telemarketing effort of

1,000 calls and sell 18 units profitably, this is a good scenario with minimal fluctuations. If you have to hire a direct sales force, what is the ramp time for your sales team and what experience level do they need, what kind of training and what sales tools are required for them to be successful? If you are going direct, what type of quota, incentive, salary, territory and customer mix are your targeting?

If you are going through distribution, who are the channels, who do the channels represent now and are they willing to spend the time to ramp up your product? If the channel sales people has 1 or 10,000 products to sell, how are they compensated? If the channel sales person is not compensated to sell your product but it is just in the catalog, you will be totally wasting your time and your projections will be complete failures; you will wish you were never in the business.

Just because a major distribution agrees to sell your product, if the sales people are on a quota and they do not have sufficient incentive to sell your product, you will languish in frustration because the sales person will sell what makes their quota. You need to understand the motivation of the sale person and build in adequate incentives and compensation to get your products attention with the sales force.

Understand your channel, what motivates them, what synergy's exist and implement a program that gives the channel an incentive to sell your product; make the numbers a part of your projected business plan. Chan-

Navigating Points:

In many instances, your supplier may not have the parts or raw materials to ship you, they may have to manufacturer them and to get the product to you faster there could, and probably will, be a premium. The lead time could cause you a delay. Success is the kind of opportunity you want to deal with but, have a plan in place otherwise you will have immense frustration. With frustration comes poor logic and decision making so plan, plan and plan some more.

nels can be fickle and the incumbent vendor can mount a campaign to undercut you or neutralize your product in the channel by offering better incentives and promising the world. Even if you do not perceive your product as being competitive with another, you are taking valuable sales time away from the incumbent vendor. Since you are trying to get equal time, you are going to have to be more innovative with your approach until you establish a track record for performance and customer need.

Marketing and channel management are essential to your success if you are attempting to sell through distribution.

2.   **What is your estimate of expenses on the profit and loss for the most probable performance of the new product?**

This is the most probable scenario for your product after you have completed your market studies. You should have determined all of the development, marketing, manufacturing, and sales costs for specific scenarios and the one that makes the most sense is the most probable.

Keep in mind, alternative methods of distribution. Depending on your Window of Opportunity, you may have to make a decision to reduce your margin and sell through distribution instead of direct. If you need to make a big splash and you are in a competitive market, co-op advertising may offer increases beyond your initial projections. Keep a finger on the pulse of the economic

If there is such a thing as good leadership, it is to give a good example.

— Ingvar Kamprad

Sometimes when you innovate, you make mistakes. It is best to admit them quickly and get on with improving your other innovations.

— Steve Jobs

You've got to say, I think that if I keep working at this and want it badly enough, I can have it. It's called perseverance.

— Lee Iacocca

conditions and be able to react pro-actively instead of re-activity.

3.   **What investments are required to make the most likely case scenario happen?**

Relying on the intelligence of your marketing and having adequate funding to support the efforts depicted in your business plan are necessary. Adequate funding is not bootstrapping the project although the majority of projects are initially begun through this method. Boot strapping can work if you are trying to develop a concept or prove a theory, this will gain the needed support and ultimate funding or purchase of your idea.

The products that I have been involved with were high tech related and the greatest weakness that I discovered was not hiring qualified and experienced engineering personnel. Personnel were hired on the assumption that they understood a technology and by the time we discovered that they were learning on the job, the project was behind schedule six months and we had just made an investment in their learning curve.

Examine the scope of the development effort and ensure that you have key people that understand the application of the technology, project management, parts procurement, finance, marketing, sales and support. If you have experienced people, it is key to have each take ownership of their part of the effort. This can be ac-

Navigating Points:

In business, it has been my experience that controls on the finances are most important to your startup or continued success. You may not like the controls but each department head should be cognizance of how budgets are prepared, why they need to be justified and what steps you have to go through in order to track them.

You need to be a person with an overall vision of the industry. Where is it heading through technology, what the growth potential is, how do we differentiate, how big a piece of the pie can we expect to have, should we consider alliances and you need the partners to achieve your goals.

complished by discussing the market need, widow of opportunity and time to bring the product to market.

Empower your people by having each person take ownership and responsibility for their part providing the resources required to make it happen in the agreed time frames. Each manager should agree with the time and resources to make their part of the project successful. After agreement, plot each milestone on a project management reporting grid or software and schedule daily, weekly or as required have meetings to discuss the status and progress of the development effort.

When bottlenecks are apparent, you will be able to identify them easily and hopefully correct the situation by a reallocation of effort, which could be personnel, equipment or budget.

4. How much longer will it take to break even in your worst case scenario as opposed to your best case scenario?

The bottom line is when development funds can no longer support the company and revenue is required to offset the startup capital things can get tough. Your worst case scenario could be caused by various conditions.

Some of the scenarios that could cause a worse case are:
• Product entry is delayed due to technology, regulatory issues, testing, parts availability, personnel, and natural disaster or economic down turn.
• Competition has entered the market and you have to reduce

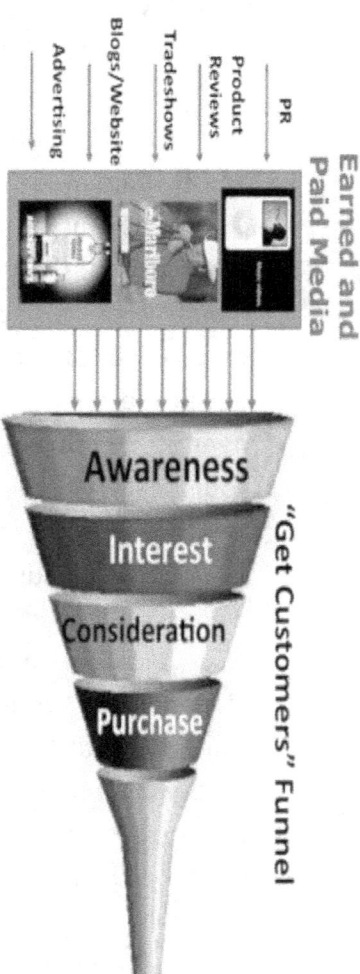

your price in order to maintain volume.

- Your channels did not come on line as projected and you have to hire direct sales people to supplement the sales ramp.

5. **What are the major assumptions that drive the forecasts in each scenario?**

This is your decision regarding the major assumptions that will drive the forecasts for each scenario.

Examples of major assumptions are:
- Product delivery is on time
- Sales channel ramp is timely
- Pricing is consistent with the forecast
- Product yield is in line with projection. If your product is manufactured, the yield is categorized as the number of products that come off the assembly line without defect and that do not require rework to make the product salable.
- Marketing was accurate in depicting the requirement
- Costs are consistent with the Business Plan

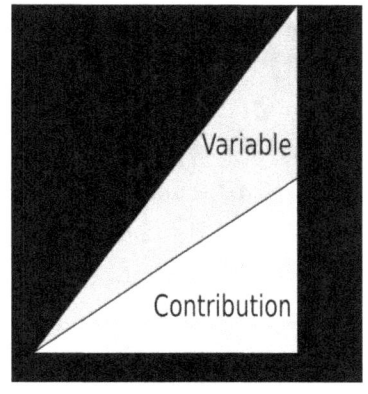

6. **What are your major assumptions about your cost structure? Address both variable and fixed expense as -sumptions, investment size, alternatives and time frames.**

Fixed costs can be categorized as capital equipment purchases such as machinery, facility, personnel and parts. You can budget these costs over a period of years with assumptions for inflation, building and equipment depreciation and parts based on purchase quantity. You can also forecast increases in overhead based on the growth of your company which is usually tied to sales.

Depending on the usage projected for your capital equipment, you may be able to lease or rent out the use of the equipment to offset some or all of the expense.

Variable costs can be material related depending on quantity and demand at the time. If you can forecast requirements for a one to three year time and negotiate a contract with your suppliers, you can ensure that your cost of goods will be stable for a greater period of time than if you can only purchase for the short term. I have seen and heard of small companies getting moved to the back of the line by some suppliers if quantities dropped below certain quantities or dollar value.

You may be the first in line and first to get your product to the market but when a major competitor starts using the part or material and begins purchasing in large quantities, you may get a price increase, delay in delivery or be charged a premium for the product due to overtime costs to manufacture your component or raw material.

Other variable costs to consider are the continuing marketing and sales costs. Most new companies underestimate the cost of marketing, advertising and promotion as well as the sales cost. Look at "what if" scenarios to increase advertising if leads are not what you expected. What if your channel or channels do not ramp up as ex-

Fixed costs can be categorized as capital equipment purchases such as machinery, facility, personnel and parts. You can budget these costs over a period of years with assumptions for inflation, building and equipment depreciation and parts based on purchase quantity. You can also forecast increases in overhead based on the growth of your company which is usually tied to sales.

Depending on the usage projected for your capital equipment, you may be able to lease or rent out the use of the equipment to offset some or all of the expense.

pected, do you add direct sales or look to other avenues of sales distribution.   Did you consider the co-op advertising that is required by outside channels, what about offsite training? Can your margins support those costs or will you have to look at revising your margin structure.

Support and warranty are often overlooked and can be two to ten times what you anticipated. How would you handle this situation? Would you use 900 calls, warranty contract, exchange of product, or hire additional support?

7.   What are the major, go/no go decision points between scenarios?

Your product development plan should depict the major milestones or pre-requisite events that need to occur before another can begin or be completed. Major decision points could start at the market requirement being steady or increasing.

Development of the prototype, bringing development costs in line per your business plan, completion of regulatory and customer testing, having agreements in place with major distribution or other means of selling your product, funding for each phase of development, parts and material availability, a theme and mission statement are all needed and are major decision points. All these decision points could mean a go or no go for continuation of the development and deployment of your product.

8.   Can you build a simple effective format to track if you are on

Navigating Points:

Absolutely essential to the success of any project is a tracking mechanism for measuring performance and keeping track of budgets. Depending on the size of your company and the breadth of your product, you may appoint a Product Manager to manage all aspects of the development process. This person should be empowered to make everyone accountable for non-performance and have to give mandatory status updates at required agreed to intervals. The Product Manager can, and should, update the project status and recommend alternative procedures or resources if the project starts to miss agreed to milestones.

target with your assumptions and forecast?

Absolutely essential to the success of any project is a tracking mechanism for measuring performance and keeping track of budgets. Depending on the size of your company and the breadth of your product, you may appoint a Product Manager to manage all aspects of the development process. This person should be empowered to make everyone accountable for non-performance and have to give mandatory status updates at required agreed to intervals. The Product Manager can, and should, update the project status and recommend alternative procedures or resources if the project starts to miss agreed to mile stones.

In most startup companies, a Project Manager is appointed and all department managers, finance, operations, sales, marketing and other executives are in attendance at every meeting along the way.

9. **Where can you get the data to answer or update the questions on our new products performance in the marketplace?**

Several methods can serve as ways to get answers as to your products performance in the marketplace. Where the market is dictates where you will get your answers on your products performance.

If you are developing a fad product, a simple toy or single level build product, you are probably selling your product through a retail chain or telemarketing. If you demonstrate your product at trade shows, or at the retail store, you can get direct feedback and draw your own conclusions. If your data is through direct mail, magazine ads or call centers/telemarketing, you can analyze the return on investment by the number of inquiries and sales made through each medium and again act accordingly.

If you piggy back on another product and are depend ent on an imbedded base or new sale in order to sell your product, you will be dependent on the base line product sales person for feedback on your products' performance. If you have an extended ramp caused by outside distribution having to get trained and promote and sell your product, you should have, in your launch plan, a method of buddy calls with your distribution partners to ensure that the benefits are being conveyed. You can get direct feedback from the end user and salesperson in this way. This also serves as a training tool and commitment to sell your product, all things being equal.

10. **What are your main sources of data needed in order to update your assumptions?**

If marketing assumptions are to be updated, your sources would be trade journals that advertise your type of product, government agencies that track market trends, consultants, competitors annual reports, product literature, trade shows, association tracking reports for your type of product, distributors and ultimate end users.

Sales figures would come from your sales sources. If you sell direct or use regional sales personnel, you should expect monthly reports on sales forecasts from their customers and prospects. Your sales order entry function should be able to track and analyze trends by customer, market, time of year, channel and product in order to update sales assumptions. Many channels send sales reports to their suppliers by region and customer.

Chapter 11
Growth Objectives

Growth Objectives with adequate research allows you to forecast what you can expect in return for your product development and execution of a well thought out marketing and sales execution strategy. If you have determined a plan through the New Product Assessment Matrix or other market assessment methodologies and you have universal agreement on a product direction, you are ready to begin the assessment of your products Growth Objectives.

Growth Objectives are questions that stimulate the thought processes associated with the immediate, short and long term potential revenue and markets that you currently believe are, or could be, in need of your product. Can your product be enhanced by making it smaller, bigger, replacing or adding parts, changing color, giving added value to another products or be purchased as an OEM to another company?

Your business plan should reflect the costs associated with enhancing your base product with time frames and markets. An investor likes to see multiple markets and growth for a product. If you can show growth in a business plan, it is one more hurdle that you will not have to overcome when your business plan is reviewed by potential investors. A solid business plan can be an effective tool in attracting key employees and also influencing potential distributors. Channel marketing and sales partners like to have multiple products from one vendor, especially if they are of quality and in demand. Having multiple products from one manufacturer minimizes the set-up of files and the need to perform the tiresome due diligence associated with bringing on new products for distribution.

I have taken the liberty of editorializing on each of the

Navigating Points:

If you are developing a fad product, a simple toy or single level build product, you are probably selling your product through a retail chain or telemarketing. If you demonstrate your product at trade shows, or at the retail store, you can get direct feedback and draw your own conclusions. If your data is through direct mail, magazine ads or call centers/ telemarketing, you can analyze the return on investment by the number of inquiries and sales made through each medium and again act accordingly.

following questions as food for thought to stimulate your thought processes on how and where your product can be focused to target multiple market opportunities.

1. **What business results are expected from new product de -velopment?**

Business results are the bottom line for any successful venture. Be prepared to present your business case with   facts that can support funding the project. Factored into the Growth Objectives section should be added from the   previous exercises.

2. **When can performance results be expected?**

Project the unexpected scenario and calculate if you have the capacity and capability to deal with the results of the unexpected. In order to project performance, you have to have all of the critical pieces in place to make an objective decision. Agree on an overall project plan by department and function and enter the results into a project management package for internal review. The project management system can be as simple as writing the projected results down by month with the necessary resources and associated expenditures.

I suggest the use of project management software to plot the activities and major milestones of each activity. Review critical milestones at a scheduled weekly or monthly meeting and adjust the objectives as necessary to keep the project on track.

Performance results are not just sales but a recognition   of the over all staff. Successful companies recognize performance in each department. Performance is a chain reaction from the idea, to marketing, fund raising,

Your business plan should reflect the costs associated with enhancing your base product with time frames and markets. An investor likes to see multiple markets and growth for a product. If you can show growth in a business plan, it is one more hurdle that you will not have to overcome when your business plan is reviewed by potential investors. A solid business plan can be an effective tool in attracting key employees and also influencing potential distributors. Channel marketing and sales partners like to have multiple products from one vendor, especially if they are of quality and in demand.

hiring people, developing the product, manufacturing, writing instructions and tutorials if necessary, training, promotion and selling. Each department manager should be responsible for developing a critical path for inclusion into a master project scheduling program to track and report on the status of each department's performance.

A designated Project Manager should be appointed and empowered to schedule and run the meetings and attendance needs to be mandatory. Hard questions will be asked if projected performance criteria are not being met and this is where team work and relying on each other's ability to develop and meet an agreed schedule plan is important. From this meeting you will ascertain who is realistic in their forecast to meet a given schedule and you will be able to be proactive instead of reactive to potential delays.

Objectively, sales performance is projected to the bottom line. Subjectively, other factors outside of your control can alter the sales performance. Sometimes you can release a version of the product that has benefit to a target market as a trial and if that trial is successful, you can produce a product for the larger target market without fear of failing because you have proven a concept. After your product is released to that field, and it does not matter if the product is late, sales better be ready to make it happen. There are a few reasons for unacceptable sales.

The biggest error that you can make as a sales or marketing manager is to project sales based on assumptions from your customer. This is a cliché but I have had many salespeople come back to me and tell me that a name distributor wants to sell our product and they will by X if we could just reduce the price or add this or that functionality. This is not selling but conversely, you are giving away the product and you're fired, as Donald Trump would say.

Why you ask, can't I rely on my customers' forecast? Books are available on the reasons why a forecast can change in the early stages of development and release of a product. Let's examine some of the reasons why a forecast can change if you are relying on a distribution channel for your sales. The domino or trickledown effect for delays can have immense results on performance. Some of the effects could be:

You were late in delivery and the impact resulted in:
•Missed field training opportunities
•Funds allocated to other products
•Your lab testing slot is given to other products because of your delay
•Customers delay the decision to purchase agreed to quantities because of the comfort factor of having missed the first deliver
•Competition tells your customers, "Told you so." about this upstart not being able to make good on the proposed delivery
•Price increased as a result of a shortage of materials or a labor strike and your distribution channel balks at accepting the increase.
•Your customer contact in marketing, sales or contract wants to re-negotiate a section of the contract.
•Key engineers, marketing or sales people left your company and the word spreads to the competition and it is used against you with your customers and prospects.

There a thousand reasons why your performance results will not be accurate, so be proactive in developing fudge factors that will ensure that your performance results will be in line with your forecast. A fudge factor in a development house could be an outside resource to help you

The Experts Speak Out...

Success in business requires training and discipline and hard work. But if you're not frightened by these things, the opportunities are just as great today as they ever were.

— *David Rockefeller*

Well, you know, I was a human being before I became a businessman.

— *George Soros*

Leadership is the art of getting someone else to do something you want done because he wants to do it.

— *Dwight Eisenhower*

meet a schedule if you fall behind for whatever reason. Marketing should have an outside contract house to assist in gathering critical marketing data to support the marketing effort. Sales could be other markets that you are developing, but not forecasted, that come through earlier than expected.

Develop relationships with raw materials, parts suppliers and manufacturers that can quickly step in and fill the need if any of the three aforementioned happen to cause a significant delay.

If possible, make your forecast from your customer or channels input and break it down to a level that meets your minimum performance criteria. Develop fudge factors that will allow you meet your forecast. Work smart and do not be naive in thinking that everyone is accurate in giving you forecasts. Take psychology into account when dealing with other people. What is in it for them, what is their risk to reward, how do you evaluate their forecast?

Remember that everyone wants to be successful and look good in management's eyes. It is your job to interpret the validity in the numbers and ask the tough questions that can throw doubt into the numbers. When doubts appear, ask for alternatives to erase the doubts or find out if the input is filled with fudge factors. Don't be combative but you need to understand where and how the numbers were derived. Perform as much due diligence on the numbers as possible. Can you get letters of intent, early contracts or even positive words from your customers or prospects as to their intentions?

Why wouldn't you believe a forecast if a prospect in good faith presented you with one and swore up and down that it was accurate within ten percent? This is all

Navigating Points:

The biggest error that you can make as a sales or marketing manager is to project sales based on assumptions from your customer. This is a cliché but I have had many salespeople come back to me and tell me that a name distributor wants to sell our product and they will by X if we could just reduce the price or add this or that functionality. This is not selling but conversely, you are giving away the product and you're fired, as Donald Trump would say.

that you will have to go on to make your forecast so be as objective in presenting your forecast as possible. After a period of time a trend will be apparent and your forecast will become much clearer and that will help you be much more accurate in developing and presenting forecast.

If the inventory is not moving, you need to be aware of this and be proactive in understanding why. Develop an open channel of communication with your customer and be creative in helping your customer move the inventory to generate more orders. Your customer will appreciate this effort and be much more lenient if you need a favor or miss a back order.

3. **Is senior management willing to go outside the bounds of your strategy to develop new products?**
Are you willing to partner with synergistic product de-velopers, sell the manufacturing rights for a royalty, or will you work in an OEM environment or private label? If your product strategy was to go it alone and only sell direct, other strategies could help you be more successful and would be outside the bounds of your initial strategy.

4. **Where should you place your product focus?**
Earlier exercises such as the New Product Assessment Matrix and New Product Customer Survey should give you input and help you focus on the direction of where development should focus. If you are already a successful company, your customers and channels will give you product direction.

As technology continues to advance, costs to develop sometimes become less expensive and products that were beyond the realm of reasonableness become reasonable. Technology advances can alter the focus of development

If possible, make your forecast from your customer or channels input and break it down to a level that meets your minimum performance criteria. Develop fudge factors that will allow you meet your forecast. Work smart and do not be naive in thinking that everyone is accurate in giving you forecasts. Take psychology into account when dealing with other people. What is in it for them, what is their risk to reward, how do you evaluate their forecast?

because of reduced costs or potential new attainable markets. You should not drastically re-focus your efforts into directions that your company is not familiar. Do consider alternatives if you are willing to partner with companies that have focus in the new markets that you are considering.

International markets are sometimes more receptive to less technology driven products than western markets so be aware of the possible opportunities for your markets in off shore markets.

5. **What is the relative priority and level of resources available for a new product?**
    If you are a startup, all of your resources are tied up on this product and it is your highest priority. Whether you are a startup or existing company looking to develop a new product, resources could be an issue.

    Level of resources could be an issue if you are dealing in high tech products that require special technical resources or manufacturing capabilities. Ensure that resources are available either on a full-time basis or on a contract basis for the time required to complete the product. Many companies are hiring resources on a contract basis and when the project is complete, they do not have the worry of releasing a person. If special manufacturing or assembly is required, the same is true here, contract to firms that have the resource.

    The most over looked resource for all companies is the resource of sales channel development and management. This is especially true of an entrepreneur that thinks that their product is the greatest thing since sliced bread. They believe that they won't be able to build them fast enough to meet the market demand. This is rarely the case and you should have a good understanding of how you expect to bring your product to market.

There instances where this is true are few and far in-between. Some examples would be the Hula Hoop, Frisbee, and Panty Hose, weight loss, cosmetics, exercise equipment, consumer electronics, fad medicines and fashion. Electronic breakthroughs usually have a small Window of Opportunity and can be quickly copied by off shore firms with cheaper labor and higher capacity manufacturing capabilities. If you perceive that you have a product that has a national market and you have your channel to market in place, be sure to time the advertising to coincide with the release of the product. Timing is everything with a high visibility product. If you cannot hit the market running and gain market share quickly, be assured that someone will copy the product and also move it though national distribution channels.

6. **This question pertains to an existing company and the mo -tives or rationale that a key executive would sponsor new product development.**

This can be analyzed from various viewpoints. If you are a Product Manager for a large company it might be nice to know why the product is being sponsored and receiving the visibility it has. If you are the entrepreneur, you understand the reason for sponsoring and mentoring because you have a vested interest in the ultimate success of the product.

If an executive is sponsoring or championing the product, and you are the designated product lead, it would be nice to know all of the reasons why the product is being sponsored. What does the research say, is it a pet project of the owner, if the company develops the product does it position itself for a takeover or does a key customer desire the product to enhance productivity or open up new distribution channels. It's food for thought.

7. Why do new products fail in your industry?

To answer this question, look at your competitors, talk with consultants and talk to customers that may have products that are no longer supported or under any type of warrantee.

Find out how many companies are in your industry and research how many could gear up to produce and distribute your type of product and in what time frame. Have a disaster plan in place to identify potential competitors that would have a possible interest in purchasing your product if you don't have the resources to complete the development or don't have the resources to take it to market. You may only get pennies on the dollar as you are depicted as road kill waiting for a vulture to pick your bones.

Products fail for a variety of reasons but the main reason for failure is lack of marketing and having a business plan that is bullet proof. No plan is fail safe but if your business plan can stand the scrutiny of bankers and venture capitalists you have a better than even chance of succeeding. I have talked to many venture capitalists and have heard it said that only one in 100 business plans ever make it to the point of funding. If you are a Product Manager in a company chartered with developing the product, the same disciplines should apply as if you were starting from scratch.

If you have a consumer product for a particular age group or if the product has electronics or new age materials, you will have severe regulatory issues to deal with. Getting your product into a lab may take longer than expected and you

Navigating Points:

Products fail for a variety of reasons but the main reason for failure is lack of marketing and having a business plan that is bullet proof. No plan is fail safe but if your business plan can stand the scrutiny of bankers and venture capitalists you have a better than even chance of succeeding. I have talked to many venture capitalists and have heard it said that only one in 100 business plans ever make it to the point of funding. If you are a Product Manager in a company chartered with developing the product, the same disciplines should apply as if you were starting from scratch.

.

probably will not pass the first time through so you will have to contend with scheduling issues that probably were not anticipated. All of this takes time and if you did not plan for this, your cash reserves can become depleted very quickly.

As the reserves are dwindling, and if this is your first product, pressure mounts on the development team. Prospects that have expected to have the product in hand for testing and resale are delayed and sales are under greater pressure to increase the forecast to make up for the short fall. The issue with sales is just the opposite of what should happen. When products are delayed, it is the sales teams' job to keep the prospects on the hook so they don't lose confidence with your company. It is vital to keep your prospects and customers informed of what the delay is all about. They have dealt with delays before and if you are up front in informing them of the issues and you are not too late in delivering the product, you should be safe with the order.

The picture that I am painting is one of realistic possibilities that happen more often than not, so be prepared for the unexpected and have a contingency plan in place.

Common reasons for product failures are:
- Insufficient market research
- Insufficient funding
- Downturn in the economy
- Patent, copyright and trademark infringement
- Overzealous forecasts
- Can't meet regulatory requirements
- Personnel leaves
- Window of Opportunity closes more rapidly than expected
- Development and testing time underestimated
- Raw materials not available

The Experts Speak Out...

The great leaders are like the best conductors – they reach beyond the notes to reach the magic in the players.

– Blaine Lee

To think creatively, we must be able to look afresh at what we normally take for granted.

– George Kneller

To the degree we're not living our dreams; our comfort zone has more control of us than we have over ourselves.

– Peter McWilliams

- Customers purchased from competitors
- Price increase caused by inflation or cost materials/labor increase and you could not make a profit

8. **Who introduces new products successfully in this industry?**

There is no reason to re-invent the wheel if there are like companies that are successful penetrating the same market that you are targeting. Talk to the customers of your competitors or call the companies that you admire and wish to emulate. If the company is public, you can go to the stock exchange and request annual reports or you can call the company and simply request a visit; you might be surprised at your reception. People like to talk about their successes and they probably would not think of you as a threat.

Another means of gathering information is to request a Dunn and Bradstreet report or go to their web page. This report will detail key officers, sales, rate the company and describe their products. You can also go to the Better Business Bureau and Chamber of Commerce to gather information. Successful companies many times will mentor a startup if the products are non-conflicting. In some cases you may get a key person to be a member of your board of directors or, at the least, an advisor.

If the company is private, information is sometimes much more difficult to obtain. I suggest going direct, researching the Contacts Influential, WWW, D&B, Better Business Bureau, Trade Journals and talking to customers.

If you can learn by someone else's mistakes or trial and error, there is no need for you to make the same mistakes. Listen and learn. Listening can be the hardest thing to do when you are excited about your product and every moment that is not used developing or selling is thought of as wasting time, however it is important to take the time to do the research.

9. **How can this product grow your business in this industry?**

    Ask yourself the following questions:
    - If this is your first product and you are a new company, have you done your market research and do you have a business plan that justifies the development?
    - What market share do you expect to get and in what period of time before competition enters?
    - Are you developing this product in order to position your company to be purchased by one of your competitors?
    - Are your customers requesting this product?
    - Can you attain greater market share and profitability by developing this product?
    - Does this product require new technology and will the product position your company in the forefront of your competitors?
    - Will the financial community give you good reviews if you make this venture?
    - If you develop this product, will channels or major customers open that were not open before?
    - Look at all of the reasons why you are making this bold step and position yourself to take the steps to achieve your goal.

10. **What alternative do you have for accomplishing your growth and development objectives?**
    Look at alternatives as fail safe methodologies to ensure that you can successfully complete the development of the product and protect your investment.

    Reasons that could impede the successful completion of the project are:

What Would John Do?

If you can learn by someone else's mistakes or trial and error, there is no need for you to make the same mistakes. Listen and learn. Listening can be the hardest thing to do when you are excited about your product and every moment that is not used developing or selling is thought of as wasting time, however it is important to take the time to do the research.

- Money wasn't budgeted for the unexpected and the unexpected happened.
- You were too early in the technology curve and could not get it to work correctly.
- Personnel quit or were not available to accomplish the tasks on time.
- The Window of Opportunity closed more rapidly than expected. Competition entered with a cheaper like product and took the majority market share.
- The company was sold and the new company wants to go in another direction.
- The product was delayed for regulatory noncompliance, lack of parts, union strikes or acts of God.
- Alternatives are not available for all of the aforementioned, but I stress again, a good plan with solid market research are some of the many reasons for having an alternative.
- If you are a privately held company and you are running low on cash, you have a number of alternatives. Pride should be discarded if it means shelving or discontinuing the development of the product for financial reasons. A few reasons are:
- You could request that the employees take pay cuts instead of stock options or gifts of stock or ownership. This will only work if the employees believe in the products' ultimate success as much as you do.
- A second method is to go to venture capitalists for money. If you do this and they agree to fund your company, be prepared to relinquish a major share of the equity. You will also have to create a Board of Directors if you do not already have one and you will have stringent reporting requirements in order to spend the new capital.
- Go public with an IPO (Initial Public Offering) - After the dot com crash, IPO's are difficult and usually companies with an established profitable earnings are successful. An IPO will only work if you have a solid, bullet proof business plan and need cash to

Navigating Points:

There is no reason to re-invent the wheel if there are like companies that are successful penetrating the same market that you are targeting. Talk to the customers of your competitors or call the companies that you admire and wish to emulate. If the company is public, you can go to the stock exchange and request annual reports or you can call the company and simply request a visit; you might be surprised at your reception. People like to talk about their successes and they probably would not think of you as a threat.

expand a proven concept. Going public to get cash to complete development is just about impossible but not completely impossible if the business plan is, again, bullet proof and can stand up the rigorous due diligence.

11. **What is the growth potential from your existing prod -ucts?**

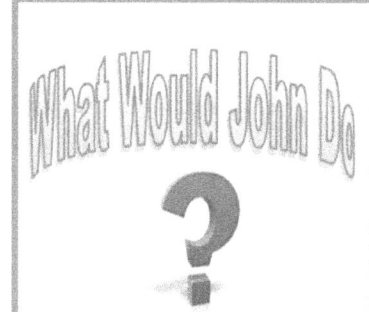

If you are a startup company, you will not have any growth potential only the potential your market research tells you on your current product. If you are a company with a track record, examine the sales trends and profitability of your current product line. Sometimes companies get complacent and when they realize that technology is passing them buy and customers are changing vendors, it is almost too late to get back in the picture.

Small family owned companies have a tendency to fall in this mode. They milk the product for all it is worth and if no one in the family wants to continue the company business, it is sold to a competitor for the base or it just dissolves.

If you have single or multiple product lines, where in the growth cycle are each of the products and where is each vulnerable?
Other questions to ask are:
- Are your products price sensitive?
- Is competition eroding your base or forcing you to lower your margins to stay competitive?
- You have no competition and price is not an issue because of the benefits derived from using the products. Who do you perceive as eventual competitors and how can you counter if competition enters the market?
- Do your products have mid-life enhancement capabilities to continue the life cycle and fund new product development?

If you are a startup company, you will not have any growth potential only the potential your market research tells you on your current product. If you are a company with a track record, examine the sales trends and profitability of your current product line. Sometimes companies get complacent and when they realize that technology is passing them buy and customers are changing vendors, it is almost too late to get back in the picture.
Small family owned companies have a tendency to fall in this mode. They milk the product for all it is worth and if no one in the family wants to continue the company business, it is sold to a competitor for the base or it just dissolves.

- Should you look to acquire synergistic companies that are in markets that you desire but have not been able to penetrate because of a lack of product?
- Do you have the right resources to develop new products?
- Can you increase the warranty, offer extended warranties, use 900 support lines or should you sell off the support?

12. **What new technologies are anticipated that may be a platform for new product development and commercialization?**
     If your products are high tech in nature, there are new disciplines and standards being developed and written daily. Do you comply or even know what the new stand-ards are? If you do not and your competition does, you will be in a catchup mode in order to be compliant.

     Fortune 500 companies and internationally, industries are conforming to specific standards and regulations to not only increase market share but to encourage cottage industries in order to enhance and give added value to a given product or family of products. Take Microsoft as an example, they have 20 times more users than Apple. On the other hand, Apple is huge but fewer applications are written for this platform because it is not as large and standards are ridiculously hard to understand let alone manage on a day to day basis. Consider your market, the competitors in your field and how you would get your product to the marketplace. Sometimes a large piece of a smaller market is better than a tiny piece of a larger market.

     If you are making a toy or a consumable, consider the materials now available and the labor to make the product. People like environmentally safe, organically grown, equality in labor and so on. For instance, telecommunications companies using web based technologies to access, process, promote and sell products are the fastest growth industry in the world.

13. **What percentage of next year's growth in revenues will come from new product development?**

     If you are a startup company, all of your growth will come from the product that you are developing. If you are an existing company, new products may be the avenue that will stem the down turn in growth and/or profitability. If you are going public or asking for venture capital -ists to invest in your company, the reasons are probably because of the new products and anticipated growth they will bring to the company.

14. **What is the earliest time that positive impact on profitability Is expected f rom new product development?**
You have a business plan based on market research that generated the money to develop the product. If you are using a Project Manage -ment package to track the progress of the development, you should be able to forecast when you expect an impact on profitability.

Daily questions will be asked from investors or executives of your company if you are chartered with the marketing and/or sales functions. They will be asking for the status of contract negotiations with companies that you forecasted to close and for the reasons the contract negotiations may have been delayed. What about new business and can investors call the prospects or customers that have signed contracts to get their reason for entering into agreement with your company?

If outside money is required to make it happen, be prepared for the hard questions and they will probably become more frequent the closer the time for product release gets.
Now that you have reviewed the Growth Objectives section, I have attached a list of fourteen (14) questions for handouts to your key decision makers. I would suggest that you hand out the materials at least a week ahead of time and schedule a meeting for a weekend or at a time where you will not be interrupted for a period of 4-8 hours.

Personnel and key officers that are mandatory include:
President   Operations Manager
Director of Marketing   Manufacturing
Director of Sales   Key Board of Directors
Product Managers   Chief Financial Officer
Comptroller

Chapter 12

Distribution, Alliance and Partner Relationships

Partnerships allow for the big to dominate and the small to be a player. The stakes are usually high to play and if you don't understand the game, you can lose your ante before you even get started.

The greed factor makes and breaks corporations whether they are a big player or an entrepreneurial startup that has second mortgages on everything they own. The little guy has to play smarter and also move faster when the decision is at hand. When the opportunity is there, play your hand and take no prisoners. This is a cliché laden paragraph but the analogy has a great deal of truth as I will explain.

Even the largest of companies, whether it is Microsoft, IBM, General Motors, General Electric, Proctor and Gamble, Standard Oil, General Mills or any name that you can find in a store, uses partner relationships to reach the broadest market possible. Why do they do this? The stores have instant feedback on the products they sell, they can reach the purchaser and keep their sales overhead down.

The manufacturer does not have the headache of infrastructure managing the site locations, and all that this entails. The manufacturer has national, regional and local marketing, sales and support personnel to support the efforts of all of their partners. The name recognition that the name manufacturers give the distribution partners attracts customers to their stores and customers buy more than just the one product.

The retail or wholesale outlets usually buy volume which allows the manufacturer to manufacture less expensively and the result is a less expensive product for the end user to purchase. Partner relationships are the best way to increase volume and gain maximum exposure to any given market.

While conducting my research marketing phase of finding out if my products filled a "hole in the market" I researched what partners would most likely have an interest in giving me feedback and ultimately selling my product. After I identified the potential partners, I used whatever means at my disposal to find the right people to talk to. If you have contacts or have business acquaintances or friends at your targeted companies, use this network first. Cold calls should be a last resort.

When you make a contact, have your pitch down to a concise, benefit laden and interest generating series of trial closes that will ask your prospect to do something positive and that will result in a face to face discussion. Be prepared to respond to all of the questions about your company's stability, where the target markets are, how you match up with competition, how you would support the product, Windows of Opportunity, future products, price and delivery.

Break your target partners into two groups, those that you know personally or have been recommended by respected colleagues and those that you are cold calling. The first group is more likely to give you feedback on your idea and what it will take to get your product into their distribution channel. The second group will probably ask you hard questions and if you are in the development stage, you will be wasting their time. The exceptions to this rule are in the high tech world where technology breakthroughs can open up a new emerging market and no one has delivered a product to fill the

Long-range planning works best in the short term.

– Doug Evelyn

The NBA is never just a business. It's always business. It's always personal. All good businesses are personal. The best businesses are very personal.

– Mark Cuban

You can fool all the people all the time if the advertising is right and the budget is big enough.

– Joseph E. Levine

A business has to be involving, it has to be fun, and it has to exercise your creative instincts.

– Richard Branson

requirement. A good tactic to use is to say that you have the technology and are interested in their view of the market relative to benefits, price and need.

I have broken ground on several products and I used the latter tactic very successfully. I try to get my prospect to take ownership of the idea, give me feedback on features for providing specific benefits and I engineer the key features into the first or next release presenting the product back to the prospect. They have ownership of the product and in all cases, I have a channel that anxiously awaits the release of the product because it has their input.

Not all distribution channels are right for every product. Look closely at the target customers of your prospective channel partners and determine what synergistic effects your product brings to the distribution strategy of the channel partner. Ask yourself, what advantages do I give this channel? Do I enhance their product? Do I make them a one stop shop for like products? Do I bring new technology? There will be many more advantages that you see that you can bring than your prospective channel partner will initially see so prioritize them and make your presentations accordingly.

There are many products that do not require channel partners but rather a direct approach because of speed in getting to a market, the cost to manufacture and lack of margin. Aa fad product with a short life span or something that can be explained during a phone call and can be closed quickly is an example of this. These types of products might be best suited for a call center, telemarketer, and a home shopping network, magazine bingo cards, WWW, direct mail, fairs or other like media that will elicit a purchase.

Navigating Points:

Partnerships allow for the big to dominate and the small to be a player. The stakes are usually high to play and if you don't understand the game, you can lose your ante before you even get started.

The greed factor makes and breaks corporations whether they are a big player or an entrepreneurial startup that has second mortgages on everything they own. The little guy has to play smarter and also move faster when the decision is at hand. When the opportunity is there, play your hand and take no prisoners.

If you have a commodity product that would be sold in consumer electronics, computer, department, pharmaceutical, or variety stores, you will need to hire and train a direct sales force and to solicit for and sell through local, regional and national distribution channels to bring your product to market.

More sophisticated or large dollar volume products usually require the manufacturer to hire a core of direct sales personnel specialized in the technology of the product and familiar with the channel partner sales technique. Cementing these relationships will require you to training their sales force and assisting in the sales process, a term called buddy or joint sales calls.

After a period of time, and as trust is built, many major distributors will allow you to call on their customers direct or pass you leads to sell compatible products that enhance their product. Another sell is where you have a high ticket item or one that justifies your direct sales force and you rely on your own efforts to promote, sell, develop, manufacture and support your product.

A final sell is where you develop a private label product for other companies and they put their name on your product. They either support the product themselves or contract for warranty through you or OEM (Original Equipment Manufacture} where your product is part of their product.

The type of product, cost to manufacture, price to consumer, technology, and sophistication are a few of the reasons to consider when begin researching for potential channel partners.

The following questions will help you think of the best route to take or promote thoughts on alternative ways to bring

While conducting my research marketing phase of finding out if my products filled a "hole in the market" I researched what partners would most likely have an interest in giving me feedback and ultimately selling my product. After I identified the potential partners, I used whatever means at my disposal to find the right people to talk to. If you have contacts or have business acquaintances or friends at your targeted companies, use this network first. Cold calls should be a last resort.

your product to market.

1. **In each instance when you have decided to sign up an outside distribution channel, why did you feel it was in the best interest of your company to do so?**

- Was it name recognition and prestige?

- National, regional or local distribution?

- Current channel partner which reduced the time to market.

- Minimal competition within the channel.

- Non-exclusive distribution requirement.

- Excellent margin.

- A channel that was targeted, we could monitor the successes, counter the objections, build credibility and move to larger markets with momentum.

- Minimized support because it was local. This reduces expenses of telephone, travel and personal support.

- Channel would perform all of the functions of advertising, safes and support and let us be an engineering and development company which is what we are good at.

These are a few reasons why you might want to sign up a distribution channel. First and foremost, consider the long term effects on your business plan. Does it meet the criteria as set forth in your business plan for consistent growth? If you start making exceptions, you will probably answer for those later down the path. Exceptions mean a turn has to be made in timing to get to a market, funds are running out, development took longer than expected, competition is entering the market sooner than expected, the Window of Opportunity is closing or a host of other manifestations could cause you to alter your strategy.

2. **Who are your prospective channels and list them in order of strategic importance?**

    This question should be answered in a brainstorming session amongst your marketing, sales, possible investors and any other personnel that could possibly offer suggestions on who might be a target market for your product.

    For this type of brainstorming session, I like to be off-site or have it take place on the weekend so that there will be no interruptions and you can be relaxed. Appoint a facilitator and someone to take notes. I have found that the best way to get the group to interact is to explain the objective of the session and that you want to explore any and all possible alternatives that will make your company successful. Use easel pads to take all of the notes and then tape them to the woodwork or walls as they fill up with ideas.

    - Brainstorm who could possibly distribute your product on one Pad.

    - Break each name out and have a separate pad for each and list what the benefits and possible objections would be for the channel to pick up you product such as,

      Benefits would be enhancing their product lines

      Opening up new markets for distribution

      New technology

      Need new products

       Makes them more of a one-stop shop for like products.

After a period of time, and as trust is built, many major distributors will allow you to call on their customers direct or pass you leads to sell compatible products that enhance their product. Another sell is where you have a high ticket item or one that justifies your direct sales force and you rely on your own efforts to promote, sell, develop, manufacture and support your product.

Customers like to go to one store or distributor and get as many products as possible. This eliminates finger pointing and saves immeasurable time when it comes time to solve a problem.

- Targets our market

- Has access to our future products markets

- A competitive advantage over another manufactuer or distributor.

- Objections or obstacles to overcome in order to get an identified channel on board.

- Long time frame to get your product approved

- Competition imbedded in the channel

- Your company is not ISO certified

- You are non-union

- You are a startup without references

- You have a brand new technology with an unproven market

- You are not equipped to support a large national distribution effort

- Only sign on exclusive manufacturers products

- Over extended with creditors

After you have listed the benefits and obstacles to overcome for each channel, prioritize them according to minimum of obstacles to overcome and make another list on the greatest potential each offers. You will probably find that the fewest obstacles to overcome are

Navigating Points:

These are a few reasons why you might want to sign up a distribution channel. First and foremost, consider the long term effects on your business plan. Does it meet the criteria as set forth in your business plan for consistent growth? If you start making exceptions, you will probably answer for those later down the path. Exceptions mean a turn has to be made in timing to get to a market, funds are running out, development took longer than expected, competition is entering the market sooner than expected, the Window of Opportunity is closing or a host of other manifestations could cause you to alter your strategy.

through the smaller of the distribution channels.

Now with the two lists in hand, brainstorm how, with the resources at your disposal, you would attack the channels and bring them to agreement. Note the added resources or necessary events that will be necessary to attract the channel.

Now that you have the two lists, you might want to mount a two or possibly three pronged attack plan. The plan would consist of calling the channels that would most likely come on board first with the minimum number of obstacles to overcome while starting the trial closing process with the larger more cumbersome channels that may have the most potential. The next attack plan would concentrate on a direct sales plan to an end user that would give your product credibility or an independent chain to prove the marketability of your product. There is nothing better than a good testimonial or solid reference that a prospect can call on. Very few like to be the first at anything so identify the risk takers or rebels and go after them to prove your products potential in the market.

3. **Who are you targeting and why?**

This is a checks and balances question that asks the question similar to the exercise you did for question two. Let us make sure that our target channels are realistic for us to attack and we have a reasonable chance for suc-cess. Do these channels meet the Mission Statement for sales of your product for your short and long term suc-cess?

4. **Identify who could be your strategic partners?**

No enterprise can exist for itself alone. It ministers to some great need, it performs some great service, not for itself, but for others...or failing therein, it ceases to be profitable and ceases to exist.

– Calvin Coolidge

Live daringly, boldly, fearlessly. Taste the relish to be found in competition – in having put forth the best within you.

– Henry J. Kaiser

Winning is not a sometime thing; it's an all time thing. You don't win once in a while, you don't do things right once in a while, you do them right all the time. Winning is a habit. Unfortunately, so is losing.

– Vince Lombardi

A strategic partner is one that buys in and supports your short and long term objectives for product development and growth. This partner will assign account or product management personnel to work with you on all issues. You can count on this partner to give you market infor -mation, support, advertising, product testing, references and competitive information.

Look at others that are strategic partners of this channel. What are they doing right and how did they gain the confidence of this channel? If your partner has non-competitive products, call up the channel partners and ask them what is key to gaining a relationship with this strategic partner. In most cases, the partners are proud of their relationship and are more than willing to share their experience. This one call could shorten your trial close tenfold.

Do not be complacent with a strategic partner. Remember that there are many others that would like to be in your position with this channel and if you stumble or consistently miss deadlines, your relationship could deteriorate very quickly. If this happens, you will find it very difficult to regain your position of credibility with this channel partner.

5. **Is it possible to have cost reductions as volumes in -crease?**

There are very few products that do not reduce in cost as the volume increases. Factors that preclude cost reductions are changes in the economy and, specifically, the cost of labor. A few years back when silicon was in scarce supply and microchips could not be manufactured fast enough, the demand was greater than the supply. The little guy needing 10,000 chips was pushed back in the queue or charged a pre

-mium because IBM was purchasing 10,000,000. Who got the most attention, the larger order? The cost of products with the lesser order of microchips had to increase or hold price to the consumer but lost margin. IBM could lower cost and increase margin. A case where the rich get richer and you try to hold your market share through support or other means.

Build into your production schedules cost decreases as volume increases. In many instances, a component manufacturer will give you the next level discount on parts based on a forecast. If you don't live up to the forecast, you most likely won't be charged the premium. This is where you need a good negotiator.

Another good point to take note of is not to have a sole source supplier. Getting locked into a sole source supplier can make you very vulnerable to price increases and others moving you back in the queue.

6. **What are your methods of communicating with your distribution channels?**

    Communication is key to your success. I cannot stress the importance of this enough. If you are a startup com -pany with a forecast of delivery on a certain date, a minimum of a weekly communication is a must. A prod -uct plan depicting all of the events that implicate the channel should be updated weekly and there should be key focal people that can make decisions so as not to cause delays.

    The channel member has other products to sell and sup-port and in order to get you ramped up for distribution, the following is being done by your channel member.

Who are you targeting and why?

This is a checks and balances question that asks the question similar to the exercise you did for question two. Let us make sure that our target channels are realistic for us to attack and we have a reasonable chance for success. Do these channels meet the Mission Statement for sales of your product for your short and long term success?

- Scheduling

- Advertising and promotions

- Sales training

- Support training

- Inventory, receiving and warranty exchange

- Product literature

- Accounts Payable

- Various levels of testing

Each of these seven points could be broken out with several sub tasks depending on the type of product. The point is that if you miss a deadline, the channel partner also loses credibility with management and their customers. Communicate on a regular scheduled basis and the reverse is true for your partner. If they are not keeping up with their end of the bargain, that is also pointed out at the update meeting and then the plan can be revised to get back on schedule.

Many times I have seen companies cater to the every whim of a channel member. I have always found that if you get assigned responsibilities up front with agreements to perform, the schedule goes much more smoothly because neither party wants to be beholding to the other.

7. **What issues need to be communicated on a regular ba -sis?**

First off, common sense issues that you would like to have communicated to you if you were the channel

Navigating Points:

A strategic partner is one that buys in and supports your short and long term objectives for product development and growth. This partner will assign account or product management personnel to work with you on all issues. You can count on this partner to give you market information, support, advertising, product testing, references and competitive information.

Look at others that are strategic partners of this channel. If your partner has non-competitive products, call up the channel partners and ask them what is key to gaining a relationship with this strategic partner.

partner working with a manufacturer or service provid -er. As I mentioned earlier, in order to keep both parties committed to a successful launch of the product, focal points should be appointed on both sides, responsibili -ties allocated, milestones decided and all of the steps written into a project plan for all to see. Periodic status meetings should be established and adhered to and it is usually the manufacturer or service provider that facili -tates the meeting and provides the timely minutes and updates the schedules.

After the launch of the product, meetings should be established with product management, sales management, and marketing and at higher executive levels to communicate successes and ward off objections or other negative comments. Customer testimonial letters, pricing, new documentation, promotional campaigns, upgrades and enhancements and new products should be communicated on a regular basis.

After an established customer base is in place and if your product warrants it, a customer focus group is a good means of getting feedback on your product both positive and negative. If you have a focus group that purchased your product, and the group would not be formed if they did not use your product, be very objective with the input provided.

I formed three focus groups and their input was invaluable in prioritizing new features, markets, pricing, where competition was relative to competing with our product. They were in the focus group because they owned the product and it made them money, their life was eas-

The first rule of any technology used in a business is that automation applied to an efficient operation will magnify the efficiency. The second is that automation applied to an inefficient operation will magnify the inefficiency.

— Bill Gates

Look well to this day. Yesterday is but a dream and tomorrow is only a vision. But today well lived makes every yesterday a dream of happiness and every tomorrow a vision of hope. Look well therefore to this day.

— Francis Gray

ier, it saved labor or a myriad of other benefits. All I had to do was listen and be responsive. Some product focus groups only get lip service for their input and as you would expect, the groups rapidly fold because they are not listened to.

8. **What feedback mechanisms do you need to maintain the manufacturer to distributor relationship?**

Regular feedback and timely reporting are the answer here. If you agreed to a co-op fund at the end of each quarter, make sure that your check is sent. If you were to send a status report on support calls to your factory, in-ventory, back orders, warranty repair or incentive pay-ments for special sales promotions, don't fail to do so as you agreed. If there are technology breakthroughs that can afford new benefits or open up new markets communicate and solicit input for new products or en-hancements.

If you agreed to attend trade shows or you generate leads that are to be passed on to the distributor, be timely and don't let the leads atrophy. If you agree to go off book for a special onetime pricing for a prestigious client or large volume deal live up to your side of the agreement.

If your product has release control for bug correc-tions or malfunctioning equipment, communicate the release notices and upgrades if required. The reverse is true in all of the aforementioned instances as well. If you don't get paid on time, get warranty trouble reports with returned goods.

9. **Do you have clear mutual goals for business with each of your distribution channels?**

In questions 2-4, we identified the strategic importance of each channel and prioritized by size, ease to penetrate and target markets for present and future distribution. Each channel has a specific target for your product and it is up to you to increase sales by selling the benefits of your prod -ucts into other markets that cover or could with reason- able ease.

Other goals are increased volume to gain lower prices, maybe you work towards a license, private label or OEM agree- ment after your product has proven itself in the market. Once a channel commits to a private label or other ownership, you have them pretty well locked up and you would have to really mess up for competition to unseat your product.

Chapter 13

Cost of Sales

Cost of Sales will determine your gross margin or profit before taxes on the product that you are developing for sales purposes. Analyzing the market for that requirement and determining the need is the first step in developing a business plan. The steps that lie ahead in determining if the product can be developed, sold and supported with a profit will determine if you can have a viable business. I should reiterate that many companies differentiate between cost of sales and cost to manufacturer. They are right, they are different disciplines but ultimately if you are to sell the product profitably, all of the costs should be less than what you are selling it for in order to justify starting a business or developing a new product.

This segment will ask you questions concerning the Cost of Sales and I have offered some ideas as food for thought when you analyze your own Cost of Sales.

1.   **Who are your sales and distribution channels?**

If you are an existing entity with established sales chan -nels, you should examine if the disciplines are in place to achieve the desired results as depicted in your busi -ness plan. Different products require different meth -ods of selling to achieve the maximum results. As an example, you would not hire a direct sales force to sell a single fad product that may have a life span of several months. You might contract with a contract Call Center to tele market your product or you would contact spe -cialty distribution channels to sell your product, those that have immediate access to your target market.

The identification, selling and training of your distribu -tion channel is one of the most critical steps in the evo-

Navigating Points:

Regular feedback and time-ly reporting are the answer here. If you agreed to a co-op fund at the end of each quarter, make sure that your check is sent. If you were to send a status report on support calls to your fac-tory, inventory, back orders, warranty repair or incen-tive payments for special sales promotions, don't fail to do so as you agreed. If there are technology breakthroughs that can afford new benefits or open up new markets com-municate and solicit input for new products or en-hancements.

lution of your products success. Many times I have found that companies spend all of their time engineering, writing documentation, marketing and when it comes to selling, they think that it will fall into place when the product is ready for release. Not true, in fact the opposite is more common than not and especially with a startup company.

I heartily recommend that you begin the sales channel identification and closing as soon as you have completed the marketing phase and are beginning the product development. Not every channel that you have identified will come on board and you will need contingency plans in case some that have agreed to come on board back out.

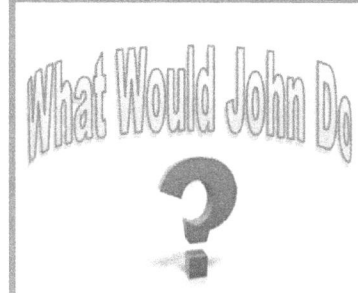

2. **Can you use existing channels or do you have to devel op new channels?**

    Careful consideration should be given to existing chan -nels, even if they are not equipped to carry out the sales of your new product. You do not want to jeopardy -ize existing sales channels unless first discussing the opportunity with the channel. Since existing channels know your company they deserve the opportunity to explore the potential and possibly make recommenda -tions on who might be better equipped to take your product to market even if they are not totally prepared to sell your product,.

3. **What are the major market segments for your new product and what channels exist?**

    During your market analysis phase, you should have de termined whether your product has global, geographic, seasonal, target or niche market potential. You should also consider if your product can be sold as a standalone, give added value to another product, has OEM potential, or could be licensed.

If you are an existing entity with established sales channels, you should examine if the disciplines are in place to achieve the desired results as depicted in your business plan. Different products require different methods of selling to achieve the maximum results. As an example, you would not hire a direct sales force to sell a single fad product that may have a life span of several months. You might contract with a contract Call Center to tele market your product or you would contact specialty distribution channels to sell your product, those that have immediate access to your target market.

A major market segment could be an industrial market identified by a SIC (Standard Industrial Code). The internet or your nearest major library have SIC directories that list every industry. After identifying your major markets, you can extract those firms that most closely resemble your target market for direct calling, telemarketing, mailings or any other contact deemed necessary to promote and sell your product.

Other methods to identify major market segments are to call the marketing, product marketing, or sales managers of those companies that could use your product or have channels to your ultimate end user or purchaser. It is very difficult to get to head buyers or the Product Managers of major international retail chains. When you do get to see them they will only have 15-30 minutes, at best, to listen to your pitch. Make it concise, to the point, explaining the benefits, markets, price and what you would do to help promote your product.

After you identify the channels and markets for your product, you may be stymied about how to best take your product to market. A simple way to identify channels to market is to call a store that sells products that you believe have access to your market and ask them if they purchase direct from the manufacturer or do they buy from a wholesaler.

4. **What are the benefits and consequences of the chan -nels selected?**

This question is designed to make you think about sup port and margin for your product. How much support is required for your product and how much margin can you afford to give away in order to get your product to market, If you are considering a large national retail chain such as Office Depot, Costco, Sam's or any of the major chains, they will want your best price and for you take on all of the support responsibilities. Another ma-jor consideration is the no fault warranty and how you negotiate the terms and conditions of a no fault. No fault means that a customer that purchases your prod-uct can bring it back to the store where they purchased it and receive another for any reason. The reasons could be the color was wrong, too hard to operate, not what I thought it was or they could have used it for six months and simply want a new one. The store may have a policy of total replacement for any reason.

If you are not prepared to take no fault responsibility and have a methodology to re-enter the returned goods back to inventory, you need to re-think your bottom line margin with the no fault clause.

This channel may sell tremendous volume which allows you to purchase parts or manufacturer less expensively which lowers your cost and allows you the luxury of carrying no fault distributors.

If you tele market your product through a call center and your product retails for $19.95 less taxes and shipping hypothetically, let's say you can manufacture the product for $8.00 and you are paying a call center $18.00 an hour, per agent to tele market your product. The call center makes an average of 25 calls per agent hour and the average time it takes to sell your product over the telephone is six minutes. Come to find out, you are experiencing only two sales per agent hour when you expected four.

Using one agent hour at $18.00 they are selling two of your products, your volume per agent is $39.90 per hour. Your cost to manufacturer is $16.00 for two units and you pay the agent another $18.00 per hour. Your gross profit on two sales per hour is $39.90 less $16.00 (cost of product), less $18.00 (agent cost per hour) for a

total gross profit of $5.90. You may have additional overhead and taxes to pay and your revenue is 50% of forecasted. If you have hundreds of agents selling two per hour, you may be fine but if your market demand is calculated wrong, you may have to re-think your channel to market strategy.

Take an example of a high tech product that requires a face to face demonstration to explain the benefits to the buyer. Consider the channels prior to or current expertise in being able to demonstrate your product properly to the potential end user. More importantly, if the channel picks up your product and the salesperson has a bag to carry with a catalog of 1,000's of items how much attention will be paid to yours. This is especially true if the salesperson is on a quota, and most are. The salesperson, feels comfortable with some products more than others and some products offer higher revenue value than others. If there is no special incentive to pitch your product, the salesperson goes where the sales are in order to make quota.

This channel may require videos for training, monthly sales meetings to train and explain, co-op funds to advertise, trade show participation, buddy calls, lead transfers and special support for before and after sales. All of this takes money and most startup companies do not budget enough marketing, sales, training and support dollars to adequately bring the product to market.

The upside to major channel distribution is access to immediate markets. The downside is the support required to bring the channel up to speed and have the sales staff have a desire to push your product. Another thing to remember is the number of other manufacturer's products that this salesperson will be carrying. The salesperson is being wined and dined or given special support by some manufacturers, possibly for years, and

Navigating Points:

Other methods to identify major market segments are to call the marketing, product marketing, or sales managers of those companies that could use your product or have channels to your ultimate end user or purchaser. It is very difficult to get to head buyers or the Product Managers of major international retail chains.

When you do get to see them they will only have 15-30 minutes, at best, to listen to your pitch. Make it concise, to the point, explaining the benefits, markets, price and what you would do to help promote your product.

they feel very comfortable with the other manufacturer's product. A good old boys network is in place and friendships are built. For you to penetrate this network even though headquarters says that you are now in their family of products, will take some work. Until you get the field sales person to want to sell your product, you will never get your expected sales result.

A true misconception of advertising is that if you advertise, they will come. Something may come but it is not always a buyer. You get a lot of potential competitors and consultants requesting information to stay abreast of the industry and as many more just collecting information. Again, your return on advertising is only as good as the research you have done to determine market demand and identified the channels that are most appropriate to bring your product to the market.

5. **What is the aggregate cost of sales for the budgeted period for each distribution channel?**

Each channel should have a General Ledger sub account number for tracking each channels expenditure. It is not easy to assimilate the cost associated with the ramp up of each channel because a channel ramp may be one year before you begin reaping the rewards as forecast-ed by you from the channel. If a channel has hundreds of offices and you are expected to train them and do joint calls to key prospects, this could take a year to complete.

What you have to do in this case is to monitor the progress of your sales training ramp and follow the progress of those already trained relative to presenting and closing customers. Be prepared to alter your training as feedback comes in from the prior trained field representatives. If input is positive, write testimonials, and reference the positive, if negative, rework the product if

The Experts Speak Out...

People are definitely a company's greatest asset. It doesn't make any difference whether the product is cars or cosmetics. A company is only as good as the people it keeps.

— Mary Kay Ash

In the business world, everyone is paid in two coins: cash and experience. Take the experience first; the cash will come later.

— Harold Geneen

necessary and alter your training to emphasize the positives.

Items that make up the aggregate cost of sales are:

- All labor costs such as sales, marketing and general office

- Benefits

- Expenses such as travel, meals, lodging, rental car, etc.

- Advertising and promotional programs

- Internal allocated labor and benefits

- Spiffs and sales incentives

- Copy expenses

- Co-op advertising funds. These are funds that you offer or are expected to give to national distribution chains to assist in the promotion of your product. In most instances and you should expect such and you approve all advertising and promotional programs.

- Trade show booth rentals or purchases and associated graphics or other equipment required for the booth.

- Promotional product pieces

- Product briefs

- Media campaigns through radio, television, Internet, telemarketing, bingo cards, coupons, etc.

6. **What is the relationship between cost of sales and the sales level in the distribution channel? Are the most expensive channels producing the most sales?**

If you track the expenses allocated to each channel, it is relatively easy to determine where you are receiving the greatest return for your investment. There are excep
-tions to every rule and the larger the channel, the more expensive to ramp up the channel and the longer it

takes for the channel to begin moving significant vol-ume. This is not always true but I have found that it is, on average, the norm. You have to consider the chan-nels window of time to devote to your product. It may not coincide with your time because you'd like it sold yesterday. You may have to wait in a queue and when your time is due, be prepared to act quickly and have everything ready to roll.

Hard decisions will have to be made if major channels are not moving significant enough volume for you to support the sales and support effort. You will have to look at the exposure and benefits that you are deriving from this channel. Now, evaluate if the channel is mar-ginally profitable, does the channel give you credibility with other channels, do you have other and more bene-ficial products to move through this channel in the fu-ture and what are you learning. There are subjective areas of learning and gaining experience that you can not necessarily quantify with dollars. You have to weigh the learning to the cost of the lesson.

7. **What are the target markets for market coverage and penetration for each selected channel?**

    After you have evaluated your target markets you need to determine:

    - Detail demographics of your selected target markets

    - Best methodologies to reach your markets by priority

    - Funds required to explore and lock in agreements for your channels

    - Decide on which channel and methodology is best to reach your greatest in demand target market

    - What competitors are already in my channels and how

What Would John Do

?

Each channel should have a General Ledger sub account number for tracking each chan-nels expenditure. It is not easy to assimilate the cost associat-ed with the ramp up of each channel because a channel ramp may be one year before you begin reaping the rewards as forecasted by you from the channel. If a channel has hun-dreds of offices and you are expected to train them and do joint calls to key prospects, this could take a year to complete.

do I counter the incumbent challenge?

- Best use of media in order to advertise and promote my product and generate interest and demand

8. **What kind of support and training are required for each channel?**

Your product will dictate the level of support and train-ing required for each channel. If you have a product that sells for $50,000 and takes days to train on, re - quires special demonstration equipment and a great deal of pre and post-sales support, be prepared to spend a great deal of time on training and support. The other considerations are the size of the market that will purchase your $50,000 product and the time to sell, in stall and support.

If you have a channel that is accustomed to your level of product sophistication, your costs will be substantially less than a channel that may sell a commodity product but thinks that they have access to your target market. The latter may require joint calls to sell your product and if you don't have direct support or channels to sup-port your resellers, they will lose their initiative very quickly. Once a channel does not get the support they think they should receive, it is near impossible to get that reseller to present your product.

Be very sure that you are prepared to support whatever channel you are going after. Remember that there are many competitors that are vying for their time to sell their products. It may be better to go slow and miss a channel than lose a channel, or channels, because you could not support them as purported in the agreement or verbally.

9. **What product objective should you select for each channel?**

Navigating Points:

If you track the expenses allocated to each channel, it is relatively easy to deter-mine where you are receiv-ing the greatest return for your investment. There are exceptions to every rule and the larger the channel, the more expensive to ramp up the channel and the longer it takes for the channel to begin moving significant volume. This is not always true but I have found that it is, on average, the norm. You have to consider the channels window of time to devote to your product. It may not coincide with your time because you'd like it sold yesterday. You may have to wait in a queue and when your time is due, be prepared to act quickly and have everything ready to roll.

Channels have varied targets of responsibility. Many have corporate sales staffs that target specific major Fortune 1000 companies and within this group they may break it down between hospitality, aerospace, defense, telecommunications, etc. They may have retail account groups that target national, local or regional chains and still another group that targets end users. The mix is de-pendent on the mass appeal, cost and complexity of your product.

Research the target markets, each of your prospective channels targets and determine the expected time and cost to bring any given channel on line to sell your product. Usually the aggressive channels are more willing to bring your products on but if they don't reach the expected volume and meet the margin requirements, they quickly move your product to a lesser position in the store or drop it all together.

10. **Do you have an agreement for the objective from the sales channel manager for your objective?**

Ownership of the objective is paramount in getting agreements with your sales manager on your sales objectives. Immediate revenue may not be the immediate goal depending upon where you are in your development. Objectives should be measurable milestones that, when accomplished, moves the sales process closer to a close.

Examples of milestones for your channel or sales managers are:

- Establishing appointments with your chosen channel market resellers
- Getting your prospects to take ownership of your product
- Discussing various markets and the potential require-

The Experts Speak Out...

To be successful, you have to have your heart in your business, and your business in your heart.

– Thomas Watson, Sr.

The absolute fundamental aim is to make money out of satisfying customers.

– John Egan

There are a lot of things that go into creating success. I don't like to do just the things I like to do. I like to do things that cause the company to succeed. I don't spend a lot of time doing my favorite activities.

– Michael Dell

ments for your product

- Finding out who and if there is competition for your product

- Testing price thresholds

- Determining the Window of Opportunity

- Pre and post-sales support requirements

- Warranty requirements

- Discussing the terms and conditions of a sales agreement

All of the above are measurable trial closes that, when communicated to the company, bring the company closer together. Nothing builds moral faster than having sales communicate that a prospect is considering reselling your product.

11.   **Are the channels that you are not targeting do you think they could be of benefit in the future?**

An example of a channel that is not a target now but could be in the future are the super store chains like Costco. Costco was originally a membership discount wholesale food and pharmacy store. As they grew, they added tires, sporting goods, books, clothing, jewelry, computers and software, automobiles, dishes, appliances, toys, camping equipment and almost anything that a department store carries only now in a warehouse environment.

A few years ago, you would have never thought of talking to a Costco to sell your consumer electronics or computer wares. Now this is a channel that sells millions of dollars' worth of electronics and computer wares. How many channels are there like this that are ready to explode on the retail side and are possibly looking for products like yours?

And then there are International markets that offer channels of distribution with almost unlimited potential for every type of product and service.

12. What is the potential?

Determining potential can be a fun exercise but it can also be heartbreaking. Heartbreaking in the sense that you know that you have a better product with more benefits and features and at a price point lower than any competitor but you can't get it to market.

More business plans fail because they did not understand how to correlate potential to the real world. Channels are basically greedy. Channels want the best technology at the lowest price, highest margin with the greatest demand and they want you to carry the burden of on time inventory, sales, support and warranty.

Most of the major channels are successful because they are in such demand by manufacturers that want them to sell their products. They can pick and choose what products will fill their shelves or be carried in their catalog or warehouses.

The process of getting chosen is not always about the best product. Getting chosen by a channel can be based solely on reputation. How well did you perform in the past relative to margin, support and inventory management. The incumbent has the upper hand in most all instances and if there is a product on the shelf that is similar to yours, or perceived similar, you will have a hard time convincing the product manager to pick yours.

Potential can be calculated through demographic research by households, income, buying habits, viewing habits, businesses by SIC and other criteria that is available through your local library. You can do the math and see that if 100% buy your product, you will be wildly successful beyond your wildest dreams. What if you only get 1/2 of 1% of the potential? Will that segment make you a viable business?

Timing, demand, cost to develop, technology availability, personnel resources, channels to market, competition, economy, staying power and the money to make it happen are all crucial elements in the equation to determine potential.

13. **In each targeted segment, what is the cost of acquiring a new customer?**

Navigating Points:

Hard decisions are required with a minimum of subjectivity. The entrepreneur tends to let the subjective cloud the decision process. The reasons that I have observed where the issue became clouded is when the engineer or idea person also holds the purse strings and thinks that everyone should buy the product based on the benefits, features and price. In an ideal world, this theory may hold some water, but in the competitive world of commerce where relationships many times outweigh logic, the hard world of reality is very confrontational.

Ownership of the objective is paramount in getting agreements with your sales manager on your sales objectives. Immediate revenue may not be the immediate goal depending upon where you are in your development. Objectives should be measurable milestones that, when accomplished, moves the sales process closer to a close. Examples of milestones for your channel or sales managers are:

If you do not have a sales force or established channels of distribution, you will need to categorize the channels by strength and understand what each channel offers your company. After identifying and categorizing the next logical things to consider are:

Establishing appointments with your chosen channel market resellers

- What is the approximate amount of time it would take to close and ramp up a given channel?

Getting your prospects to take ownership of your product

- What obstacles would we have to overcome in order to bring a channel on board?

Discussing various markets and the potential requirements for your product

- Your own company's strength in the market. Why will you be successful, your financial statement, personnel, quality of product, R&D support, etc.

- Competition in the channel.

- Endorsements by trade journals, industry consultants and satisfied customers.

- What channels can we logically expect to sign with the resources at our disposal?

- Do we consider private labels, OEM agreements, technology licenses or exclusive territory agreements in order to attract distribution channels?

Time is money and the larger the distribution channel, the longer it takes to ramp. You are probably not much different than most entrepreneurs if you do not work for an established manufacturer or distributor. You may need immediate revenue because you didn't budget for the marketing and sales expense it takes in order to bring on a national distribution channel. You will probably advertise, have a small direct sales force, and go after the direct leads and save the margin that you would pay to a channel partner. While in this mode, you will have identified channels and need to try to move to closure while your direct sales force keeps the doors open with direct sales.

14. **In each targeted segment, what is the value of a new customer?**

A new satisfied customer could be an end user or distri-bution channel. A single well nurtured seed can yield a thousand fold. I have started many companies and been the first to sell new products. The key to my suc-cess was to nurture the end user through all phases of the decision process and then follow through on all lev-els of support. My customer owned my product and would tell our story to other prospects looking at similar products.

If your product is a toy and you watch the children, as

What Would John Do

?

The process of getting chosen is not always about the best product. Getting chosen by a channel can be based solely on reputation. How well did you perform in the past relative to margin, support and inventory management. The incumbent has the upper hand in most all instances and if there is a product on the shelf that is similar to yours, or perceived similar, you will have a hard time convincing the product manager to pick yours.

yourself, are they laughing, intrigued and are other children wanting to play with or use the product. If they are, you have a winner. If they leave it aside or only look at it for a few minutes and then lay it aside, you probably have a loser.

An analogy can be drawn between how a child views

and uses a product and how an adult or company uses a product. If they are satisfied, they tell their friends, if not, they also tell their friends or possibly worse, they don't tell their friends and send the product back.

Another value is the credibility you receive when you penetrate a prestige channel and they sell your product. Other channels notice and it makes it easier to penetrate new channels and it paves the way to other, and potentially more lucrative, markets. After you have proven yourself in a channel, future products will be readily accepted and you will not have to go through the arduous process of waiting in line and getting stamps of approval.

Satisfied customers can lead to free editorials in major

trade journals, free advertising or preferred placement in stores and trade shows. Awards such as the prestigious Malcolm Baldridge award for quality can be bestowed on your product or company; this helps.   Complying with various regulatory requirements aid in satisfied customers and in many cases, you have to adhere to specific requirements in order to sell your products.

Chapter 14
Setting Pricing Policies

How do we not leave money on the table but still price our product competitively and gain market share in the quickest possible time? A little luck is involved but with market research on customer needs, economy, competition, where the technology curve is, how you will distribute or sell your product and what your costs are, you should be able to find a price that is close to what the market will bear.

I have had experiences where I have negotiated a private label contract with one of the largest telecommunications companies in the world for a fair price. A fair price is one where we achieved our target margin and the distributor felt that they could sell our product for a fair price. Come time to sign the contract, my CEO asked if he could come down to the contract signing and ask a few questions about why they selected us and how we could do business in the future. This was a fair request and I agreed to have him come along. Come time to sign the contract, the CEO lowers the price $200 per unit for no reason other than to say that I was priced to high. Needless to say the purchasing company Vice President looked at me and couldn't believe his ears as my mouth dropped open. Once I recovered my eyes squinted, mouth pursed and I was upset.

The deal was signed and what the CEO was not aware of was all of the testing that would be required, the special packaging, documentation, pre and post-sales support and co-op

Navigating Points:

Time is money and the larger the distribution channel, the longer it takes to ramp. You are probably not much different than most entrepreneurs if you do not work for an established manufacturer or distributor. You may need immediate revenue because you didn't budget for the marketing and sales expense it takes in order to bring on a national distribution channel. You will probably advertise, have a small direct sales force, and go after the direct leads and save the margin that you would pay to a channel partner.

advertising. We landed the contract and over the five years of the contract, we lost money and he repeatedly asked me to re-negotiate a new contract with price increases. Needless to say, I never let him go on another contract signing with me.

Pricing your product is easier if you have an established benchmark price that your industry feels is fair for the product. When you enter a market where you are another product in a field of many, you better be sure that your targeted market share is worthwhile and that you can break even on development and deployment. Where you can make better margin in a market with existing competitors is where you use or develop new technology.

If the technology allows you make the product less expensively, combine functions that were separate, reduce costs and time and thus increase productivity or open up new markets not previously open due to the price, you will have a competitive Window of Opportunity. It might be that your product increases productivity or cost and justifies itself, allowing for you to set a price higher than the competition for the advantages that technology offers.

When pricing your product, you have to look at the capital equipment costs, labor and all of the overheads associated with manufacturing a product and then add in the sales and marketing and support expenses. If you had to go to venture capitalists, banks or other outside investors, how was the financing structured for break even and return on investment? This time frame may be six months or six years. Being held accountable for the cash applies pressure but you should not be in the business if you cannot stand a little heat. My experience with high tech products or software is one of not making deadlines so there is a track record of delayed releases. When you build your business plan build in fudge factors for development, marketing, manufacturing and selling to give you enough cushions to be a hero and bring your product in on time. This is good budgeting and most engineers that develop a schedule are more likely to underestimate that overestimate because of the pride factor. If you are the person with overall responsibility for the project, ensure that you critique each event and review what could possibly go wrong and then have the engineer modify the schedule for a second and third review.

The price of your product should not be cast in concrete until you know the cost to engineer, manufacturer, test as well as where competition is positioned and if you can sell the product in sufficient quantities to get a reasonable return investment in an agreed to time frame. Pricing is also dependent on the methodology that you are going use to sell your product. Here are five examples:

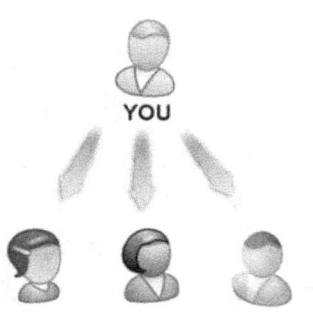

1. **Direct sales**

    Direct means that you will have a sales force that calls on customers directly or by other means that puts you in direct contact with your target market. This is gener -ally the most expensive way to sell your product if you are selling on a national basis. On the other hand, when you sell direct, you do not have to give away margin to other resellers and this will enable you to give special incentives and promotional programs for developing sales for your product. TV/QVC, WWW and other inter net avenues are great ways to sell single tier products.

2. **Distribution sales (Single Tier)**

Distribution or channel sales means that you do not sell direct or if you do, you have specific accounts or target markets that your distributors or channels do not sell into. When you sell to distribution, and this channel sells direct to the end user, you will need to adjust your margin in order to support your channels required oper -ating margin. Is your product unique enough or manu -factured inexpensively enough to support selling to a reseller?

3. **Distribution sales (Two Tier)**

Large distributors that have a national presence usually sell to other resellers that sell to the consumer. In this instance, you will have sales people that sell to the ma -jor distributors and the major distributors sell to re-gional or local resellers that have the presence to sell to the consumer. Your product has to support your inter -nal sales operation, the master distributor and the ac -tual reseller to the consumer.

An example would be that you have a product that will retail for $100. Your cost to manufacturer is $35 and you require a 100% markup or $70 to the next level of distribution. Depending on the type of product you are selling, your distributor may require 5-100% mark up. When they sell the product to the reseller that sells to the consumer, they may also require 5-100% mark up when it is sold to the consumer.

I have found no greater satis-faction than achieving success through honest dealing and strict adherence to the view that, for you to gain, those you deal with should gain as well.

—*Alan Greenspan*

Let's be honest. There's not a business anywhere that is without problems. Business is complicated and imperfect. Every business everywhere is staffed with imperfect human beings and exists by providing a product or service to other imperfect human beings.

– *Bob Parsons*

If you have this two tiered markup after your own, your list price product of $100 with all of the mark ups now sells to the consumer for $280 if each person took a 100% mark up on your $35 cost to manufacturer item. Needless to say you would not sell many items at this price. You need to examine the channel margin requirements, volume discounts to bring your costs down and determine if your product can or should be sold through this type of sales process.

4. **Telemarketing/Call Centers**

Telemarketing is not right for every product but is excel-lent for generating leads, selling low end products, re newing sales to co-existing channels, hospitality prod-ucts, catalog sales, insurance, and periodicals as well as to markets that have defined demographics that compa-nies can target for their products.

Telemarketing requires in-house or a contract house call center that is trained to call and respond in a positive manner to the respondents' question. A call center uses what is called a predictive dialer where thousands of telephone numbers are loaded into a computer and then calls are made and when a contact is made, the caller is directed instantaneously to a voice that re-sponds to the caller.

Products that are tele marketed have detailed statistical analysis done on the average time it takes to make a call, the cost of the call list and how many purchases via

Navigating Points:

When pricing your product, you have to look at the capi-tal equipment costs, labor and all of the overheads associated with manufactur-ing a product and then add in the sales and marketing and support expenses. If you had to go to venture capitalists, banks or other outside investors, how was the financing structured for break even and return on investment? Being held accountable for the cash applies pressure but you should not be in the busi-ness if you cannot stand a little heat. My experience with high tech products or software is one of not mak-ing deadlines so there is a track record of delayed re-leases.

this technique to a demographic that typically would purchase your product. As an example if I purchase a list of 50,000 names for $5,000 and it costs me $15 per hour for one telemarketing person and I have 10 assigned to sell my product, and my contract would be for 21 days at 12 hours per day. My cost to sell this product, without any guarantee that I will, is $37,800.

If your product sells for $100 you will need 378 of the 50,000 names to purchase in order to break even on the cost to just tele market. That is 7.5% of the 50,000 names and the national average is right around 1-2%. So I would be wary about this strategy in spending my money.

Bingo cards, coupons, 1-800 numbers, radio, and TV are all ways to generate leads and sell products. These are methods to sell products and to generate leads. You will have to have in-house personnel to handle the calls generated from these types of leads, so look at the cost to sell your product and price accordingly.

Pricing your product is not an easy task and in order to ensure that you are pricing your product correctly, examine all of the variables that could affect your pricing strategy and then compare it against your business plan. If you cannot make a reasonable profit selling the product yourself, examine selling the technology to someone who is established in the market or look to another product idea.

Direct means that you will have a sales force that calls on customers directly or by other means that puts you in direct contact with your target market. This is generally the most expensive way to sell your product if you are selling on a national basis. On the other hand, when you sell direct, you do not have to give away margin to other resellers and this will enable you to give special incentives and promotional programs for developing sales for your product. TV/QVC, WWW and other internet avenues are great ways to sell single tier products.

If you can sell your product as an add-on to another line of products and have your item be a line item, this could be very productive and possibly lucrative if the products are synergistic or seasonable.

I have outlined questions with ideas that can be of help in deciding how to price your product. The next series of questions asks you to analysis the benefits your products offer your customers in order to justify your pricing.

5. **You have a new product, what are the benefits to the consumer?**

This is a multi-step process. First of all, do a brainstorm -ing session with others familiar with your idea or per -ceived new product. Write down all of the possible benefits. Also write down what markets or de mographics you believe that the product will benefit. After you have done both of these exercises, list the benefits on the left hand side of spread sheet or Excel program and then write down the target markets along the top of the page. Check the benefits for each target market. You now have baseline of benefits for various target markets. Taking this process to its logical conclu -sion, I would recommend that you research the target market segments for real need, size and accessibility and means to access.

6. **What are the competitive alternatives to your prod -uct?**

Using the matrix that you developed in question 1, de-velop a competitive matrix, if appropriate, and list your competitors on the extreme right of the page and again, check off their strengths that compare against your tar get markets, strengths and weaknesses. This task is disc-ussed in more detail when we examine our competitors more closely.

7. **Does your product increase sales or make your customer's job easier?**

Not all products make our customers' job easier but all products should increase sales. Products for the fashion, toy, medical and fad markets could be products that make life more fun. I am big on matrices and would suggest that you have another brainstorming session with your colleagues or employees and list the benefits for which you will target markets to ensure that you are on target. Take your product to the field and talk to the possible consumers and resellers of the proposed prod -uct and verify that your benefits are on target before you take the next step in your development process.

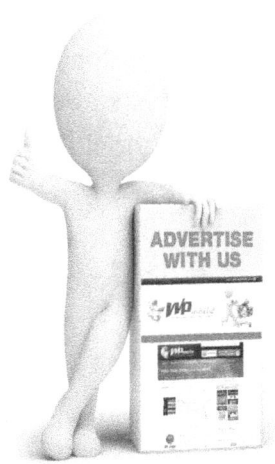

If you are developing a standalone product that does not rely on the sale of another in order for yours to be productive or useful, market research has to be in place to tell you that your product is in demand and will increase sales. If it does not increase sales or make your product line you should rethink the reasons for develop-ing and selling a product that will not increase sales.

If you are an alliance partner, OEM (Original Equipment

Manufacturer) or private label manufacturer for a major manufacturer or distribution chain, you are manufacturing a product to your reseller's specifications in order to be compatible or have a degree of synergism with your customer's main product. This practice is very common as most companies do not have the distribution in place to sell nationally so they negotiate an agreement with a major distributor that has an interest in their product. If you can increase their sales, make their flagship product easier to use or broaden their market, you probably have a winner.

Navigating Points:

If you are developing a standalone product that does not rely on the sale of another in order for yours to be productive or useful, market research has to be in place to tell you that your product is in demand and will increase sales. If it does not increase sales or make your product line you should rethink the reasons for developing and selling a product that will not increase sales.

8. **Roll up all of the costs to bring your product to market and estimate the breakeven point**

     After you have discussed and researched every possible market for your product, how you will bring it to market as well as engineer and manufacturer your product? You should have all of the costs available to begin the process of writing your business plan. In your business plan, you will have a spread sheet for one to five years, or whatever is most appropriate, to justify the develop -ment of your product to an investor or yourself.

     I recommend using the Stanford Business Plan as a model for writing your plan because it is a good model and is accepted by the investment community for funding new projects. You will have all of your one time, and recurring monthly costs by department for the one to five years of your business plan which is the expense side of the ledger. On the bottom of the ledger, you will have the revenue by product with supporting documentation on who you are selling to over this period of time. You will need letters of intent, contracts or industry consultant reassurance to justify your revenue numbers for credibility with your potential investors. After entering your costs and revenue numbers, you should have a break-even point somewhere in the future and show a revenue curve of increasing profitability. If you do not, cost are out of line with margin, there is not enough volume or too much competition.

9. **What margin is acceptable for you to be successful?**
Gross margin, gross profit margin or gross profit rate is the difference between the production costs excluding, overhead, payroll, taxes, interest payments and sales revenue. Gross margin can be defined as the amount of contribution to the business enterprise after paying for direct-fixed and direct-variable unit costs required to cover fixed overheads and provide a buffer for unknown items. It expresses the relationship between gross profit and cost of goods. Gross margin is equal net sales less cost of goods sold plus annual sales return.

(COGS) Cost of Goods Sold includes variable costs and fixed costs directly linked to the sale, such as material costs, labor, supplier profit, shipping costs, etc. It does not include indirect fixed costs like office expenses, rent and administrative costs.

Higher gross margins for a manufacturer reflect greater

I recommend using the Stanford Business Plan as a model for writing your plan because it is a good model and is accepted by the investment community for funding new projects. You will have all of your one time, and recurring monthly costs by department for the one to five years of your business plan which is the expense side of the ledger. On the bottom of the ledger, you will have the revenue by product with supporting documentation on who you are selling to over this period of time. You will need letters of intent, contracts or industry consultant reassurance to justify your revenue numbers for credibility with your potential investors.

efficiency in turning raw materials into income. For a retailer it will be their markup over wholesale. Larger gross margins are generally considered ideal for most companies with the exception of discount retailers who instead rely on operational efficiency and strategic financing to remain competitive at lower margins.

So how is gross margin used in sales? Retailers can measure their profit by using two methods, markup and or margin, both give a description of the gross profit. The markup expresses profit as a percentage of the retailers cost for the product. The margin expresses profit as a percentage of the retailer's sales price for the product. The two methods give different percentages but both percentages are valid descriptions of the retailer's profit. It is important to specify which method you are using when you refer to a retailers profit as a percentage.

Some retailers use margins because you can easily calculate profits from a sales total. If your margin is 30%, then 30% of your sales total is profit. If your markup is 30%, the percentage of your daily sales that are profit will not be the same percentage.

Some retailers use markups because it is easier to calculate a sales price from a cost using markups. If your markup is 40%, then your sales price will be 40% above the item cost. If your margin is 40%, your sales price will be equal to 40% over the cost or 60% above the item cost.

10. **Markup as a percent of cost**

If a product costs you $100 to make and you want to make a 50% profit on the sale of the product, you would have to use a markup of 100%. To calculate the price to the customer which could be an end user or a channel partner, you simply take the product cost of $100 and multiply by one plus the markup arriving at the selling price of $200. The equation for calculating gross margin is gross margin equal sales less cost of goods sold. A simple way to keep markup and gross margin factors straight is to remember that:

- Percent of gross profit is 100 times the price difference divided by the cost.
- Percent of gross margin is 100 times the price difference divided by the selling price.

11. **Gross margin as a percentage of revenue**

Most people find it easier to work with gross margin be cause it directly tells you how much of the sales revenue or price is profit. In reference to the two aforement -ioned examples, the $200 price that includes a 100% markup represents a 50% gross margin. Gross margin is just the percentage of the selling price that is profit. In this case 50% of the price is profit or $100.

In a more complex example of a selling price of $339, a markup of 66% represents approximately a 40% gross margin. This means that 40% of the $339 is profit. In accounting, the gross margin refers to sales minus cost of goods sold.

12. Using gross margin to calculate selling price

Given the cost of an item, one can compute the selling price required to achieve a specific gross margin. For example, if your product costs $100 and the required gross margin s 40%, then: Selling price equal $100 / (1-40%) = $100 / 0.60 = $166.67

13. Difference between industries

An industries profit margins differ, for example, clothing profit margins expect to be in the 40% range as goods need to be bought from suppliers at a certain cost be-fore they are resold. In other industries, such as soft-ware product development, since the cost of duplica-tion is negligible, the gross profit margin can be as high as 80% in many cases.

Commonly, when setting prices, a retailer will add a markup to the price they paid for a stock item; this will usually be a percentage increase.   A product company that purchases apples in bulk for .20 may sell them indi-vidually with a markup of 50%. A .20 marked up by 50% gives the selling price of .30. This is the percentage of the sales resulting from the markup (.10 per apple divid-ed by the .30 selling price gives a gross margin of 33.33%.) After the produce company sells all of their apples they can expect to be able to keep one third of the money and the remainder will be paid to the whole-saler. Any error in this calculation is a measure of pilfer-age, spoilage, gifts, till error or unsold product.

Navigating Points:

Most people find it easier to work with gross margin be-cause it directly tells you how much of the sales reve-nue or price is profit. In reference to the two afore-mentioned examples, the $200 price that includes a 100% markup represents a 50% gross margin. Gross margin is just the percentage of the selling price that is profit. In this case 50% of the price is profit or $100. In a more complex example of a selling price of $339, a markup of 66% represents approximately a 40% gross margin.

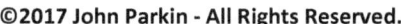

A misguided owner may expect that they can keep 5% of the money in the till after all that is the markup used. It is very important, no matter what industry you are in, to understand the difference between markup percentage and gross margin. Here is another simple calculator to help you understand the difference between gross profit margin and markup.

If markup equals 1/n gross profit equals 1(n=1) where n equals any number. For instance if markup equals 50% (1/2) then gross profit equals 33.3% (1/3). Another example is if markup equals 25% (1/4) then gross profit equals 20% (1/5). Importantly, this also works in reverse. If gross profit equals 20% (1/5) then markup equals 25% (1/4)

The gross profit P is the difference between the cost to make the product C and the selling price or revenue R. $P = R - C$. The markup percentage M is the profit P divided by the cost C to make the product. $M = P/C = (R-C) / C$

The gross margin percentage G is the profit P divided by the selling price or revenue R. $G + P / R = (R-C) / R$

You need to closely examine your sales cost, storage costs, raw materials, spoilage waste, interest cost and support cost. Only then can you justify that the 50% markup is sufficient to sell and be profitable on a specific piece of merchandise.

If you use resellers, you will have to give away part of

The man who does not work for the love of work but only for money is likely to neither make money nor find much fun in life.

– Charles M. Schwab

You must remain focused on your journey to greatness.

– Les Brown

Far and away the best prize that life offers is the chance to work hard at work worth doing.

– Theodore Roosevelt

your markup. You do this for volume, greater market penetration and to keep your direct sales expense low. Even though it looks like you are giving away valuable margin, calculate what the direct sales expense would be if you had to have a direct sales force in place to sell the volume forecasted by your channel to market partners.

14.   **Are we delivering more or less value than our compete tors for a similar product?**
Delivering less value than your competitors for a similar product can be done by a major manufacturer because of name and reputation. The garment industry is famous for this ploy. If you have a Nordstrom or Saks la -bel on a garment made of cotton and it costs $75, you can often go to Kmart for the same product made of cotton in the same style and it will cost $15. People pay for labels, support, name and reputation.

If you are an upstart trying to compete in this market, you should have distribution outlets or have enough money to open your own chain of retail outlets to grow your name and reputation. Using a spreadsheet that depicts your competition, markets strengths and weaknesses, add price to the equation and compare. Do not fall into the trap of thinking that because you have the best product for the best price that you should have the market share in X months. Relationship selling, support and reputation have to be brought into the equation. You need to determine a methodology of being accepted by a target market channel as a secondary choice. Second choice does not mean second best in this case. Second means that you are positioning yourself as an alternate vendor in case the primary vendor cannot provide the product or service or you have a benefit that the primary vendor cannot provide. As you continue this positioning process, you will be training salespeople for your product and building relationships. This process will be successful if the primary vendor defaults or can't deliver then you will have the opportunity to supplant the incumbent manufacturer and the reseller will default to your product.

Another methodology to gain entrance into your resellers channel is to support rural branches that the major manufacturers may not have enough time to cover adequately. Support is key and if you support other than main stream, this is a good way to get your product recognized and make inroads into the main line distribution of your channel to market partners.

The value that you deliver may take away margin in the short term but if you support your customers and they are other than the main distribution network, you are positioning yourself for greater rewards in the future.

15. **Can you price the product more attractively at a lower margin and capitalize with upgrades or enter the mar -ket with complementary products?**
The type of product dictates whether or not you have

the capability to add value at a later date. Examples are almost any software product, Barbie Dolls, Lionel Trains, CD's, Mr. Potato Head, Lego Blocks, coins, plates, shot glasses, flags, pennants, bobble heads or first in a series of dolls, pictures or figurines. People are lured into pur chasing one and the promotions and advertising pres -sures them in to purchasing the complete set.

Many times music or figurine resellers offer the first in the set for a penny and consumers are then obligated to purchase six more during the next twelve months at the regular price. They may think that they are purchasing a good deal and if they truly want the product and can enjoy it, it is a good deal. What they don't know is that their name is placed in a special demographic category of people that purchase this type of product and their name, address and telephone number may be sold a hundred times over to other companies wanting to sell like products.

One popular set of companies that do this include those who sell computer hardware and software such as Microsoft with Windows, Intel. They offer special high speed processing chips and IBM, Toshiba, Apple and Compaq offer up-gradable personal computers that use the high speed chips and Windows. A multibillion dollar market was created as a result of this standardization and thousands of cottage industries have sprung up to offer added value in terms of special software, high speed links to tie systems together and peripherals to

Navigating Points:

One popular set of companies that do this include those who sell computer hardware and software such as Microsoft with Windows, Intel. They offer special high speed processing chips and IBM, Toshiba, Apple and Compaq offer up-gradable personal computers that use the high speed chips and Windows. A multibillion dollar market was created as a result of this standardization and thousands of cottage industries have sprung up to offer added value in terms of special software, high speed links to tie systems together and peripherals to store different media and at in greater volumes at less cost.

store different media and at in greater volumes at less cost.

16. **Can you structure your price low enough to gain mar -ket share and high enough to target a return on total investment?**

Market share is a relative term and it is dependent on the size of your target market. It is also dependent on whether you are offering a brand new product with or without new technology, or offering a look alike be cause you believe that the market can support another product in your target market. The cost to bring your product to market is dependent on the volume and that drives your cost lower so that you can be more compete -tive. This is especially true if you are offering a look alike product but you will need something to draw your target market to your product.

When you draw up your business plan, you should have several scenarios with different "what if" and/or cost and margin scenarios with different channel to market partners. From these "what if" scenarios, you should be able to make a quantitative best guess decision on a channel to market strategy that enables you to realize your market share and, at a margin, justify a solid ROI (Return On Investment).

17. **Is your price high enough to generate target profitabil -ity and yet low enough to compress the time required to get volume up and costs down?**

Target marketing of your distribution and/or potential

Market share is a relative term and it is dependent on the size of your target market. It is also dependent on whether you are offering a brand new product with or without new technology, or offering a look alike because you believe that the market can support another product in your target market. The cost to bring your product to market is de-pendent on the volume and that drives your cost lower so that you can be more competitive. This is especially true if you are offering a look alike product but you will need something to draw your target market to your prod-uct.

consumers will tell you if your price is attractive enough to get a high initial sales volume. Again, several factors have to be weighed when considering you price. Compe-tition, uniqueness, size of the market, usefulness, ease of use, technology, fad or business product and cost to develop and deploy.

Channel to market is key to your success in order to cap-italize on the Window of Opportunity. If you do not have the channels primed for the product prior to intro-duction, the window will close rapidly.

18.   How does raising your initial price affect the invest -ment required to develop the product?
Raising your price will affect the timeframe in realizing a return on investment. Price raising before taking your product to market should be based on some immediate research that says that you are unique, there is no com petition in the near future, there is a great demand and/ or you have a lock on the market. If this is your situa -tion, you are unique and you will possibly be very suc -cessful. It is important to note that it can be very diffi cult to raise your price without some clause in your con -tract if you are going through distribution.

If you are in a position to pre-sell your product where there are customers that are willing to pay X dollars for the right to be first on the market with your product, you can reduce the initial investment to develop the product. This is sometimes true with new technology, pharmaceuticals or with companies that have a reputation for successful product launches.

19. How does lowering the price affect investment?

Price lowering or discounting is done for many reasons. Attracting customers to read your brochure or catalog or come into your store is one reason for lowering a price. By lowering a price on a commodity item that people buy every day, week, month or year, you get a captive audience with hopes of having them purchase something that has a greater margin or just having them get acquainted with your store or product mix. After reading your catalog or visiting your store, the customer has a better understanding of what you offer and will come back when needing the same or like product again. If your product has good value, word of mouth advertising spreads about your products and you gain by lowering your price. Eliminating the competition is another reason for lowering your price. If it is a fair trade item, you could potentially get into trouble if you go beyond the bounds of reasonableness though.

Technology also forces companies to lower price for fear of having slow or no moving inventory on items that are being outdated or improved with technology. If customers' warehouses are filled with potentially obso-lete goods, it is the job of marketing to keep informed of where technology and your competition is heading relative to making your product becoming obsolete.

The Experts Speak Out...

The new source of power is not money in the hands of a few, but information in the hands of many.

– John Naisbitt

The man who will use his skill and constructive imagination to see how much he can give for a dollar, instead of how little he can give for a dollar, is bound to succeed.

– Henry Ford

It's through curiosity and looking at opportunities in new ways that we've always mapped our path at Dell. There's always an opportunity to make a difference.

– Michael Dell

Buying the market or capturing early market share is another reason for lowering your price. If you are late in releasing your product you may want to consider lowering your price as a special incentive, launching your product for X months until sales match manufacturing capabilities to produce the product when you are established in the channel with a demand, than you can go back to your original price.

Lowering your price affects your investment and your customer's investment by allowing for slow moving, technology or price vulnerable items to be sold at a faster rate. Price lowering also can get you to the market at a faster rate because a customer on the fence at a higher price will come off the fence and purchase at the new lower price. You can also minimize your competitions erosion of your market and you can use the lower price to attract customers to purchase other higher margin items.

20. **How does your pricing level and structure relate to the anticipated experience curve effect? How does it relate to any planned cost reduction based on the number of products produced?**

If you anticipate that you will be manufacturing in large volumes and you only have experience in lower volumes where you can control yields, a price change could increase demand. If this occurs, it could place undue pressures on manufacturing which may decrease yields and increase rework which causes higher costs.

In order to minimize the downside from lack of experience, you should ramp up to full production for a short period of time to better understand how you can cope with the increased demand and where your line needs improvement. You need to do this before mass production is critical and there is not enough time to perfect your process. All areas of production are affected when the volume increases, including testing, packaging, shipping and rework.

I have seen instances where increased manufacturing has caused a higher price for component parts, it was with memory chips. There was a shortage of Motorola chips and the large volume manufacturers that required millions had first right of refusal on all products.

Even though we had a contract for X number, we were delayed and could not increase the demand because of the pressure exerted by the major buyers. We were forced to pay a premium in order to get our allocated order and/or wait until the larger orders were filled. It was worth the risk to Motorola to put us off since we were a $100,000 a year company as opposed to a $100,000,000 a year company in orders.

21. **Should you change your pricing policy to increase cumulative volume and thereby increase accumulated experience? Should you set your price low enough to get high initial sales and lower unit costs?**
These are very valid questions. There are solid reasons to change your policy and experience is one of them. If you are trying to ramp up your manufacturing facility to test capacity or yield, if you have new channels coming on line that have a requirement for X months of product in reserve for safety stock reasons, you will need to increase volume.

If you lower price and volume increases, your volume purchasing power increases enabling you to purchase parts at a lower price which ultimately gives you a greater margin on sales. Incentive pricing for product an -nouncements can increase the order volume from your customers which has the same effect on lower costs because of higher volume require -ments.

22. **Can you predict changes in market share based on anticipated price changes by your competitors?**
If your products are unique or commodity and prices are dramatically re-

duced, you could experience a change in anticipated market share. Usually market share takes a period of time and does not happen overnight or in a few months. Your product has to be distributed nationally and ac   companied by a mass advertising, direct mail, telemarketing or other method to alert the consumer that a price change is coming. Through promoting, your competition is causing a delay or fear in your mind; what if I purchase your item, I may be wasting my money if I can purchase a like item at a greatly reduced price in a week or month from now.

You should have relationships with your customers that sell your competitors version of your product and be aware of your customers stocking levels of competitive products. If your stock is not moving, you can bet that some incentive should or will be coming down to help move the stock on hand.

If your competitors are drastically lowering prices, maybe the cost of manufacturing is lowered because of volume purchasing is allowing for a price reduction. Just maybe new technology is about to be announced that will make the current product obsolete so they want to make sure that all current product is sold before announcing the new replacement product. I have seen it happen many times, a company will announce a new product to replace an existing one due to technology improvements and the company did not take into consideration the inventory on hand and/or in their customers warehouses; the result can be devastating in many ways. You cannot move your current inventory nor can your customers move theirs because you have announced a new replacement product.

If your customers were smart, they will have a clause written into their contract that protects them from such a blunder by their manufacturer whereby the manufacturer has to credit obsolete inventory on new products. You had better know how much inventory you have in the field before you announce a product that makes an existing one obsolete or you could be in for quite a sizable hit on your bottom line with no place to move the old inventory except to write it off.

Chapter 15
Financial Performance

The bottom line is financial performance. A solid business plan depicting all costs and time frames is paramount in predicting the financial performance of any venture. You usually can't begin a project unless you have a plan that forecasts the financial performance. If you have to raise money, you are required to have a plan that can stand the test of due diligence from the potential lending or investing source. If you are funding the project yourself, your accountant would advise you to have a solid financial plan because it just makes good sense.

I recommend using Excel or one of the more popular spreadsheet programs that is easy to modify and model "what if " scenarios for pricing, units and cost of sales. You will probably end with a hundred different models and if you are smart you should always use the most conservative model and the most conservative should meet the financial performance of your business plan.

If you go to an outside lending/investing source, they are experts in doing due diligence and they will tear your plan to shreds if it is not substantiated with solid costs and forecasts. You will end up doing the plan several times over in order to meet their criteria. Also remember that for every 100 business plans presented only one or two will get the attention and investment from the lending source. Venture Capitalists are inundated with business plans every day so when you make a presentation, make it good and have the facts to back up every number in the plan.

I have listed 15 questions that you should answer when making your "financial plan". If you do your due diligence on these 15 questions, you will have a done the planning to ade-

I have seen instances where increased manufacturing has caused a higher price for component parts, it was with memory chips. There was a shortage of Motorola chips and the large volume manufacturers that required millions had first right of refusal on all products.

Even though we had a contract for X number, we were delayed and could not increase the demand because of the pressure exerted by the major buyers. We were forced to pay a premium in order to get our allocated order and/or wait until the larger orders were filled.

quately project the performance of your product or service.

1. **What is the price?**

The price of the product is the sell price to your custom -er. If you are selling through resellers, calculate the price based on the tiers that your product has to go through to get to the end user or purchaser.

Example:

•Direct sales are made from your company to the end user at an established "Customer List Price", (CLP). If you are selling through distribution, you will be asked to establish a published CLP for your product.

•One tier distribution sales are where you sell to a customer that sells directly to the end user, such as a retail outlet. The price they sell your product for will probably be close to the CLP that you have established. Remember that you have to give away margin in order to sell to this tier. If your product is selling for CLP at $100 and your costs are $50 to bring to the market, you have a markup of 100%. The reseller will have a markup of 10-50% and that is the percentage that you will have to give up in order for them to sell your product. Depending on the volume, you will probably have 2-4 different price breaks for your customers. Calculate their volume and your margin when making your financial plan.

•A three tiered price schedule is not uncommon. This is where you sell to a major supply house and they sell to localized or regional resellers. If this is your strategy to sell in this channel, your product should support the margins for a three tiered markup that will not exceed the suggested CLP.

This scenario has you selling to the distributor, they take their mark, they sell to a local reseller, and they take their mark and sell to the end user. As the manufactur-

er, you have to calculate the margin that you can afford to give up and still be successful. Your marketing effort should uncover the best strategy for bringing your product to market and the best margin that you can expect for selling to the various channels.

2. **How many units do you expect to sell by quarter?**
    This sounds so easy but is the most difficult thing to forecast. You will find that your numbers will be torn to shreds by your own people if you are a marketing per-son in a company or an entrepreneur trying to raise money by the investor or banker. I have had numbers that I thought were solid as a rock and circumstances beyond my control skewed the numbers sometimes back to zero. The best way to get solid numbers is to get ownership of the product by your potential reseller. Get commitments in writing such as a letter of intent or a contract. This serves as a forcing function for your com-pany to deliver against a firm commitment and gives you ammunition with potential investors to do due dili-gence on your numbers with real buyers.

    When you put your numbers down on paper, you are on the line. If the numbers look to high, you will be ques-tioned about the validity and be seen as being too opti-mistic. If your numbers look to low, you are conserva-tive and not imaginative enough or don't know how to sell. It takes a tough skin to put numbers down on a spreadsheet that will pass due diligence. Remember, if there were not numbers that could be scrutinized, you would never get the funding or authorization to start the project.

3. **What level of support expense will be incurred and list these by category?**
    The more technical the product, and especially if hard

ware such as computer or telephony related or soft ware, the more support is required to be successful. If you are manufacturing something that is hardware re -lated, you need to calculate the failure rate and fore -cast a warranty repair of less than .02% returns of the product. This translates, for example, into you giving a one year warranty under the initial purchase agreement for the product. If you sell 10,000, and you have a fail -ure rate of .02%, you will have to replace 200 at no charge.

Will you offer telephone support at no charge for N months after purchase? What do you expect the cost of each call to be in terms of line and personnel time? If you have a recall or the documentation or instructions for operation are unclear, this cost can be prohibitive.

Examine closely the support that your products will conceivably need; what you are willing to offer under the initial purchase agreement. Will you offer telephone support at a 900 cost, 800 at no cost, specific time at no cost, depot change out, mail in and ship out. There are a myriad of ways to handle support and the support is dependent on the product and the image that you wish to convey. Think this issue through clearly and don't leave money on the table if you can charge for the support and make the support function a profit center or zero cost drain.

4.   **What is the cost to be incurred to manufacture the product?**

- Service oriented businesses
- If consultative in nature or software, the costs to consider are personnel, computer equipment and supplies, facility and utilities. Personnel could be contractors that

Navigating Points:

This sounds so easy but is the most difficult thing to forecast. You will find that your numbers will be torn to shreds by your own people if you are a marketing person in a company or an entrepreneur trying to raise money by the investor or banker. I have had numbers that I thought were solid as a rock and circumstances beyond my control skewed the numbers sometimes back to zero. The best way to get solid numbers is to get ownership of the product by your potential reseller. Get commitments in writing such as a letter of intent or a contract.

work on a time and materials basis or project. Equipment could be leased, purchased or lease purchase agreements. Once the product is complete, the cost to duplicate should be factored into the equation.

- Hardware oriented business, which I will classify as anything other than the written word
- In my experience the personnel that runs the manufacturing process is the most expensive recurring expense that a manufacturer can have. If forecasted numbers for production and they are less than forecasted, you will have to lay off people and you can get a reputation for having an unsecure work environment. You have to pay your fulltime people more than the going rate. If you forecasted numbers that are cyclical and not smooth, you may have to hire many part time people and work shifts. If your numbers are just around the corner, you can't afford not to have the personnel to manufacture the product because the order is coming tomorrow.

You need good people who will take care to build the product to the tested standard and give yield that is greater than 98% coming off of the line. Yield is the percent of the products that go through the line that are 100% and do not require rework prior to shipping. Rework can absolutely ruin the profitability of a company.

Equipment
- Manufacturing equipment can be leased, purchased or you can negotiate dead time with another manufacturer making a manufacturer to manufacturer deal to produce your product until you have the volume to justify your own manufacturing facility. Most new companies go off shore to have products manufactured due to the average cost of labor, stringent standards are in place and/or they can buy in volume and have other like prod-

What Would John Do ?

I recommend using Excel or one of the more popular spreadsheet programs that is easy to modify and model "what if" scenarios for pricing, units and cost of sales. You will probably end with a hundred different models and if you are smart you should always use the most conservative model and the most conservative should meet the financial performance of your business plan.

ucts that use the same type of components which in turn will make your cost to manufacturer less expensive.
Facility

- Look at your product or service and analyze the customer. If you have to bring your customer in for on-hands demonstration and training, you may require a better facility than if you are making clothes, parts or other machinery that will simply be shipped to the end user or reseller.

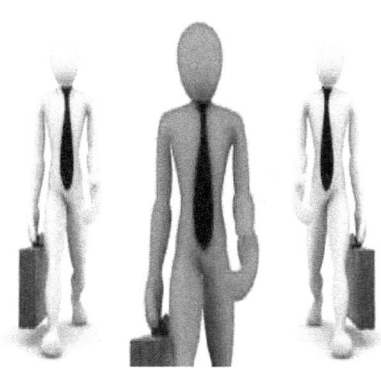

If you are not opposed to relocation, look at areas where they give tax breaks for new industry or have labor ready pools, good work ethics and not a lot of competition with other major manufacturers.

An example of this is a large Southern California defense contractor that had to an average of $30 an hour for union labor and benefits and had a labor force that was constantly moving. This movement caused poor quality which in turn caused reworking and more inspectors. The result for the manufacturer was a higher priced product to the consumer and a less competition. The contractor received a large defense order from the government that would cover 10 years and employ 2,000 people. The contractor did not want to expand the Southern California plant because of the costs and union problems so they embarked on expansion where there would be tax breaks, good labor pools and no unions. They settled in Mississippi, built a plant, hired a labor force and the productivity was almost three time greater than in Southern California. Why? The land was almost given away for the opportunity to offer more jobs in the area. Tax breaks were given the employer, there was not a union and there was a labor ready pool.

5.   **What are the sources of cash and when can cash be**

forecasted?

You have the product, the market is waiting and now you need the cash as promised by the investor. Some times everything falls in place but more often than not cash is just out of your reach and you get frustrated be -cause you were promised the cash. You have people to hire, people to pay, equipment to purchase, facilities to lease, prospects and customers to keep on the line and everyone is asking for money.

All I can say is that until you get a revenue producing product spend what you have and forecast cash as though it will not be there for three months because this is possible. This means that you have to have a re- serve of three months cash to continue operation and you can't spend what you don't have. How can I get cash and where are some potential sources?

- SBA - Small Business Association
- Friends and Family
- Venture Capitalists
- Banks and Lending Institutions
- Minority Government Lending Associations
- Potential customers for your product or service
- IPO's (Initial Public Offerings)

6. **What are the revenue projections, expense, invest- ment and cash management budgets for the first year?**
On your spreadsheet, create categories that can be transferred to your General Ledger for tracking and re porting. Itemize all significant expense categories for a minimum of one year but preferably for three years.

7. **What are the key ratios to measure financial perfor -mance?**
Financial performance of a given product is dependent on many factors and only you can determine those fac

The Experts Speak Out...

In all realms of life, it takes courage to stretch your lim- its, express your power, and fulfill your potential. It's no different in the financial realm.

– Suze Orman

The expectations of life de- pend upon diligence; the me- chanic that would perfect his work must first sharpen his tools.

– Confucius

The first one gets the oyster; the second gets the shell.

– Andrew Carnegie

Hire character. Train skill.

– Peter Schutz

-tors which will directly lead to your success. In order to be able to measure your financial performance, you have to have enough cash to engineer and bring the product to market.

I recommend that you use a project management spreadsheet software program which depicts the activities of each department and milestones for completion. This is the single most important step in measuring the performance of your people in meeting the goals of delivering a product. This is an area which I will address in future chapters but without this measurement guideline, your project will more than like fail, not meet deadlines or, at best, be well over budget, the Window of Opportunity closes or the competition will beat you to the punch.

A schedule should be written, agreed to and updated weekly or daily in order to meet the established goals of the company for releasing the product.

Moneys are allocated to specific work groups for completion of specific tasks, and with project management, you can measure financial performance of the development phase.

After product completion, you can examine the cash reserves to bring the product to market and begin the process of ramping up your sales channels. A rude awakening could slam you right in the face when you ask your customers for their forecasted orders. Rarely does a customer take the amount they originally forecasted. If you are the sales manager, you will be scrutinized unmercifully because revenues were forecasted and now they won't be there. Money will have to be taken from other departments, personnel may have to be laid off or new people can't be hired, equipment purchases delayed, lesser Christmas party and on and on.

Know your customers, cultivate an inside champion, monitor the pulse, build enthusiasm for your product, schedule the release with promotions, sales and product training. All of these activities will keep your company and product in the forefront of your customer and help ensure that your product order will come in on time.

The best ratio is to meet or beat the forecasted numbers on the business plan. The standard ratio for most successful companies is about $110,000 per employee in annual revenue and this should be outlined within that plan.

8. **What is the break-even model and when is the pro-
    -jected time frame?**
    Using your spreadsheet, project when you expect to break even. Identifying product to customer is the best methodology for presenting the model. Be sure to include support and warranty revenue and any projected enhancements that are forecasted.

    Look at equipment and facility depreciation and the cost of goods if quantities are ordered which will reduce the cost to manufacturer and increase the margin.

    At some point in time, the business should begin to operate on the generated revenues and not have to depend on seed capital. As an investor, they want to know when they can begin seeing a return on their investment.

9. **Can you increase price the first year if you enhance the**

product?

Price increases need careful consideration. You never want to obsolete your own product. If you have a prod-uct and slightly modify it to increase the marketability but it is not significant enough to differentiate from your original product, all of your customers will want to exchange or have credit on the existing product in their warehouse. If they send all of the old product back and you can't retrofit it with the new enhancement, you have to swallow the loss and hopefully you will be smarter when you decide to make a new product or en-hance the old one next time.

If you enhance the product, make it a module that is external to the original so that it can be inventoried and sold on its own merit. If it is software, make it a module that can be purchased and downloaded into the pro-gram for more benefit.

If you decide to increase the price, did you have the price increase capability built into the contract for infla-tionary reasons or for parts increases? You will more than likely also have clauses that stipulate that a 60-180 day notice prior to any price increases.

A national distribution company can't change prices on a whim. Catalogs have to be printed, notices have to be sent, bar codes or stickers have to be changed and you will have to honor the old price for who knows how long because some salesperson promised the product to a customer for N months at the old price. You will proba-bly concede the request for fear of losing the customer.

10. **What do your assumptions on inflation and exchange rate do to this model?**

When using a spreadsheet, you can readily create a for-mula that allows for altering the model based on infla

Navigating Points:

Know your customers, culti-vate an inside champion, monitor the pulse, build en-thusiasm for your product, schedule the release with promotions, sales and prod-uct training. All of these activities will keep your com-pany and product in the forefront of your customer and help ensure that your product order will come in on time.

The best ratio is to meet or beat the forecasted numbers on the business plan. The standard ratio for most suc-cessful companies is about $110,000 per employee in annual revenue and this should be outlined within that plan.

-tion and currency exchange.

11. **What percentage of market share will be needed to achieve a positive cash flow?**
This is where a thorough understanding of the market requirements comes into play. Know your market and ask the tough questions to all of potential influencers. This includes consultants, regulatory agencies, EPA, cus-tomers, prospects and competitors.

Examine the market; is it a niche with few or no com-petitors? Are there enough requirements for the prod-uct to support a business? Will there be competitors if you are successful? If the market has global impact will you be able to compete with major manufacturers with channel to markets in place? Should you consider an alliance and accept a lesser margin but with the oppor-tunity to gain market share to support the business case?

12. **What percentage of market share do your three top competitors have in the market that you are entering?**
This is a question that can be answered very simply; with X, Y and Z as your top three competitors with each having N share of the market how do you stack up? This information may be interesting but what does it reveal?

If there are no competitors in your market, why not? Are you a pioneer? If you are the first entrant in this market are you experienced in introducing new prod-ucts? Do you have the right kind of personnel to sell the product and are the channels attuned to selling new products from unknown entities?

New products require more scrutiny from potential re-sellers and customers. Both will show interest and may-

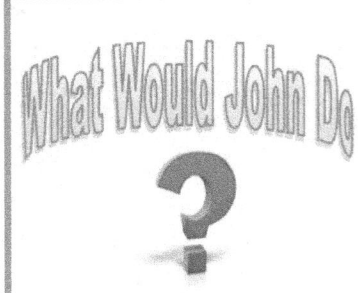

I recommend that you use a project management spread-sheet software program which depicts the activities of each department and milestones for completion. This is the single most important step in meas-uring the performance of your people in meeting the goals of delivering a product. This is an area which I will address in future chapters but without this measurement guideline, your project will more than like fail, not meet deadlines or, at best, be well over budget, the Window of Opportunity closes or the competition will beat you to the punch.

be run to the table with the order. Be prepared that to actually get the order in your hand from the table might be very time consuming and require a great deal of negotiation. Negotiation might be the wrong choice of words here, you will more than likely be giving concessions to get quality test sites and references so that future sales will be made easier. This is a more realistic view of the reception many new products receive when entering the market.

Another viewpoint to analyze is if there are few or no competitors but many were in the industry but dropped out. Ask yourself, why did they drop out? This is especially pertinent if some major players made a big splash and then dropped out or sold the division. What can you learn from their entrance and subsequent dissolution of the division?

Could it be that the market was not mature at the time of their entrance, technology did not support it or give a superior enough benefit over the current solution? Or could it be that even if the price was less expensive over the current solution, the replacement, retraining and support were probably over riding factors to stay with the current solution? If possible, talk to the personnel that were involved in the product development of the failed company and learn from their error in judgment.

If there are many competitors selling like products and the largest competitor has a market share of 10% with the next having less than 5% what does this reveal? Maybe there is no universal standard, everybody has a niche market they target or the product is so specialized it can't cross over multiple markets. On the other hand, there could be a standard so rigid that the development is so costly that companies can't afford to enter the market unless they are forced to be in order to stay competitive.

If there are no major companies over $100,000,000 in gross sales in the market, maybe the margin would have to be too high to justify the Research and Development and sales expense for the size of the market. Ask yourself if your competitors are selling direct or through alliances with other major resellers. Also ask yourself if the product is a flagship of your competitors or an ancillary product to support the sales effort of the flagship product. This is food for thought to help you better understand the reason there are few or a great number of competitors in your chosen industry.

13. **What is the relationship between price and market share?**

When examining your competitor's size and approach to the market, a possible strategy of growth will reveal itself with each of your major competitors. Three approaches are usually apparent with almost all companies.

- The company started with a hybrid or custom design for a single customer and someone thought that the application, product or service could have universal or niche market appeal. The entrepreneur attempts to place a shell around the product to make it appealing to a universal or niche market and a new business is formed.
- The company is formed with a universal product in mind that solves a problem or gives a benefit as a standalone product or service or compliments an existing service or product. If the belief of the founder is correct, the company believes that, as a universal product or service, they will sell great numbers and, as a result, they can reduce the price to gain an immediate market share.

The possible fallacy to this thinking is that the development to provide a universal product is usually much more costly than to provide a hybrid or custom product or service. If the volume does not materialize as projected, the company is in a deficit spending position greater than forecasted and one of three things happen. The first is to salvage the operation with an influx of new capital based on the potential and the current ramp of product acceptance, the second is to sell the company and get what you can and the third is to close the doors.

- The company is formed to solve a specific problem in a niche market. This is the usual case and I believe it has the greatest chance of success given that your market research is valid. A niche market company has the greatest chance to succeed because you can target an industry and leverage your customer's success. In a niche market there are tight association which, if you can become an associate member, will allow you to be a guest speaker, give white papers, write articles in their newsletter or demonstrate your wares at various conventions.

Niche marketing offers a better chance of success because of who your target customers are and if you are successful word travel fast and it is easier to saturate the Window of Opportunity before competition.

14. **What is the relationship between size and timing of investment and market share?**
This question goes back to #13 with a specific emphasis on the size of the market, emerging technology, cost to develop, channel to market, pro motional and support considerations. If you are in the software business, you are not going to develop an operating system or new programming language because you couldn't compete with the likes of Microsoft. Even high level programming languages are few and far between but applica -tions using a new language on Windows, as an example, could have a niche market appeal if not universal appeal.

A great example of this is Boeing. Boeing Airplane enters a market based on the trends of flyers and builds smaller planes and more economical engines to gain entrance in the short haul routes. As nations such as China emerge as major markets, Boeing researches the market, gains confidence of the country and ensures the success of investing in the Chinese transportation market. International stocks or companies that are opening up markets in Asia are hot right now because of the size of the market and the expected return on their investment.

Success is in the eyes of the entrepreneur. Making a successful business out of an idea has its rewards but if a business fails but develops new technology, is that a failure? It is monetarily, but the developers may be recognized by another company and a new career could emerge.

Sales
&
Account
Management

Chapter 16

Account Management

So many times I have been asked about how to manage an account or sell into an account. What the bottom line always boils down to is, how can you maximize the revenue potential from a specific account? Sometimes bringing the customer from a prospect through closing is easier than long term account management. This section deals with the psychology of managing an account. The psychology of managing an account is understanding the industry demographics, mission statements, culture and intrinsic values of the customer and key managers. This is accomplished through listening and application.

Let's examine listening and understand its importance. Listening in its simplest terms is exactly that, listening. When you are not listening you are vulnerable.

Listening is watching body language

Listening is sensing a change in a tone of voice.

You listen and watch the atmosphere of the office. Is it busy, is there white noise, closed doors, open bull pens, phones off the hook, people dashing to and from, piped music, traffic noise, industrial noise, cell phones ringing, how are they dressed, how you are greeted, is there promptness and how is desk is organized and are there pictures in the main office. All of these points are relevant in understanding the account management process.

We are constantly listening but are we taking in what we hear and understanding how that can be used to better manage your account. When you listen to your accounts, you

Navigating Points:

New products require more scrutiny from potential resellers and customers. Both will show interest and maybe run to the table with the order. Be prepared that to actually get the order in your hand from the table might be very time consuming and require a great deal of negotiation. Negotiation might be the wrong choice of words here, you will more than likely be giving concessions to get quality test sites and references so that future sales will be made easier. This is a more realistic view of the reception many new products receive when entering the market.

know what is important to them and understand why you were selected over your competitor. Listening and application of your products benefits to your customers' needs brought you the account and the same process will be successful through account management. Listening tells you how to respond and talking before you listen is one of the biggest errors salespeople make. As an old adage goes, "he who speaks first loses". When you ask for a response and the room goes silent, "he who speaks first loses".

As an example, you have just completed a presentation of a new product, service or idea and sense the customer is ready to buy. You ask the question, the room goes silent and you can't stand the silence so you speak about an additional discount or say you will call later or ask your prospect to call when they are ready. You really lose. The customer would re-spond if you were quiet. The worst they would say is we don't want the product for some reason. The best case is they accept your offer and a contract is signed.

In the worst case scenario your customers have an ob-jection that requires an answer but this is another opportunity to close the deal. Always remember that in every deal there are going to be two winners. The buyer and the seller. You are there because you offered the best product, service, warranty, technology, etc. The buyer needs to have a concession from the seller and if you recognize this during your negotiations, you should be prepared to make the best deal for your company but also be prepared to back down on a specific points. The customer will recognize that you are listening because you agreed to inventory one week of product at your local facility in return for their business. This concession was offered by you as a goodwill gesture to gain your customers business and it worked but only because you listened and anticipated the customers' needs.

Remember, the customer bought your product for the benefits you provided for their needs. Understand that you were the chosen one out of many, first of all because you listened and secondly, because your product offered a benefit that was equal or superior to the current or competitors product or services. You had to be doing something right or you wouldn't be in the position of managing the account. The benefits you can leverage to your advantage range from:

- You have a name known for quality and support

- You cultivated an inside champion

- You were aggressive in applying the benefits of your product to their needs

- Your product was superior in every area including cost

- You gave away the farm to win the account

- You hold the patent or copyright and the customer needs your product to open up new markets and expand the base.

- You are a division of the customer and they feel obligated to purchase your product even though your product is not quite to the level of your competitors.

- Your product opens up new markets and or channels.

- Your product enhances the value of the flagship product.

- Your product gives a midlife kicker to the flagship product and buys time to develop a product with the latest technology.

Whatever the reason the customer selected you, it is now your job to continue to listen, and nurture the seeds of ideas and manage the account with orderly and consistent dis-

Navigating Points:

Listening is watching body language

Listening is sensing a change in a tone of voice.

You listen and watch the atmosphere of the office. Is it busy, is there white noise, closed doors, open bull pens, phones off the hook, people dashing to and from, piped music, traffic noise, industrial noise, cell phones ringing, how are they dressed, how you are greeted, is there promptness and how is desk is organized and are there pictures in the main office. All of these points are relevant in understanding the account management process.

cipline. The following questions will help you understand the attributes that constitute quality account management.

1. **What is Account Management?**

Account management is the application of a consistent discipline in caring for the client's needs. This discipline is the manner in which you communicate, schedule and follow through. One of the biggest mistakes I see in Account Management is making the wrong assumptions.

Some examples where assuming can be very costly are:

•Making an assumption that because they have always ordered at the end of each month, they will continue.

•Product training will be asked for when required.

•I will always get a good reference from this customer.

•This customer will buy any products that we offer.

•We're solidly entrenched in this account.

•Competition could never get into this account.

•I have solid inside product champions that will always keep me informed.

•They always promote our product in all of their catalogs and at trade shows.

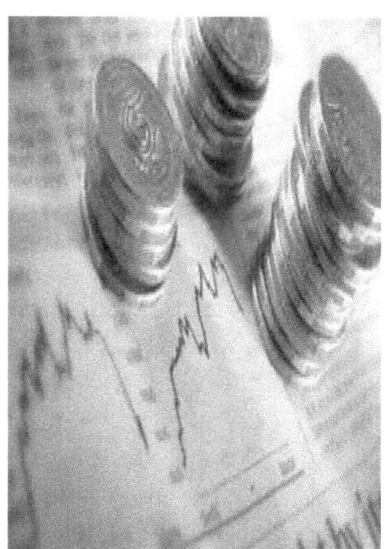

Account Management is not assuming or taking anything for granted. Items A-H are just a few of the many things that need to be discussed, assigned responsibility and planned for in order for them not to fall through the cracks through wrong assumptions. If you are dealing with a major account, you may have to deal with many department managers and the more personnel you deal with, the more thought processes and personalities you have to manage. The more managers that you deal with the more vacations, leaves of absences, promotions, firings and resignations there are. Each of these situations requires that you make sure that your project is followed through from one manager to another and that you assume nothing.

When you maintain the discipline, you are forced to review each of the objectives of Account Management. This discipline forces you to stay informed and plan with each of the managers that have anything to do with marketing, ordering, selling or supporting your product.

Account Management can be accomplished through trial and error or you can strategize internally the best way to grow the account in order to maximize the revenue potential. The best method that I have found to manage an account is to develop one or more inside champions depending on the branches, departments or divisions that are actively involved with the use or sale of your product.

Account Management opportunities can evolve through a salesperson closing a deal and the opportunities become so lucrative that the salesperson is required to develop an Account Management program to maximize the account potential. Other reasons accounts are assigned a manager is to reward a salesperson for a job well done. The account is considered a plum and helps to make the quota for the salesperson. In other instances, salespersons leave and the accounts turn into house accounts for upper level management to manage. The reasons of why a customer requires an account manager are many, the objective is singular. Keep the customer happy and continue to grow the opportunity.

My successes in selling and ultimately managing accounts follow these disciplines to one degree or another depending on the size and nature of the business.

2. **What are the demographics of the account?**

Years ago, and even today, a simple form can be used to

236

draw up an organizational chart depicting the depart-ment, manager, key personnel and benefit derived through the use of your product.

Other things to consider are:

- What are the ages of the management?

- What are the target markets of the account?

- Are they aggressive in marketing and selling?

- Are they leaders or followers?

- Are they a good credit risk? (You can check Dunn and Bradstreet.)

- If they are traded, how has their stock performed and what is their price to earnings ratio?

3.   Key decision makers

Who are they, how do I maintain contact and what in fluences do they have over my product? Find out as much as you can about habits, other competitors that they deal with and how they are thought of in the com-pany. Most importantly, what are their intrinsic values? Are they free thinkers or calculated risk takers? Maybe they only go with the flow and never make a decision without a committee so all decisions are group made with little risk.

4.   Competitive environment

What is the business that your customer is in and who are their key competitors. By understanding this ele-ment, you can aid in brainstorming new ideas to im prove or develop new products to help the customer gain a larger market share. If you are selling to the cus-tomers competitors, you will have to be careful and up front in how you deal with these issues.

5.   Marketing

What Would John Do?

Account Management is not assuming or taking anything for granted. Items A-H are just a few of the many things that need to be discussed, assigned responsibility and planned for in order for them not to fall through the cracks through wrong assumptions. If you are dealing with a major account, you may have to deal with many department managers and the more personnel you deal with, the more thought processes and personalities you have to manage. The more managers that you deal with the more vacations, leaves of absences, promotions, firings and resignations there are. Each of these situations requires that you make sure that your project is followed through from one manager to another and that you assume nothing.

Marketing is all of the issues dealing with promotions and advertising, focus groups, technology, product re search and introduction and all relate to staying ahead of the competition and gaining a larger market share.

Stay in tune with the product direction and that in which your customer is heading. You may uncover additional product opportunities that are synergistic with your current offerings and open up new markets. Stay plugged into promotional activities that can aid in the pulling through of your product or the growing your products presence in the account. Are there trade shows that you can jointly attend, co-op advertising programs or other activities that can aid in promoting market awareness of your product?

Navigating Points:

Account Management can be accomplished through trial and error or you can strategize internally the best way to grow the account in order to maximize the revenue potential. The best method that I have found to manage an account is to develop one or more inside champions depending on the branches, departments or divisions that are actively involved with the use or sale of your product.

6.   Training requirements

Sometimes overlooked after the initial product launch, training should be your most consistent activity with your customer. How you train can be expensive. Consid -er charging for training if appropriate and especially if a precedent is set in your industry. Offer training at cen -tral locations where several or all of the branches in a region can be accommodated. Offer to attend branch, regional or national sales meetings. If your product is a flag ship, you will probably have access to these types of meetings. If not, you will probably have to spend more time and money and train as branches or sales repre -sentatives can be made available.

Training gets you face time. Face time is when you can get in front of your customer and expound on the bene-fits of your product. You can also listen and hear the reasons why your product sells and also the objections. The objections are where you can make the greatest inroads in improving customer satisfaction. If you respond positively to an objection with a new feature that answers that objection, you will gain immediate respect from the person that raised the objection. Objections usually come from two groups, the sales person because they lost a deal to the competition or the product manager that manages your product for their company.

7. Post-sales support and warranty

Post-sales support involves product training and also buddy calls or joint customer calls where you travel along with the sales representative and either assist in presenting the benefits of your product or supports the primary contact as required in presenting or demon -strating your product.

Post-sales support sets the tone from the leaders. Ensuring that you have personnel available to answer questions on pricing, configurations, delivery, operations and warranty are helpful and impressive to the customer. If your product requires computer support, have the tools available that allow you to dial into the system to analyze the problem and download changes.

If you offer warranty exchange, make sure that you have adequate parts or replacement units for a rapid turnaround. Many times customers will purchase products that are not the latest technology but, because the company has a reputation for quality support, the customer will not change suppliers.

If you employ a CRM product, you can possibly track all of the contacts issues from inception to close, all location and contact information, products, orders, pricing special discounts, latest stock quotes, web page information, key dates to remember, forecasts and much more.

Many CRM products allow you off load all pertinent information and let you take the PC on the road, call on the account, bring up the account information, update and synchronize the information back to home office from your hotel line and back to the office.

8. **Pricing**

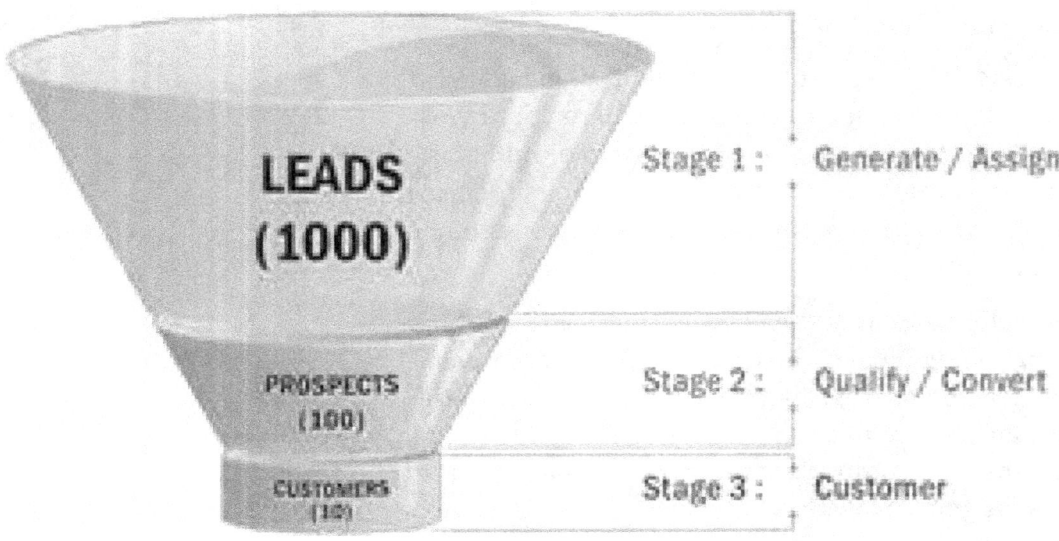

Always a hot item. Written into your contract are arti -cles about pricing and how they can go up or down. Even with a contract, a price increase is never taken lightly. Inform the customer of the impending price in crease and use it to your advantage. Allow for orders to be placed for next year at the old price if the order comes in before a scheduled price increase is due.

A good contact manager program provides you with the ability to track and update personnel as required, provide chronological reporting, schedule meetings, telephone directory, word processor with form letters as well as a whole host of other capabilities. Most packages are equipped with automatic dialers from your personal computer and, if you have Automatic Number Identification in your area, the telephone number will automatically bring up the customer on your screen as you answer the telephone. These are all things that will help make your account management the best it can be.

CHAPTER 17

Territory Management

Wouldn't it be great if all of the potential users of your product would light up so we could pluck them off one by one? Well, they don't and if you are a company with limited resources in terms of Regional or Home Office Sales Personnel, you have to work smarter in generating prospects, qualifying prospects and ultimately bringing to closure prospects that will purchase your product or service.

Some studies discuss the methodologies of generating qualified leads and developing sales channels that serve those needs depending on the type of product you are offering for sale. The following study gives a few examples of how companies can cover a large territory effectively with just a few personnel.

Territory Management

Territory Management is not just having hired guns in territories with quotas for new sales, upgrade sales and account growth. Territory Management is knowing your personnel, channel management, the potential for sales in a territory, your competitions strengths and weaknesses, your customers' loyalties and ultimately bring sales to the bottom line.

Qualified, experienced salespeople in a territory that have an entrepreneurial spirit, that can work independently with minimal direction is the number one pre-requisite for sales in remote territories outside of the home office region. If you

Post-sales support sets the tone from the leaders. Ensuring that you have personnel available to answer questions on pricing, configurations, delivery, operations and warranty are helpful and impressive to the customer. If your product requires computer support, have the tools available that allow you to dial into the system to analyze the problem and download changes.

are in the Mid-Atlantic, Northeast, Southeast or anywhere where there is a distinct work ethic way of doing business or accent, find the people that walk the walk, talk the talk and have a good old boys network that you can tap into for instant product credibility.

After you have developed the product or service, advertised, generated leads and hired the staff required to cover the territory and make sales, you will need effective ways to understand the potential business and close ratio for the territory. Sales people don't like to have reams of paperwork to fill out reporting on customer and prospect status. Things such as forecasts with percent of close ratios and conference calls are necessary for the Sales Manager, or whoever is in charge of sales, to be able to report to the Senior Management team on the progress of sales. Usually, everything that a company does is predicated on sales.

Manufacturing builds from sales forecasts, Research and Development is funded from sales, hiring and firing is regulated on sales, stock goes up or down from sales and the company 401K, profit sharing and bonus participation is regulated on sales. If you have ever been a sales person or Sales Manager, you should have some idea of the requirement for a sales reporting system that will give you the input on a regular base from which you can formulate a sales forecast.

As a rule of thumb, the more expensive or technical an item is, the more need for an experienced sales and support staff to train, support and make the sale. Again, depending on

Navigating Points:

Territory Management is not just having hired guns in territories with quotas for new sales, upgrade sales and account growth. Territory Management is knowing your personnel, channel management, the potential for sales in a territory, your competitions strengths and weaknesses, your customers' loyalties and ultimately bring sales to the bottom line.

Qualified, experienced salespeople in a territory that have an entrepreneurial spirit, that can work independently with minimal direction is the number one pre-requisite for sales in remote territories outside of the home office region.

the simplicity or complexity of your product, your low prospective accounts may only require a questionnaire or telephone call twice a year. Others will require quarterly or monthly calls and more intensive week to week activity. If you sell through distribution, sales channel management may be your most important source to sell your products and services. Not unlike a direct sale customer, they could be more demanding, especially if your product represents a flagship or high volume, high margin product. Channel Management is covered in another study which is also available from a number at the end of this publication.

Step one in territory management is to know where the high priority prospects are. These are prospects that have an immediate interest or application for your product and don't need to be sold on the concept. It is a wise person that understands the demographics of the users of your product because this will aid in concentrating your advertising dollars in media that will reach the greatest target segments for your products.

Territory management also concentrates on the channels that can reach the greatest number of buyers for your product. A sales channel could be a local, regional, national or international distribution or manufacturing company that has many times more sales personnel than you and, as a result, can penetrate an area faster and get quicker results. If your business plan calls for great numbers of product sales to make the numbers, don't forget that your price will have to be tiered in order for your channel to sell competitively.

Tiered pricing simply means that if you are selling direct for a price of $100.00 and you have a two times cost of sales to justify being in business and you need to sell through other than direct channels, can your product still sell if you have to mark it up to sell to distribution? Distribution may then sell direct or they may sell to dealers or stores and they, in turn, will have to place a markup on the product to meet the demand of their business plan. Tiered pricing and selling through distribution is also covered in another study which is also available.

Tracking the Pipeline

Are you making great strides in generating interest for you product and closing outside distribution channels but not getting the desired results? There are many methods of keeping track of the pipeline. Pipeline simply means the numbers of prospects that you have that are in some phase of purchasing or selling your product. Tracking your top 5, 10, 20 or 100 prospects or customers and bringing to their deals to closure will be your most profitable function. A simple formula for tracking your top prospects is as follows:

(Sale $S X % of chance to close) X (Number of work days per year = Days allowed on the account per year.
Annual quota (Use $1,000,000 as a sample quota)

Use the PERCENT OF CLOSE INDICATION along with your Major Account Planning Guide to track the status of your accounts. Every prospect and customer should have a series of action items planned to bring the account to closure. In place of a paper trail involving a Major Account Planning Guide, there are computer applications such as ACT for Windows that allow you to enter all customer and prospect demographic information along with the capability to plan and report on various milestones. Many also have the capability to remind you of appointments, letter and label writing and printing as well as other nice features.

Using the formula along with the PERCENT OF CLOSE INDICATION for a prospect with a 70% chance of close, it looks like this.
$10,000 X 70% = $7,000 X 260 = 1.820.000 = 1.82 days
1,000.000

In this example, a prospect with a 70% chance of close should not have more than 1.82 days of effort spent on closing the prospect. Taking into consideration reality, if you're a new company or the prospect is key to new sales, you may spend considerably more effort in closing this prospect than 1.82 days. If you look at the pipeline and track the closure time for all sales, the effort will probably be close to the allocated time.

If the prospect is a $500,000 account and the formula says three weeks, this time is not spent serially but spread out over many months and with many resources to bring to closure.

Most of the prospects that initially show interest may have a 10% close factor allowing a minimum amount of time to be spent. This time is trial closing and used to set an appointment or get some type of action where the prospect has committed time and resources to closer examine or hear your presentation. After you have taken this next step, the probability goes up and you are afforded the luxury of spending more time on the account to closure.

As a sales manager with salespeople turning in territory management reports with a percentage of closures, it will be easy to identify and track the high profile accounts and assist your personnel in closing the required business. It will also be an aid to track the number of prospects in the pipeline and determine if there are too many prospects to cover and concentrate on closing not prospecting.

Some salespeople are great at prospecting but poor on closing and you, as the manager, will be gung ho on the salesperson that brings in a full sheet of prospects with closure percentages. On the other hand, a salesperson with few prospects but high closure could be the salesperson that makes numbers and has a handle on territory management and understands the close cycle.

Be aware of the trends in territory reporting and call on prospects with your people to verify the validity of the reporting as well as to take the pulse of the prospect community. The prospects will tell you about competition, where you are weak and strong, and what it will take to close business. After the salesperson spends the allocated time and the prospect probability goes up, use your own judgment as to the amount of time to spend since this isn't an exact science.

Navigating Points:

Territory management also concentrates on the channels that can reach the greatest number of buyers for your product. A sales channel could be a local, regional, national or international distribution or manufacturing company that has many times more sales personnel than you and, as a result, can penetrate an area faster and get quicker results. If your business plan calls for great numbers of product sales to make the numbers, don't forget that your price will have to be tiered in order for your channel to sell competitively.

We are dealing with relationships, likes and dislikes and a lot of subjectivity. Decimal one and one will always add up to two but in sales, you can win the battle and lose the war. Other reasons that you may spend more time closing an account that are deemed profitable are the nature or influence the account has. The account might be a leader in the industry and recognizable so you could leverage the account through reference sales and advertising. You might also have to buy an account to get you started. Again, depending on type of product, you might consider special incentives for geographic territories in order to get your product some momentum. So don't be afraid to spend money to get key accounts as long as it is not a habit and a crutch for your salespeople.

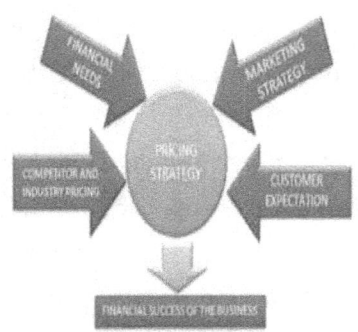

When your salespeople turn in their territory management reports on a weekly or monthly basis, an exception in reporting the pipeline would be those prospects that they are leveraging through incentives to land a key account. It should not be unlike dominos if you have done your marketing. When you land a key prospect that will allow you to reference them, your product is in demand, you have differentiated from competition and are priced competitively. All things being equal, with good pre and post-sales support, the pipeline will fill up. When the pipeline is full, many of the accounts will take less time to sell because you have leveraged key regional and national accounts and have promoted the product in markets that can use your product.

Dual File Prospecting

Keep good files if you are manually tracking prospect activity in your territory. If you are computerized, use one of the prospect/customer management programs to track prospects and customer activity. They are available for your tablet and laptop and it is a good idea to use the voice activated feature to record ideas for future use.

The prospects are the ones that you are spending your serious time on and arranged in percentage of close sequence by alphabet, state, county and city. This is important in order optimize your time in a region. Normally, and again the value of the account will dictate the time and resources you spend to bring to closure, we would call on many prospects in a region to get the most out of your money and especially if you have to fly and be there overnight.

The suspect files are the tire kickers and want you to call them when you are in their region. You call on these prospects as fill-in when you don't have appointments for a given time slot or you finish earlier than expected.

Many of the suspects could be tele marketed or direct mailed to keep them informed on the status or your product and as the interest is moved forward, the prospect is passed to you for more direct involvement.

Sales Channel Development

One of the greatest pitfalls is when a company believes that the only way to sell is to sell direct. This is a great philosophy if dollars are unlimited, the product is unique and the margins are terrific. But this is not the norm so marketing has to develop a strategy that will allow a minimum number of salespeople to cover a vast territory. This task is usually accom-

Navigating Points:

Be aware of the trends in territory reporting and call on prospects with your people to verify the validity of the reporting as well as to take the pulse of the prospect community. The prospects will tell you about competition, where you are weak and strong, and what it will take to close business. After the salesperson spends the allocated time and the prospect probability goes up, use your own judgment as to the amount of time to spend since this isn't an exact science.

plished by identifying wholesale or retail distribution firms that have synergistic product lines where your product could compliment the sale, give added value or solve a problem that can't be solved with their current line of products.

Identifying the Channel

This is the easiest part of the equation. Some ways to identify potential channels for the sale of your product are:

- Look in trade journals for distribution and supply companies that sell your type of product line.
- Go to trade shows and gather information about companies that sell your type of products.
- Ask your prospects and customers who would be a candidate to sell your product.
- Talk to manufacturers' representatives that are geographic in scope.
- Talk to other manufacturers that find added value in your product when sold in conjunction with theirs. A firm may want to private label your product or they may want to OEM your product. A private label means that they buy in quantity, place their name on the product and sell it. If they OEM the product, they usually integrate the product into theirs and it gives added value that they otherwise would not have. In many cases, your product could be the tie breaker to win the sale.
- Advertise for distribution and follow up accordingly

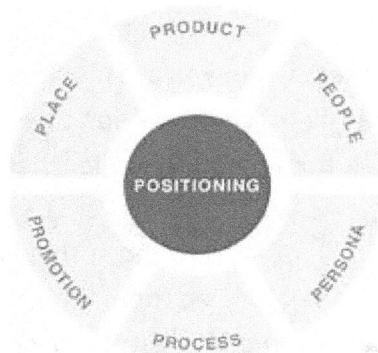

Channel Sales Requirements

After the identification of a sales channel, the closing of the channel can make or break your company. A fine-tuned, well thought out strategy needs to be in place and executed for both parties to be successful. An example is an excited company with interest from a national distribution firm that says it can sell thousands. Everyone jumps on the band wagon only to find out that in order to sell thousands the following has to be agreed to.

- Exclusive distribution rights
- Comprehensive promotional and sales aids
- 24 hour support
- Train the trainer support
- Margin enough for three tiers of sales. You, the manufacturer, have to have a margin to support your business plan. The sales channel does not sell direct but to other resellers so they have to have a decent margin and the ultimate reseller has to have enough margin to make the product attractive to the ultimate customer.
- Inventory buy backs, credit or replacement for slow moving products
- No fault warranty where the customer can return any product for any reason and the channel expects you to honor the return.
- Advertising a suggested list price
- Co-op advertising
- Buddy calls

These are a few of the many requirements that your sales channel may request in order for you to do business with them. Doing business with a channel is great if your strategy for developing and selling your product was always geared for tiered distribution.

As an example, if you knew from your marketing efforts

Navigating Points:

Keep good files if you are manually tracking prospect activity in your territory. If you are computerized, use one of the prospect/customer management programs to track prospects and customer activity. They are available for your tablet and laptop and it is a good idea to use the voice activated feature to record ideas for future use.

The prospects are the ones that you are spending your serious time on and arranged in percentage of close sequence by alphabet, state, county and city. This is important in order optimize your time in a region. Normally, and again the value of the account will dictate the time and resources you spend to bring to closure, we would call on many prospects in a region.

that for a given product it could be sold for $65 and you could develop, manufacture and have a decent margin in X were sold at $25 through distribution. If you sell to distribution for $25 and they add 25% or $6.25, the product goes to the ultimate reseller at $31.25. The reseller sells the product at a 100% mark up for a customer price of $62.50.

Did you think of the requirements of the channel and the impact to your margin they will have if you sell to them. Most manufacturers don't think of the many pitfalls that there are in doing business with a major distribution chain; all they think about is the quantity that could be sold if the deal can be made.

What about pricing incentives as the product ages or midlife kickers or enhancements to keep your product state of the art. What if competition moves in with new technology at a lower price? All of these possible scenarios need to be thought out and a proactive plan needs to be ready. If you are always in a reactive mode, you will always be scrambling to implement programs and strategies that will not have as a great a chance of being successful as if you were pro-active to begin with.

Channel Management

In order to manage a sales channel effectively, how you sell your product will make or break the relationship with the channel.

Things that Complement

Developing an effective and profitable outside sales channel can be your most valuable resource for achieving your

One of the greatest pitfalls is when a company believes that the only way to sell is to sell direct. This is a great philosophy if dollars are unlimited, the product is unique and the margins are terrific. But this is not the norm so marketing has to develop a strategy that will allow a minimum number of salespeople to cover a vast territory. This task is usually accomplished by identifying wholesale or retail distribution firms that have synergistic product lines where your product could compliment the sale, give added value or solve a problem that can't be solved with their current line of products.

revenue objectives. Channels can have 10, 100's or 1,000's of products in their catalog and the 80-20 rule usually applies. Twenty percent of the products represent eighty percent of their sales. The sales persons for the major channels have quotas and if your product does not have the necessary collateral, promotions, incentives, avenues to generate considerable revenue, is competitive and offers pre and post-sales support you will not get more than a token look from the bag carrying, quota compensated sales person.

One of the most over looked expense items in bringing a product to revenue producing is the development of sales channels. Don't be so excited about the enthusiasm that a product manager of a sales channel may have for your product. Don't forget that this product manager is deluged with new products every day and has a commitment to the incumbent vendor to continue promoting their product because they have revenue goals to maintain the profitability of their company.

Navigating Points:

What about pricing incentives as the product ages or midlife kickers or enhancements to keep your product state of the art. What if competition moves in with new technology at a lower price? All of these possible scenarios need to be thought out and a proactive plan needs to be ready. If you are always in a reactive mode, you will always be scrambling to implement programs and strategies that will not have as a great a chance of being successful as if you were proactive to begin with.

Things to Do Right

- Never sell direct to a sales channels customer. If the sales channels customer calls you for a direct price quotation for a great volume, explain your position and get the sales channel involved. An example of involvement for a major sale would involve going "Off Book" for a special price to the customer. In most cases, the sales channel will give up margin along with the manufacturer in order to make the sale and keep the channel, the customer and give you, the manufacturer the sale
- Never advertise a "Suggested List Price" without first involv-

ing all of your resellers. Your "Suggested List Price" may be less than they have been selling the product for and you will need to give your reseller a chance to reposition the product in order to maintain their required margin.

- Solicit for enhancements to your product and add them if at all possible. This shows that you care about their input and also gives your reseller ownership of your product. If you are a small manufacturer or a startup, it is usually easier to meet the needs of your resellers than if you are a mega million dollar manufacturer. This could be your competitive advantage.

- Ask about co-op advertising and actively pursue joint marketing activities. These activities could be supplying press releases, collateral material, offering to participate in regional and national trade shows, buddy calls for major prospects and other lead generation activities.

- Many times, if your product can attain flagship status with your channel, they may wish to private label and commit to larger volumes. When you get to this status, you have a solid customer that competition will find difficult to unseat.

- Don't be a burden, but maintain a close relationship with the decision makers for your family of products. Use your own judgment about the relationship and in many instances, the channel will publish a policy on doing business with them.

- Live up to your warranty commitments and if your product malfunctions, be proactive in working the problem. You were given the opportunity to sell through this channel and an un-worked problem can bring months of effort to a grinding halt in days. You may or may not be able to recover

Surviving a failure gives you more self-confidence. Failures are great learning tools.. but they must be kept to a minimum.

— Jeffrey Immelt

Whatever the mind of man can conceive and believe, it can achieve. Thoughts are things! And powerful things at that, when mixed with definiteness of purpose, and burning desire, can be translated into riches.

— Napoleon Hill

It is not the strongest of the species that survive, nor the most intelligent, but the one most responsive to change.

— Charles Darwin

depending on how you respond to the problem.

Stay In Touch

I am convinced that to effectively manage a group of salespeople that you have to stay in touch. Your personality, product, level of activity and profitability will dictate how in touch you are with your sales people. I have always maintained an open door policy that I could be called at any time for any valid reason. How you stay in touch is dependent on where your salespeople are located. Take an example of salespeople located in key metropolitan areas of the United States.

An old cliché "Success Breeds Success" is so true and I wanted all to hear of a success as soon as it occurred. One method that works very effectively is a daily, weekly or monthly conference call with a prearranged agenda that stipulates that each salesperson speaks to the success of their region, potential obstacles due to competition, pricing or personality of the account. This allows everyone to communicate on a formal basis and brings the team closer together.

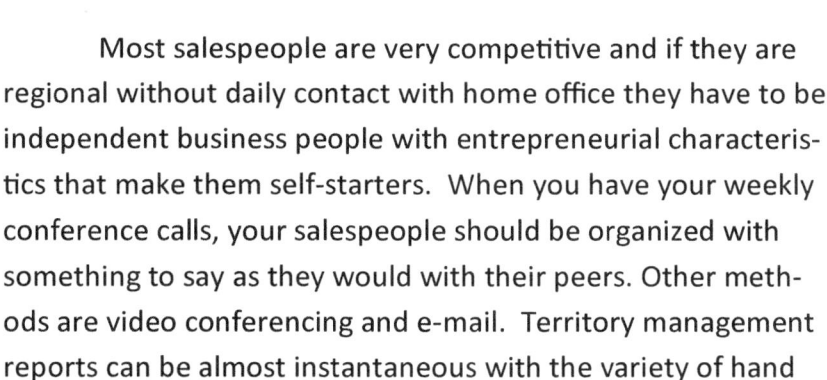

Most salespeople are very competitive and if they are regional without daily contact with home office they have to be independent business people with entrepreneurial characteristics that make them self-starters. When you have your weekly conference calls, your salespeople should be organized with something to say as they would with their peers. Other methods are video conferencing and e-mail. Territory management reports can be almost instantaneous with the variety of hand held devices on the market.

If you can afford the expense, it is wise to have quarterly, bi-yearly or yearly kick off meetings where your salespeople and other interested parties interact with each other. The salespeople are there to report on their plan to make the numbers, discuss obstacles and hear how the company will support them to make it happen in their territory.

These meetings are invaluable in letting the rest of the company understand the progress that sales is making from the efforts they have put forth to develop the products. These meetings bring the company together and allow for a direct interchange of information from the group that deals with the prospects and customers on a daily basis. Other invaluable methods to stay in touch are periodic company meetings, a newsletter and celebrating major sales or profitability.

Credibility

Sales people can win or lose credibility in the blink of an eye with many companies; especially companies that are engineer driven. Staying in touch can be immeasurable in maintaining the credibility of the salesperson. A regional sales person does not have the luxury of daily contact with developers, engineers and senior level management so be cognizance of the effort that is being put forth.

If there are product delays, warranty problems, competitive issues, pricing or other issues, remember that the sales person has only their person-

CHAPTER 18

Cold Calling Techniques

Navigating Points:

Sales people can win or lose credibility in the blink of an eye with many companies; especially companies that are engineer driven. Staying in touch can be immeasurable in maintaining the credibility of the salesperson. A regional sales person does not have the luxury of daily contact with developers, engineers and senior level management so be cognizance of the effort that is being put forth.

Objective—

Generate immediate interest to meet your objective

Goal—

Your goal for each call is to meet the first objective, "generate immediate interest." It is almost impossible to generate immediate interest if your cold call list has not been previously qualified with the demographics that could be a requirement for your product or service. Considerable thought should be given when selecting a cold call list, otherwise your close ratio could be zero. A far out example would be cold calling to sell airplanes from a residential phone book. The odds are pretty definite that you would not get any interest from such a call.

A list that contained names of previous or current owners of aircraft would be much more suitable to call from in order to generate interest. Calling into specific demographics for your product is a targeted methodology. Rural areas tend to be much more suitable for selling MLM, Amway, Tupperware, pots and pans, books, brushes, sundries, health and beauty products. Jewelry, travel, and cutlery tend to cross over demographics.

Examples of types of cold calling are:

- Surveying for product interest
- Promoting political candidates
- Soliciting for donations and services
- Appointment setting
- Closing

time proven way to generate leads and ultimately close business. The recipient of the cold call is usually not adverse to answering or listening to your pitch as long as the product or service has an application to the business or to them personally.

It is imperative that your list be selected carefully and that as you call from your list you continually monitor the responses for trends that can make the list more productive for future telemarketing.

Calling Methodology, Automatic Dialers and ACD's

The product or service that you are selling dictates the type of cold calling that will be made to the potential recipient. Automated dialers with sophisticated Automatic Call Distributors are used by the large telemarketers and call centers in order to reach the mass population. Examples of types of firms that use automatic dialers are magazine sellers, credit card sellers, and book publishing agencies, insurance and hospitality/vacations agencies.

Millions of names are stored in a computer with a software program tied into the telephone system that systematically dials each name based on the time zone of where a particular individual lives and will be home. The system dials the name and when a connection is made, the Automatic Call Distributor routes the call to a live telemarketer that gives the recipient the pitch on the product or service that is being sold.

The sophistication of the telephone system coupled with the computer hardware and software makes it almost impossible for any individual or business not be targeted for some type of telemarketing call for a product or service. The government asks your demographic information on the census or IRS for any reason. They sell this information to telemarketing firms for mass calling. As contacts are made with a prospect for a product or service, this information is recorded in a data base for future calling and this information is also sold to other like product and service providers.

If you wish to have your name excluded from further calls, you can request it when you are called. You can have your name taken off of the list and eventually you calls will diminish; most of the time.

Service Bureaus

- Referencing
- Warranties for products
- Confirming appointments
- You won something
- Selected for a giveaway
- Bingo cards
- Direct mail
- E-mail
- Your web page
- Referral Web Pages
- Cookies
- Fairs
- Trade shows
- Word of mouth

I have had a great deal of success cold calling because I targeted my list with names of businesses that could make money if they used or sold my product or service. I went in armed with a benefit list and discussed business potential. Most of the time the introduction focused on finding out what they do and asking if they had access to my type of product and what and how would it benefit them and their customers.

When I get a prospect engaged in a discussion, I found out what they were interested in and worked my product introduction around their work schedule and usually got a trial and at the least feedback that I could use for the next call.

Cold calling from a selected list to people or businesses that have used or could possibly use your product or service is a

I have experienced companies that invested thousands of dollars in getting the right salesperson with the right experience, excellent contacts and a real quota maker only to let them leave or fire them because the company could not deliver or support the committed product. The company then hires a new coach and sales people only to begin anew what was already a sound basis for continuing the sales effort when the product was capable of being delivered and supported as claimed. Examine the circumstances before making a decision on replacing the coach and sales-people. You could save yourself not only time but dollars and credibility.

For local, regional or national telemarketing, any business can contract with and purchase a list for lead generation or product/service sales; these are called service bureaus. Look in your local telephone book for telemarketing services.

Cold Calling

Let's set the stage, let us examine a typical copy machine salespersons cold call. The company usually gives the salesperson a territory so that salespersons to do not overlap or call on the same prospect. A salesperson has to have an ego, not be afraid of rejection, be outgoing, astute at reading body language and verbal interest signs and, I believe, that you have to sell your solution to the person's problem or requirement.

The Context of the Call

Prior to making the cold call, visualize the flow of the conversation in a positive format.

If you can picture the building, see an advertisement, see one of their trucks, know someone that works there, and know the business or anything else that can make you feel more comfortable prior to making the call.

- Have a note pad, voice activated tape recorder, your lap top or tablet to write down key issues or objections that might be brought up during the call.

- Have a specific name, if possible, to talk to. Having a reference name for someone in a business that asked you to call them can be very positive. People like to know that they are not the first to purchase your product and it gives them a comfort zone.

- Keep a check list of the main benefits you want to cover with the prospect until you get to know your subject manner thoroughly.

- Be acquainted with the nature of their business i.e. distribution, manufacturing, retail, etc.

- Have a goal in mind when you make the call. If they responded to a bingo card ad, called for information, attended a trade show and showed interest, they have an interest in pursuing the dialog you probably have a one in 10 chance of closing a sale of this kind.

Other cold calls types may be to find out the name of the decision person, invite them to a seminar or discover who your competition are and/or what products do they currently use.

Salespeople are motivated by results. I ask everyone, when they have what appears to be an overwhelming number of tasks to do, to write them down and then check them off as they are accomplished. You can see the positive steps towards achieving your objectives if you have a tool to chart your progress.

After a call that you thought was not particularly meaningful, jot down notes in catalog form about specific points that were brought up by the type of business. During the next call to a like company, you will be that much more knowledgeable.

When you have a caller on the line, be positive at all times and try not to be aloof. Always put yourself on the level of the person you are talking to. If you can't answer their question, tell them you will get right back to them; this builds credibility. If the person is not acquainted with your product, service or the technology, don't make assumptions; explain about your product and draw analogies to their business.

Examples of contacts made when the person is not available and contact made when the person is available.

Contact made, person not available

Introduce yourself to the person and ask for a specific name. Depending upon how high you are calling in the organization, the more likely that your contact will not be available. You will have to generate a dialogue with the receptionist to

Navigating Points:

The product or service that you are selling dictates the type of cold calling that will be made to the potential recipient. Automated dialers with sophisticated Automatic Call Distributors are used by the large telemarketers and call centers in order to reach the mass population. Examples of types of firms that use automatic dialers are magazine sellers, credit card sellers, and book publishing agencies, insurance and hospitality/vacations agencies.

find out another person to talk to. Find out the receptionists' name, thank her and ask to be transferred. If the person is not in, ask for the name (correct spelling), title, and extension and find out if they have a staff, size of organization and anything that might be useful when you get the right person on the call. You have to play it by ear to see how far you can go in asking questions.

Contact made and person is available

Introduce yourself, your company and your purpose for the call. From this point forward use all of your skills in reading body language. If your call is a person to person and if the call is on the telephone, be aware of urgency, interest and time available. Remember the interest grabber/lead point; after your introduction, you need an attention getting statement. This statement is predicated on the type of product or service that you are selling and how you present yourself if you are requesting information for a survey. It is also heavily dependent on the demographics of your audience.

Examples of Interest Grabbers when selling copiers, computers, software or other high tech-products or services are...

Hello my name is John Doe from the Widget Company and Jack Barns suggested that I give you a call about your copier requirements.

This grabber accomplishes your objectives of introducing yourself, your company and gives credibility that Jack Barns thought enough of your product to introduce you to a business associate that may have the same requirement.

Hello my name is John Doe from the Widget Company and we spoke at the
national Widget trade show in Atlanta and you asked that I give you a call after
the show to discuss your Widget requirements.

This is a pre-qualified lead to a greater extent than that of Jack Barns but the difference between this lead and lead A is that you should have knowledge of this persons' interest and should take this prospect to your next closing step.

Hello my name is John Doe from the Widget Company and I am calling you as a result of your inquiry through the Widget Trade Journal of August. There is definitely interest or the person would not have taken the time to cut out the coupon from the magazine and mail it in requesting further information.

Hello my name is John Doe from the Widget Company and I am calling local businesses to introduce our new line of copier products offering 30 day free trials with 1,000 free copies.

Having a hook such as a free trial and/or copies gives you more credibility with your cold call and should increase your chances of having the person accept your free trial and ultimately purchase or at least recommend it to another business.

Motivating yourself

How do I motivate myself when my boss has me on a quota for X cold calls a day and I am not in the right frame of mind?

Answer: Not all people are cut out for cold calling because of all the rejection they receive.

How do we motivate buyers?

- By being practical – This is how our product can help you.

- Saving Time—Everyone wants to save time.

- Avoid Effort—Make your job easier so that you can get on to bigger and better things.

- Cleanliness—Not necessarily sanitary but make your job run smoother.

Navigating Points:

Salespeople are motivated by results. I ask everyone, when they have what appears to be an overwhelming number of tasks to do, to write them down and then check them off as they are accomplished. You can see the positive steps towards achieving your objectives if you have a tool to chart your progress.

After a call that you thought was not particularly meaningful, jot down notes in catalog form about specific points that were brought up by the type of business. During the next call to a like company, you will be that much more knowledgeable.

- Money—To save, make or spend when the budget has not been depleted.

- Health-Ease stress

- Emotional

- Comfort-Selling - name recognition, service and product.

- Stylish-Latest development, technology and benefit.

- Popularity—Make your caller a hero.

- Enjoyment-How much fun you can have by using or giving it away.

- Satisfy Curiosity—Others have it, now you can have it to

- Satisfy Appetite-Looking for something new. Attract the opposite sex.

- Makes you look, feel or smell better.

- Individualism-Helps control not be dependent.

- Emulate others-Did you know that your competitor or friend bought this item.

- Possessions-Empire building.

- Avoid Criticism by purchasing, you can't go wrong with this buy for these reasons.

- Love-Loved ones, peers and superiors will love you for selecting this.

- Pride—Explain how the already good running business, home can be ran better or improved on by adding this product or service.

- Belonging-Selling by name association into a club, credit card, organization, etc.

- Self-Preservation-You can't do without it.

- Self-Indulgence-You can really get into it.

What Would John Do?

I have had a great deal of success cold calling because I targeted my list with names of businesses that could make money if they used or sold my product or service. I went in armed with a benefit list and discussed business potential. Most of the time the introduction focused on finding out what they do and asking if they had access to my type of product and what and how would it benefit them and their customers.

When I get a prospect engaged in a discussion, I found out what they were interested in and worked my product introduction around their work schedule and usually got a trial and at the least feedback that I could use for the next call.

- Duty-Doing the right thing.

- Self-Image-Winning by responding.

After making your pitch and getting their interest, you need to develop ownership by getting the prospect to either object where you can answer the objection and trial close or have the prospect agree and trial close. The close could be to get a credit card for purchase, pledge by asking for amount, name address, etc., referral or agree to attend, agree to accept written information or establish an in person visit.

Cold Calling has to have a clearly defined objective. Keeping spirits high can only be accomplished by successes so you need clearly defined hourly, daily, weekly, monthly, quarterly and yearly incentives for your telemarketers. You need to think of the tele marketers' family and include incentives that the significant other can also reap some benefit.

What worked well for me was to call a meeting with all of my telemarketers and discuss what they realistically thought they could sell and, based on their input, I would set incentives accordingly. I would only raise the quotas, and sometimes not at all, depending on what the people came up. When you have a group of people competing for spiffs or incentives, they tend to be more aggressive than if their manager gave them a quota without their input. You need to use psychology and reward everyone with the best incentives if they all achieve the goal.

Examples of incentives that I used for cold calling on daily, weekly and monthly were:

- Gas tank fill up per week for making X calls with X appointments

- Movie or concert tickets

- Weekend vacations at local resorts for X appointments per month

- Video equipment for number of closes

- Spa treatments.

I often let the women and men choose their own types of incentives for making specific goals. When your telemarketers or sales people can get immediate rewards for effort and take it home and show their spouses, it generates competition and helps motivation from the home front.

Chapter 19

Reasons to Lose an Order

Almost as important in winning a deal is why you lost the deal. Losses can be very important to your ultimate success if you analyze them and learn from them. Talk to other salespersons and find out why they lost a deal and keep a journal or log of the transactions and try to categorize the reasons for a given loss.   The next time you are in the midst of sale try to analyze the flow of the sales cycle against some of the reasons that you or your associates have won or lost. If a red flag goes up try to neutralize the objection into a positive and get the sale back on track.

You should never, as a rule, bring up religion, politics or race as those topics are pitfalls waiting to swallow your time and blow your credibility, Don't be baited into discussing or debating those three subjects. Some of the reasons why I have lost an order, heard about or read about are:

- I let my ego get in the way and tried to sell something that they didn't need.
- I didn't satisfy the prospects objections.
- I neglected the prospect and procrastinated with them and competition moved in and grabbed the order.
- I merely presented the product, I didn't sell it.
- I let myself argue with the prospect, won the argument and lost the deal.
- I talked too much about the features and not the benefits that could be derived by the customer.
- The prospect was ready to sign, but I kept on talking and I

Navigating Points:

Introduce yourself to the person and ask for a specific name. Depending upon how high you are calling in the organization, the more likely that your contact will not be available. You will have to generate a dialogue with the receptionist to find out another person to talk to. Find out the receptionists' name, thank her and ask to be transferred. If the person is not in, ask for the name (correct spelling), title, and extension and find out if they have a staff, size of organization and anything that might be useful when you get the right person on the call. You have to play it by ear to see how far you can go in asking questions.

talked myself right out of the order.

- I never asked for the order, I only hinted at the order.
- I tried to hide the objections instead of answering them and turning them into a positive.
- I totally ignored the economic and cost justifications of the product.
- I knocked my competition instead of making an objective comparison and lost the respect of my prospect.
- I lost my prospects confidence because I never did a thorough enough job on my homework and couldn't give adequate answers to the management team.
- I displayed my technical brilliance but the prospect was more interested in what the product could do for him and his company.
- I never convinced the prospect to buy now rather than later.
- When the prospect asked a question, I tried to answer a question that I couldn't and lost credibility instead of saying that I didn't know and would get back to him with the answer.
- I tried to go over the known decision makers head to the CEO and lost total credibility.
- I forgot my presentation.
- I left my product at home, in the car or it got lost.
- Never made the appointment.
- I shipped it here and you were supposed to have it in receiving, didn't you get it? (Note—This is never an excuse unless you are sending a truckload that has to be set up prior to your arrival.)

What worked well for me was to call a meeting with all of my telemarketers and discuss what they realistically thought they could sell and, based on their input, I would set incentives accordingly. I would only raise the quotas, and sometimes not at all, depending on what the people came up. When you have a group of people competing for spiffs or incentives, they tend to be more aggressive than if their manager gave them a quota without their input. You need to use psychology and reward.

CHAPTER 20
Handling Objections

Everybody is a salesperson to some degree and we get objections almost every day of our life. How we handle those objections is key to our well-being and in the personal selling process. The first sell each of us ever made was getting fed at birth. We probably cried which was very objectionable, but sold your mother on the need to be fed to quiet the crying. That is an example of an elementary handling an objection and it was very obvious, feed the baby and it will quit crying. It was a win-win situation.

Often the buyer will not volunteer an objection, but simply say they are not interested. This early objection should be recognized on the telephone and not on an actual prospect visit. If the disinterest is at the prospect premises, you misinformed the prospect on your intention or they totally misunderstood the reason for the meeting.

In the case where the prospect is disinterested, the salesperson has to be skilled in direct and indirect questioning techniques to pull these objections out. Examples of buyers disinterest statements are:

- I just don't feel right about it.
- I already have a widget that works.
- Could we postpone until next week.

All of these statements could be considered stalling statements more than objections. Each statement represents an opportunity for the salesperson to move closer to the sale by asking indirect questions like:

Statement number 1 -

Why?

A simple word that can evoke a response from your prospect. The prospect may say, "I am not sure,' to the first statement so you can ask a more direct question such as, Are the benefits not clear? or you can say, can we sit down and clarify the benefits so that you will be more at ease.

Statement number 2 -

In your response, you asked for further information.

Repeat the reason that you are present or talking to the prospect to refresh his memory on why you are calling him. The prospect will probably tell you why he called and when he does, you have the opportunity to further probe for interest and closing statements.

Statement number 3 -

A postponement could mean many things, a personal requirement, a crisis or simply a rescheduling to give you the proper time to explain your product.

Show a sincere interest in the buyers' needs and once that trust is developed, the prospect will usually open up like an old friend. Begin with indirect questions like "Why?" or 'What's the problem?" If you don't get the results that you are looking for, move on to more direct questions. Either way, you have to get to the heart of the matter and not have any open objections. You have to have a clean slate of no objections in order to close the deal.

One of the most difficult things a salesperson has to do is humble him or herself by letting the prospect or customer have all of the credit for the sale. This technique is "Seed

The Experts Speak Out...

Industry is the soul of business and the keystone of prosperity.

— *Charles Dickens*

I don't pay good wages because I have a lot of money; I have a lot of money because I pay good wages.

— *Robert Bosch*

People are definitely a company's greatest asset. It doesn't make any difference whether the product is cars or cosmetics. A company is only as good as the people it keeps.

— *Mary Kay Ash*

Planting for Future Closure" and can be one of your greatest assets of a salesperson if done right.

Seed planting can be as simple as stating that you can have your logo on the product so that when your product is in use, your customer will always have your name in front of them. As an example, in a meeting, the person that you planted the seed with brings this capability up in front of his boss and his boss says, "Great idea Jack, let's do it, It shouldn't cost that much extra." Some salespeople might say, "I told Jack that he could do that with our product Mr. Boss." Jack feels bad because he made some points and you took the credit. You did plant the seed, but you didn't water the seed for more fruit, it died on the vine and never more to bear fruit.

Planting seeds and watering them can make everyone feel good and you, as a salesperson, are ultimately concerned with winning the deal, so let the other person take the credit for the idea. If you were to say, "Great idea Jack and we could use your corporate colors for the logo." The boss will think that Jack is very resourceful and you are working well with his decision team.

Never make the prospect feel dumb or that any question is too dumb to ask. Your job as a salesperson is to be a professional educator. Always humble yourself to the buyer and try not to show superiority with answers that come with an attitude. Remember that you are selling a product and you should know most of the answers to questions that a prospect asks.

I have, in many situations, said that I do not have the answer to a specific question but that I will get right back with the answer or I will have an expert back at the office assist me when I call. This puts me in a position of credibility with the customer because I care about his concerns and I react promptly in getting the right answers. Another thing, including members at home office helps your credibility because it is team building and shows that you need the other members of the organization to help you be successful.

You may hear the same objection a hundred times but remember, to the prospect, this is the most important question or concern that he has and you should take the objection as the first time that you have heard it. You could also explain that Mr. Smith, CEO of Smith & Company asked the same question and was pleasantly surprised with the answer.

Objections should always be welcomed by the seller because it gives you, the seller, the opportunity to trial close and move closer to the sale. Never push aside an objection, because it won't go away. You will always know that it is there and if you don't have an answer, you will always fear that it will resurface. Remember that your competition probably answered the objection, so address all objections and you will move closer to the sale.

Trial closes are easier to find for higher ticket items and longer sales cycle products and services. Remember a trial close asks for a commitment. You probably won't get more than two or three chances to trial close on retail products or over the counter items.

If the prospects body language is comfortable when you make a call or he asks you about your family, sports or local news

Often the buyer will not volunteer an objection, but simply say they are not interested. This early objection should be recognized on the telephone and not on an actual prospect visit. If the disinterest is at the prospect premises, you misinformed the prospect on your intention or they totally misunderstood the reason for the meeting.

when you first meet, then the prospect probably feels good meeting with you and you can trial close more readily. I have had many instances where I would ask a trial close question or begin answering an objection and the buyer will answer his own question. As a seasoned professional, you should just sit back, listen intently and move the sale further to the close. The following is an example.

Prospect:

"I just don't know if I would have enough time to tear down and train on the new equipment without interrupting the daily work flow. Well, I could have the department come in on a weekend. That's it, we will work the weekend."

Salesperson:

"Mr. Prospect, we work weekends often to assist our customers in bringing up a new system. Do you have a time when we could schedule the effort?"

The key to any sale is to get the prospect to take ownership of your product. Ownership is only carried out when the prospect is sold on you, the company, the cost savings, increased production and the competitive advantage that your products or services will bring to his company.

Every company has some objections that a prospect could bring up. I would suggest that before your next sales meeting, you request that each salesperson jot down a list of objections and review them during a sales meeting.

After you have completed the review, write down an answer to each objection, type it up and give it to each salesperson

Navigating Points:

You may hear the same objection a hundred times but remember, to the prospect, this is the most important question or concern that he has and you should take the objection as the first time that you have heard it. You could also explain that Mr. Smith, CEO of Smith & Company asked the same question and was pleasantly surprised with the answer. Objections should always be welcomed by the seller because it gives you, the seller, the opportunity to trial close and move closer to the sale. Never push aside an objection, because it won't go away.

Chapter 21
Promotional Planner

Haphazard advertising and promotional planning can be some of the most costly mistakes a company can make. Costly because the message was not complete when it was released and did not convey the worth of the product or service that you are trying to advertise and, worst of all, the prospects that you are trying to attract will be turned off by your message.

Advertising and promotions can be very expensive if you do not know the demographics of your target audience. Shotgun mailings, advertising in trade journals, television, radio and newspaper ads, telemarketing, bingo cards, cold calling and trade shows can consume your advertising and promotional dollars without much return if not targeted to attract your desired customer.

The Promotional Planner is designed to be a tool to help you produce a given promotional piece with salient terminology to convey a message to a given target audience. The Planner should depict a worst case, the objective of the promotion you are trying to achieve and, at best case, depict the overall campaign be it a onetime deal or a five year campaign.

The Planner could convey a teaser campaign to build up anticipation, a big splash with benefits, features and price with outlets that will sell or distribute. You can depict a family of products that will be produced as the product matures. You can also portray demographics of people who will use the product. You can depict cures, fun, excitement, love, security and maturity depending on the audience you are trying to attract. The Planner is a good tool to get feedback from associates, customers and prospects and then can be used to refine your in-house promotions or outside ad agency promotions in order to construct the campaign.

Key points that any promotional piece representing your company and product should have should, at the very least, explain the benefits, features and in some way visually depict the product or service you are selling. It needs to have -

- Name of the product or service
- Product Definition (What is the product?)
- Target Audience (Who are you targeting this piece to and why?)
- Theme (Is it a first release, is it the beginning of a family of products, cost savings?)
- Principal Sales Points (What are the benefits to your target customer?)
- Competitive Advantage (Does your product give a competitive advantage or are you revolutionary?)
- Primary and Secondary Audiences (Do you potentially have additional tiers of customers?)
- Selling Strategy and Sales Cycle (What is the message you want to convey to make your customer purchase your product?)

All of your sales and technical material should be coded with the revision number, type of document, name of document and date in order to reference and update as your product changes. It is essential for your customers to stay informed

Navigating Points:

Haphazard advertising and promotional planning can be some of the most costly mistakes a company can make. Costly because the message was not complete when it was released and did not convey the worth of the product or service that you are trying to advertise and, worst of all, the prospects that you are trying to attract will be turned off by your message.

on your products or services. It used to be that paper was sent to all of your customers and they had to update their files. With the web, you can give passwords and let your customers have access to the latest changes in documentation and promotional materials within minutes of release.

What you say on your web page, your voice or e-mail greeting, business card, company logo, documentation, sales brochures, product literature or media commercial conveys a message that will attract or detract someone. Your message needs to be consistent but be alterable depending on customer or viewer feedback. All materials that a prospect or customer could possibly see should have your URL, company name, phone number or contact page with names and contact numbers or e-mail addresses. Constantly massage your feedback and place your money where you get the most bang for your buck.

Chapter 22

Business Case Development

Business Case Development should be at the heart of beginning your new company or beginning the development of a product from an idea. I have formulated my business cases over the years from a report written by Steven Carl Brandt of the Graduate School of Business at Stanford University. I have included a copy of his report for your review and included a copy of how to develop a business plan for both a startup and an already existing operating company.

The two product surveys included here are foundations for input into the business plan and coupled with the following 13 planning exercises, you will have a solid source of feedback on all aspects of developing a business plan for your product.

1.   The Development Process

History has described the monumental failures of Ford with the Edsel, Howard Hughes with his flying boat, British Airways with the Concord and the list goes on. All were ideas where huge amounts of money were ex -pended only to find out that, when the product was complete, there was not a significant market to justify continued production. In my humble opinion, it was a lack of marketing that brought these products to failure. Radical, to be sure, will draw attention but when you are spending billions on new design without testing the market, your chance for success is diminished. The rea -son that some successes are greater than others is not necessarily because the product is better, it can, in - stead, be because of a reputation for quality, name recognition, established distribution and sales channels and, more often than not, enough money to advertise and promote, which will create a demand for the prod

Navigating Points:

The Promotional Planner is designed to be a tool to help you produce a given promotional piece with salient terminology to convey a message to a given target audience. The Planner should depict a worst case, the objective of the promotion you are trying to achieve and, at best case, depict the overall campaign be it a onetime deal or a five year campaign.

The Planner could convey a teaser campaign to build up anticipation, a big splash with benefits, features and price with outlets that will sell or distribute.

-uct.

Every day, companies fail because of a lack of understanding of the New Product Development Process. Large companies have a better chance of continuing in business if a product fails than a small or startup business. The big company allocates a budget for various phases of the development process and, if they are smart, they review each phase and ensure that the specific targets for performance are met before continuing to the next phase. This review process is termed a checks and balances process. The startup company usually has less experience in developing new products and services, is tight on capital and can't afford to make a critical error in judgment. The errors in judgment usually come up front in not thoroughly understanding the market need and equating the need to the economic environment. You may have a great idea but, believe me, there are thousands of great ideas that never get off the ground for any number of reasons.

This book is not written for the business that is successful in developing and bringing new products to distribution because they are obviously doing something right or are very lucky. This book is written for the small business that has a limited amount of funds and can ill afford to have a product idea developed and produced and ultimately not be as salable as required to meet the business plan. This book is also written for the entrepreneur with an idea to make millions but does not have experience of developing a marketing plan to see if the idea warrants development.

Depression, not bankruptcy or suicide, is usually the worst that can happen if your marketing effort determines that your idea is too costly to produce, competition is already there, the window is closing or the host of other reasons that can doom an idea.

History has described the monumental failures of Ford with the Edsel, Howard Hughes with his flying boat, British Airways with the Concord and the list goes on. All were ideas where huge amounts of money were expended only to find out that, when the product was complete, there was not a significant market to justify continued production. In my humble opinion, it was a lack of marketing that brought these products to failure. Radical, to be sure, will draw attention but when you are spending billions on new design without testing the market, your chance for success is diminished.

The bright side of finding out that your idea is not salable is the understanding and education that you have gained knowledge of how to determine if your idea has a value to a market. If your idea is too costly to produce or requires mass distribution, you may find out that you can license your technology, sell the rights to the patent if patentable, negotiate a position with the company that takes your idea and you have the satisfaction of knowing that your idea has value to a market.

The best case is having an idea like a Hula Hoop, Frisbee, Pantyhose, Shake and Bake or one of the products that Popiel or George Forman used to sell on television that make a million and then you can retire and take in the royalties. Those kinds of products are few and far between so if you are like the rest of us would be millionaires, you are going to have to do it the hard way and confirm your idea through the steps of marketing.

2.   **Reasons for Developing Products**

Much has been written about the reasons for develop -ing new products and most are fairly obvious. Businesses are trying to keep ahead or abreast of their com -petitors by developing new products to meet the de -mands of the market place. Look at Bill Gates, one of the founders of Microsoft, he and others chose to be -proactive and developed an idea that now has global inertia and has changed the way that the world looks at computing. He brought not only computing to the desk top, but the information highway is in your home or business now.

You can access the Internet, buy and sell, learn, play games, network and pass information at speeds never before imagined. The successful auto makers listened and produced cars that are more luxurious, faster and sportier than the previous model. These successful businesses are proactive and anticipated the needs and demands of the market and developed products to meet and/or exceed the demands which led to highly successful businesses. These are examples of companies that are proactive and take initiative and set their own direction through intuition and actively look for ways to make an impact.

The second type of company is reactive and through external forces such as competition, distribution or customers will seek to deliver a product that has a requirement to keep it abreast of the competition and maintain market share.

I was affiliated with a company that was proactive due to technology pricing making the idea practical for home and business use. The technology was integrating voice mail and other applications into a telephone using memory chips. We were able to purchase memory in increments of one to ten megabytes and eliminate the need for mechanical parts which made the product more reliable and capable of more functions than ever before. A case in point, one of the products that I was involved with. Even though we had the technology, we lacked the engineering capability and could not pass the government regulatory tests and were late in delivering the product by almost two years. If we had done more marketing in the regulatory area, we would have known to build in the requirements to meet the government regulatory tests and the Window of Opportunity would have been open by another two years.

A reactive company is usually one that is already established and enhances current offerings through technology breakthroughs such as higher speed, cheaper energy, more capacity, durability or any of the hundreds of technology break thru products that make futuristic products available to populace.

In summary, the proactive company is probably more successful and will spend more time examining ideas because they have no immediate threat from competition or erosion of market share or profitability. Proactive companies look to grow into new markets and that is usually the motivating force for developing new products. Reactive companies usually develop products to survive, maintain profitability and market share and keep the competition out of their market niche. Whichever of these categories you are in, marketing before developing will be your best use of time.

3. **Product Definition**

The problem of definition is that it is a relative term de-pending on the situation or position that the company or individual is in pertaining to the problem of define-tion. It has been said that there are four, and probably more, reasons for developing a product. One is diversi-fication, two is expansion, three is differentiating in the market and four is technology.

4. **Differentiating Between Consumer and Industrial Prod--ucts**

The process of product development is usually multi-functional, meaning that there are many sources from which to gather and make an objective decision on whether a product should be developed. If I differenti-ate between products that are consumer related and those that are industrial related, there are different ob-jectives. Usually consumer related products are more market driven than industrial which are R&D or Re-search and Development driven.

The personnel and businesses that are consumer orient-ed are usually driven by monitoring the needs of the consumers and even the fads. If you are in on the front end of a fad such as clothes, even a non-label can some-

Navigating Points:

Much has been written about the reasons for developing new products and most are fairly obvious. Businesses are trying to keep ahead or abreast of their competitors by developing new products to meet the demands of the market place. Look at Bill Gates, one of the founders of Microsoft, he and others chose to be proactive and developed an idea that now has global inertia and has changed the way that the world looks at computing. He brought not only computing to the desk top, but the infor-mation highway is in your home or business now.

times grab onto the coat tails (no pun intended) of a major brand and ride the wave until it fades away. Other consumer related products are in the multi-media and personal computer arena. People want new games, new ways to access different media and more automation. A billion dollar industry has erupted around personal computing and telecommunications software and hardware providers.

Industrial products which are Research and Development driven are not given to the whims of the consumer but rely more on technological breakthroughs which can reduce the price of a component and thus broadens the scope of buyer of the product. Usually more time is required to conduct a thorough marketing study before an industrial product is given the approval and funding for development.

It is usually easier, and is almost the prerequisite, that consumer goods be developed and test marketed before embarking on a large scale development and sales effort. Since consumer goods have a shorter life span and Window of Opportunity, exact costs, defined markets, sales channels and margin requirements are an absolute necessity. Whereas with industrial products, technology usually drives the development with more time and greater margin flexibility.

5.   **Your Business, Your Mission and Strategy**

It is so vital to your success that you, if you are a startup, and your senior management team create a company Mission Statement and Product Strategy for growing and positioning your company to gain credibil-ity and market share in your targeted market segment or segments.

The Mission Statement should pertain to having the highest quality with the best support offering the most

I was affiliated with a company that was proactive due to technology pricing making the idea practical for home and business use. The technology was integrating voice mail and other applications into a telephone using memory chips. We were able to purchase memory in increments of one to ten megabytes and eliminate the need for mechanical parts which made the product more reliable and capable of more functions than ever before. A case in point, one of the products that I was involved with. Even though we had the technology, we lacked the engineering capability and could not pass the government regulatory tests and were late in delivering the product by almost two years.

benefits for the dollar for a product or family of products.

Your Strategy outlines the methodology for attaining the objectives of the mission statement. Both the mission statement and strategy should be communicated openly with all employees so that all may participate and take ownership of the new development process. Participating in the decision and development process makes the long hours and delays more bearable and brings out the best in all of your employees. Reward systems should be in place to recognize those that give outstanding contributions and the rewards and accolades should be given in front of the company. Building a team from the inside makes the weakest link that much stronger because the employees feel part of the team and are all working towards a common goal.

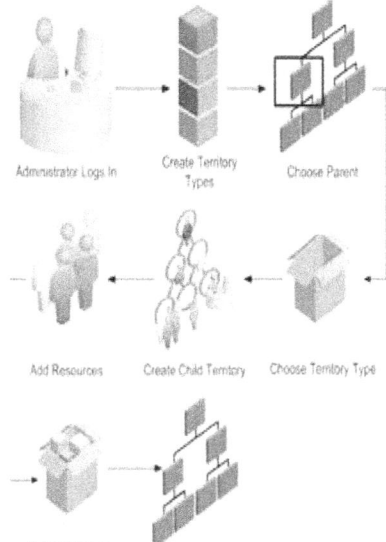

6.   **Market Positioning**

Marketplace positioning is a matter of ego, how much market share, timing and available capital it takes to bring your product to market. All things being equal, the smaller business that has the where with all to bring new products to market is sometimes better off to be second rather than first to enter a new market.

7.   **Business Case Development Task List**

The Project Leader will develop a Customer Survey for the proposed product and distribute to the appropriate Customer/Prospect Group to solicit their input, this will be the core document to support the Business Case.

At the same time as the customer/prospect input is being solicited, the Project Leader will form a team to develop the Business Case. The Business Case Project Team will complete the following activities and use the responsible departments as necessary.

Task	Responsible Department
Define the product and its deliverables	Marketing
Create/maintain the reporting /communications	Marketing
Conduct mkt/prd research and Customer Surveys	Marketing
Conduct an industry comparison	Marketing
Develop competitive assessment	Marketing
Identify regulatory issues	Marketing
Identify training requirements	Prod. Mktg.
Determine pricing strategy	Marketing
Choosing target markets	Marketing
Develop demand forecast	Marketing
Identify support and maintenance Support Support/Sales/Mfg Depts.	Customer All
Develop basic budget needs in capital, expenses and revenue budgets Marketing/Finance	
Begin costing analysis	Finance
Determine billing requirements	Accounting
Finalize demand forecasts	Marketing
Develop marketing plan	Marketing
Develop implementation plan	Project Team
Write the Business Case	Marketing

If you are a startup company, you will not have assigned departments for the specific functions as outlined here so you will have to make your best guess estimates with the resources that are available to you and your team. Any investor will require that you address all of the steps outlined in this document. This document will give you credibility when you present your Business Case. Included should be....

- Business Case Development (Operating Company)
- The main body of the business case should be 5-15 pages and at a minimum include the following:
- Product Description
- Major features and functions
- Applications and benefits for the product
- Proposed positioning in the marketplace
- Market Assessment
- The target market segment for the product
- The specific customer segment
- The target market segment's needs and how the product will meet or exceed those needs
- Who will offer the product?
- The results of the customer survey independent consultants, potential customers and results of any market research or trials
- Cross - Elastic Effects
- Does the proposed new product complement other products within our proposed target market?

8. **Situation Analysis**

Examine and research any regulatory issues that could have an effect on the development and deployment of your product. Roadblocks could be unforeseen such as patent related, government regulatory requirements, competition, distribution, technology, raw materials, social trends, global conflicts or disasters.

Navigating Points:

The Mission Statement should pertain to having the highest quality with the best support offering the most benefits for the dollar for a product or family of products.

Your Strategy outlines the methodology for attaining the objectives of the mission statement. Both the mission statement and strategy should be communicated openly with all employees so that all may participate and take ownership of the new development process. Participating in the decision and development process makes the long hours and delays more bearable and brings out the best in all of your employees. Reward systems should be in place to recognize those that give outstanding contributions and the rewards and accolades should be given in front of the company.

9. **Competition**

Never underestimate your competition. Find out who your potential competitors are and what their strengths and weaknesses and act accordingly.

10. **Market Plan**

The marketing strategy to be employed should include:

- Market objectives

- Pricing

- Distribution channels and including co-op advertising and special incentives

- Promotional strategies

- Regulatory Assessment

- Are there any regulatory issues that have to be addressed

- Financial Analysis

- Revenue and demand forecast

11. **Costs**

- Revenue requirements

- Performa income statements

- Net present value and cash flow analysis

- Technical Requirements

- Facilities, systems, hardware, software, etc.

- Programming, engineering resource requirements

- Resource Requirements

- Capital investment and working capital

12.   Human resource requirements

- Contending projects and recommended solutions

- Training requirements

- Implementation Plan Outline

- Major milestones for implementation, test lab approvals, all levels of product verification and training

- Promotional and advertising

13.   General availability

A copy of the Stanford Business Planning guidelines is attached for your review. This planning guideline is gen   -erally accepted as a standard for presenting a business case for the purposes of raising capital for new projects and startup companies. I have used this plan suc-cessfully for every new company and product launch. After Business Case submission and approval are given, the   implementation process is to begin.

Chapter 23

Guide to Preparing a Business Plan

By STEVEN CARL BRANDT

GRADUATE SCHOOL OF BUSINESS

STANFORD UNIVERSITY

Copyright 1980

Introduction

The basics for writing a business plan have not changed, just the buzz words and methodologies. A solid idea is a solid idea whether in the 1940's or in 2030. Your business plan is foremost to helping you raise the capital to get started and I believe that the following format is excellent in providing guidelines for an investor or bank to your review your requests. I first started using Mr. Brandt's "Guide to Preparing a Business Plan" back in the early 1980's and it is as good today as it was back when I started my first company. I think you will find the guide very instrumental in preparing your business plan as have I.

A business plan is a blueprint for building a business. As discussed in this guide, it is an internal, operating document, not a show piece for raising money or influencing creditors. Written business plans are useful whenever the efforts of two or more people need to be organized and synchronized over time to achieve specified results im-

Navigating Points:

Much has been written about the reasons for developing new products and most are fairly obvious. Businesses are trying to keep ahead or abreast of their competitors by developing new products to meet the demands of the market place. Look at Bill Gates, one of the founders of Microsoft, he and others chose to be proactive and developed an idea that now has global inertia and has changed the way that the world looks at computing. He brought not only computing to the desk top, but the information highway is in your home or business now.

portant to the writers of the plan. Business plans should be prepared for starting a new enterprise, directing an established one toward improved performance, diversifying a business; or introducing a relatively major new product or service to the chosen marketplace.

New Businesses

Starting a new enterprise is usually a high risk proposition. If the venture is successful, i.e., economically viable in a projected length of time, everyone is happy. If the venture is unsuccessful, careers, money, reputations, spouses, and even lives can be lost. The height of risk tends to be proportional to the presence of two prime ingredients. The directly applicable experience and managing ability of the team responsible for the venture, and the thoroughness of the thinking that goes into the undertaking before it starts. To some extent, one can substitute for the other.

Directing an Established Business

The alternative to operating a business from a written document of some kind, from a road map so to speak, is to operate it by intuition. Many success stories have been written with intuition and many business failures could have been prevented if less reliance had been placed on it. You can take your choice. One thing is clear, in the absence of a comprehensive, agreed upon plan, outside events tend to control management rather than vice versa, and the coordination of any kind of team effort for very long is difficult. An established business of any size without a plan is like an orchestra without sheet music, the results may be interesting, even good, but the probability of a favorable

A business plan in one of the single most important things you will ever do for your business. Having a plan that lays it all out allows you to create your own checks and balances by which to judge your failures and successes by.

The alternative to operating a business from a written document of some kind, from a road map so to speak, is to operate it by intuition. Many success stories have been written with intuition and many business failures could have been prevented if less reliance had been placed on it. You can take your choice.

performance is lower than need be.

Diversifying a Business

An established business has customers, creditors, employees, cash flow and, in short, it has momentum; not necessarily forward momentum but momentum that carries in a certain direction. Attempts to change the direction through diversification of some sort can be additive. The net result should be a positive and an impact of the old and new forces. They can also be subtractive and drag the established business downward. Serious diversification deserves a proper business plan.

Introducing Major New Products or Services

Minor additions to the activities of an ongoing enterprise do not normally require the rigor of a complete business plan as outlined in this guide. When the product or service requires a large commitment of resources and has a potentially large impact on the health of the enterprise, the same arguments for a plan apply as in the case of diversification. Few owners would try to add a room on their homes without a blueprint. A growing business concern requires no less of a planning effort.

Summary

In summary, after preparing a business plan, the management team should have an agreed program for action and results to which it will willingly commit itself. After reading the plan, a director, potential investor or other interested party should know precisely what the management intends to do, by when, with the human and financial resources called for in the plan.

Contents

The length and sequence of contents in a business plan will vary with the complexity of the proposed venture. A few key elements are almost always needed, however, to describe just why, how and when economic viability will be accomplished. While other objectives may exist and even be of senior importance to the writers of a given plan, economic viability is the one necessary condition around which this guide is molded. Without economic viability, few ventures, no matter how noble, survive for long.

"Why" is normally addressed by first identifying precisely who outside the enterprise is interested and qualified to buy whatever it is in the enterprise has to sell and the way it will sell it. "How" is indicated by a complete coverage of the human, production, organizational, and monetary requirements for providing the product or service on a timely and continuing basis consistent with the pricing and quality demands of the chosen marketplace. "When" is reflected by a thorough presentation of the financial implications over time of each important event called for in the plan.

1.0 The Concept

Many argue that the act of committing an idea to paper is a critical step in its development. Certainly the possi-bility of confusion, misunderstanding, or shallowness is reduced if the agony of writing it down in black and white is endured. The foundation of a business plan, is a description of the business idea from which the plan will be developed.

2.0   Objectives

A close second is the process of orderly thinking and verbalization of what it is the writer or writers wish to personally achieve. Particularly in the case of a startup, there is a great value in articulating the order of driving forces behind the entrepreneurial effort. Everybody wants to make money, of course and at least enough to get along. But there is a big difference between pursu-ing a $1,000,000 in capital gains in five years and pursu-ing a steady net income of $50,000 a year for life. Driv-ing forces such as personal freedom, professional ex-pression, financial independence, or return on invest-ment may be of prime importance. It is helpful to eve-ryone concerned to know the relative ranking of the end results sought.

3.0   Analysis of the Market

The total population of potential buyers for a given product or service is a certain size, X. within X, there are subgroups called segments that vary in characteris-tics such as the reason for buying, financial ability to buy, ease of reaching, etc. Most new enterprises need to select a limited number of segments upon which to concentrate available selling efforts. The business plan should spell out the selection process and describe, in detail, the targeted segment or segments plus precisely how they will be sold and/or serviced. Elements of this analysis section of a Plan should typically include:

3.1   General description of the entire marketplace

Navigating Points:

An established business has customers, creditors, em-ployees, cash flow and, in short, it has momentum; not necessarily forward momen-tum but momentum that carries in a certain direction. Attempts to change the di-rection through diversifica-tion of some sort can be ad-ditive. The net result should be a positive and an impact of the old and new forces. They can also be subtractive and drag the established business downward. Serious diversification deserves a proper business plan.

.

for the production service

3.2　Precise description of the segment or segments to be pursued

3.3　Description of intermediate influences on buy-ers such as dealers, distributors, sales repre-sentatives, associations, etc.

3.4　Competitive conditions both present and antici-pated

3.5　Pricing conditions both present and anticipated

3.6　Governmental influences both present and an--ticipated

3.7　History of similar products services or business--es

Break-even point estimates, i.e., how many units and or how much of the market has to be sold to cover costs.

4.0　Marketing

The aforementioned descriptive elements then set the stage for the action elements below which will cover how management plans to go about creating customers, the grand purpose of business, as Peter Drucker puts it. The marketing action elements include:

4.1　Method(s) of selling and advertising to be employed

4.2　Product or service features and benefits to be emphasized

4.3　Program for initial time period

"Why" is normally a dressed by first identifying precisely who outside the enterprise is interested and qualified to buy what-ever it is in the enterprise has to sell and the way it will sell it. "How" is indicat-ed by a complete coverage of the human, production, organizational, and mone-tary requirements for providing the product or service on a timely and continuing basis consistent with the pricing and quality demands of the chosen marketplace. "When" is reflected by a thorough presentation of the finan-cial implications over time of each important event called for in the plan.

4.4   Schedule of who is to do what by when

4.5   Budget

4.6   Results expected

4.7   Contingency plans

There is always an element of guesswork in predicting what is going to happen in the marketplace. This is one reason why management's experience base is of prime importance to an outsider evaluating a proposed busi-ness, the only antidote for uncertainty about future is homework and planning.

5.0 Production

Production of your product or service can be as simple as working out of your home or purchasing a factory to manufacture the required goods to meet the require-ments of the business plan. The elements too consider for production are:

5.1   Equipment requirements

5.2   Facility requirements

5.3   Raw material, labor and supplies requirements and sources

5.4   Quality control, packaging, transportation

5.6   Program for initial time period

5.7   Schedule of who is do what by when

5.8   Budget

5.9   Results expected

5.9.1 Contingency plans

6.0 Organization

As indicated at the start of this guide, management is a prime ingredient for success. The ability of the management team to do what it says it will do in the future is usually predictable by assessing what the individual members have accomplished in the past. The quality of the planning effort is frequently a proper re   flection of the collective experience although resumes are often attached to business plans that are to be reviewed by outsiders. As a general rule, between the members of the management team and the board, the primary functional skills, marketing, production, and finance should be well represented.

One or more technical specialists, an engineer, artist, programmer, machine operator, designer, scientist, salesperson or whatever are usually essential to a new venture. The identification, recruitment, compensation, and motivation of any such persons without whom the business could virtually not proceed is a matter to be thought through and covered in the plan.

Key individuals make up the forth layer. They are people who, because of their vision, tenacity, energy, contacts, money, interests or sheer mental capability, can make the difference between a roaring success and something less. He or she may be positioned anywhere in the organization, or even outside as, for example, an investor. But plans to keep the individuals aboard and interested may be just as important as plans for advertising or raw materials purchased. In the organization section of the plan, the main points to be covered are these:

6.1   Staffing program for initial time period

6.2   Schedule

6.3   Budget

6.4   Results expected

6.5   Contingency plans

Capable people with clear ideas of what they are to accomplish and incentives to invest their energies in the organization are the basic building blocks management has.

7.0 Funds Flow and Ownership

Money is the mortar that attracts the building blocks and holds them together until the merit of the output of the organization is widely enough recognized and valued in the marketplace to finance the business on a continuing basis, the amount and timing of the money needed is calculated from the marketing, production and organizational sections of the business plan. If outside debt or equity money is required to carry out the plan, the type, character and objectives of the investor (s) needs to be given as careful attention as the rest of the planning elements. Even if no outside capital is required, careful monitoring and control of the funds of the business is manda-

Navigating Points:

A close second is the process of orderly thinking and verbalization of what it is the writer or writers wish to personally achieve. Particularly in the case of a startup, there is a great value in articulating the order of driving forces behind the entrepreneurial effort. Everybody wants to make money, of course and at least enough to get along. But there is a big difference between pursuing a $1,000,000 in capital gains in five years and pursuing a steady net income of $50,000 a year for life. Driving forces such as personal freedom, professional expression, financial independence, or return on investment may be of prime importance.

tory.

From other sections outlined earlier in this Guide, the following should be collected:

7.1   Projected cash flows from operations; i.e., total funds in and out for the initial time period

7.2   Performa profit and loss statement

7.3   Performa balance sheets

7.4   Program for raising equity and or debt money required, if any

7.5   Program for monitoring and controlling funds with people and systems in the organizational planning

With this information, projections about the future value of the equity of the enterprise can be made, further, the magnitude of any investment required and the objectives of those people who, out of necessity must be involved such as managers, investors, guarantors and specialists, will, in large part, dictate the form of structure most suitable such as corporation, subchapter S corporation, partnership or proprietorship. Legal assistance may or may not be useful at this point, depending on the finality of the total plan which has evolved starting with the market.

Conclusion

Preparation of a business plan may turn out to be nothing more than an exercise. Done properly, a

Key individuals make up the forth layer. They are people who, because of their vision, tenacity, energy, contacts, money, interests or sheer mental capability, can make the difference between a roaring success and something less. He or she may be positioned anywhere in the organization, or even outside as, for example, an investor. But plans to keep the individuals aboard and interested may be just as important as plans for advertising or raw materials purchased.

business plan is really a simulation of the business process. By completing the plan in advance and using your best available information and objective judgment, the results may prove to be negative or the requirements for successful economic viability so enormously high that to proceed would be foolhardy.   More likely than not, the very effort required to prepare such a complete blueprint for a new enterprise will dissuade most potential entrepreneurs and thereby save them the agony of failure that, in most cases, they would have surely followed.

If on the other hand, if your business plan and its worst case scenario for success shows promise you are in for an exhilarating and sometimes emotional ride that will either make you stronger or make you realize that you should seek a secure career with a stable company.

Chapter 24

Tips to Raise Money

The task of raising money for a business is not as difficult as most people seem to think. This is especially true when you have an idea that can make you and your backers rich. Actually, there's more money available for new business ventures than there are good business ideas.

A very important rule of the game to learn is that anytime you want to raise money, your first move should be to put together a proper prospectus.

The prospectus should include:

- A description of your idea, product or service including the benefits and features. The benefits should be targeted to the end user and explained clearly. Explain what the product will be used for. Is the product a toy? If it is, what demographic age group is it targeted towards and is it educational or sports related? Can the product be a family and be evolutionary and would a buyer want to collect them all? Does the product have a cost savings, or enhance other products, lengthen a life cycle or be a tie breaker in a deal? What are the benefits of your product?

- What is the size of the target market and why would they want to purchase your product?

- What are the estimated time frames to develop, manufacture, ramp up and take it to market?

- How will you sell the product? Will you sell direct, through call centers, web pages, MLM, channel to market partners and is the product saleable internationally?

- Who are your potential competitors?

- What is the estimated cost for overhead including personnel, raw materials, components, equipment, manufacturing and facilities over a three year period?

- Do you anticipate that your company could be acquired or merged into another company?

- What are the regulatory and compliance issues for your product?

- What about support and warranty and can either be a profit center?

Include resumes for all of your key people and hopefully they have a background in some phase of the business. Include customer surveys, letter of intent, channel to market commitments and the key contacts to validate what you have stated in your prospectus. Check with the key people to make sure that it is OK to use their names in your prospectus. If you can complete this phase of the prospectus, funding will be much less of an issue. Put together forecasts in three month increments over three years or whatever your investors request.

Most investors buy the person. Investors want to believe in the person they are giving their money to. They look at you and do due diligence on you the person. Can you deliver what you say, are you believable, can you present the idea, and are you willing to risk? These are all qualities that an investor looks for when considering investing in a new venture. You may only get one shot to make a good impression so be prepared in such a fashion that you can make you point in less than 30 minutes. The norm is 15 minutes but if there is perceived interest, the time could be up to an hour with questions.

Remember that investors get deluged with proposals every day and they take about 1 in 100. Of the 100 proposals that cross their desk, they might invite their investment clientele in to hear 4-6 presentations per year. It has been my experience that when I give a presentation to a group of potential investors, if I have a product that is of interest, I will either be invited back for further presentations or a group will break out that have a keen interest in what I have to say and I may follow on for up to two hours.

Know how many potential investors will be attending your presentation. Have enough materials available to give to each but don't give the information out in written form until you have had the opportunity to present it verbally. If you pass out all of your information ahead of time, papers rustle, people jump forward and ask questions that you will cover in your presentation.

The information that you would pass out would be a promotional piece that gives the features and benefits of your product. Your business plan supports your prospectus with hard facts about the market, competition, channels, manufacturing, etc... If you have sold yourself and presented the benefits and features, now you have to have proof positive that you have done your marketing homework to justify the investor's investment in your product. The business plan has to be verifiable.

Navigating Points:

Include resumes for all of your key people and hopefully they have a background in some phase of the business. Include customer surveys, letter of intent, channel to market commitments and the key contacts to validate what you have stated in your prospectus. Check with the key people to make sure that it is OK to use their names in your prospectus. If you can complete this phase of the prospectus, funding will be much less of an issue. Put together forecasts in three month increments over three years or whatever your investors request.

For example, I had testimonials from major Fortune 100 company's product managers and other large national distributors that said that they would purchase N quantities in X time frame if they were priced at X and available in N time frame. The totals were 200,000 units at $95 each. Gross revenues were $18,100,000 for those verbal commitments.

The investors were most interested in the fact that I had already confirmed that there was a need and customers were willing to commit to purchase via a letter of intent. They did not just want to take my word for the commitment and they wanted to talk to the customer first hand. I had it set up with the customer that I would possibly have investors call them to verify what I quoted. When the investor called the customer, I was golden, as the customer corroborated what I had written in the business plan. The rest, as they say, is history.

You'll have to explain in detail how the money you want is going to be used. If it's for an existing business, you'll need a profit and loss record for at least the preceding 12 months and a plan showing how this additional money will produce greater profits. If it's a new business, you will have to show your proposed business plan, marketing research, projected costs, and anticipated income with a summary for each year broken down by quarters over a three year period.

It will be advantageous to you to base your cost estimates high and your income projections on minimal returns. If you can show a reasonable profit with what you believe to be conservative projections, you should be in good shape. By being conservative, you will be able to ride through the ups and down inherent in starting up a new business. You should also describe what makes your business unique and how it differs from your competition and the opportunities for expansion or secondary products.

The business plan/prospectus will have to state precisely what you are offering the investor in return for the use of their money. Investors will want to know the percentage of interest you are willing to pay, what amount of stock they will receive, percentage of profits, percentage of the business and/or a seat on the board. You will have to decide what is best for you to do in return for the use of the investor's money. You will state what you want but in 99% of the cases, you will fall in line with what the investors are willing to offer. In order to get the biggest slice of the pie, you need to sell yourself and understand how the game is played.

Investors use their money to make more money. They want to make as much as they can, regardless of whether it's a short term or a long term deal. In order to attract the right investor and get the money you need, you will have to spell it out in detail, and further, back up your claims with proof from your marketing research.

Venture capital investors are usually quite familiar with "high risk" proposals, yet they all want to minimize that risk as much as possible. Therefore your business plan/prospectus should include a listing of your business and personal assets with documentation on your personal tax returns for the past three years. Your prospective investor may not know anything about you or your business but if they want to know, they can pick up the telephone and know everything there is to know about you within 24 hours. The point here is don't ever try to

Navigating Points:

Know how many potential investors will be attending your presentation. Have enough materials available to give to each but don't give the information out in written form until you have had the opportunity to present it verbally. If you pass out all of your information ahead of time, papers rustle, people jump forward and ask questions that you will cover in your presentation.

"con" a potential investor; be honest with them. Lay out all the facts on the table for them and in most cases, if you have got a good idea and you have done your homework properly, an interested investor will understand your position and offer more help than you dared to ask for.

When you have your prospectus prepared, know how much money you want, exactly how it will be used and how you intend to repay it, you are ready to start looking for investors.

As simple as it seems, one of the easiest ways of raising money is by advertising in a newspaper of a national publication featuring such ads. Your ad should state the amount of money you want, and always ask for more than you need so that you have room for negotiation. Your ad should also state the type of business involved in order to separate the curious from the truly interested and the kind of return you are promising on the investment.

A first step in getting comfortable with presenting a plan to raise money is by setting up a party with friends and associates. Explain your business plan, the profit potentials and how much you need. Give them each a copy of your prospectus and ask that they pledge an increment that you know that they would feel comfortable risking as a nonparticipating partner in your business. Check with the current tax regulations. You may be allowed up to 25 partners in a Sub chapter S enterprise, opening the door for anyone to gather a group of friends around himself with something to offer them in return for their assistance in capitalizing his business.

It is always a good idea to have an attorney and an accountant help you make up your business prospectus. As you

Features of Finance

1. Investment Opportunities

2. Profitable Opportunities

3. Optimal Mix of Funds

4. System of Internal Controls

5. Future Decision Making

explain your plan to them and ask for their advice, casually ask them if they would mind letting you know of or steer your way to, any potential investor they might happen to meet. Do the same with your banker. Give him a copy of your prospectus and ask him if he would look it over and offer any suggestions for improving it, and, of course, let you know of any potential investors. In either case, it is always a good idea to let them know that you are willing to pay a finder's fee if you can be directed to the right investor.

Professional people such as doctors and dentists are known to have a tendency to join occupational investment groups. The next time you talk with your doctor or dentist, give him a copy of your prospectus and explain your plan. He may want to invest on his own or perhaps set up an appointment for your to talk with the manger of his investment group. Either way, you win because when you are looking for money, it is essential that you get the word out to as many potential investors as possible.

Don't overlook the possibilities of the small business investment companies in your area. Look them up in your telephone directory under "Investment Services." These companies exist for the sole purpose of lending money to businesses which they feel have a good chance of making money. In many instances, they trade their help for a small interest in your company.

Many states have Business Development Commissions whose goal it is to assist in the establishment and growth of new business. Not only do they offer favorable tax incentives but they also give business expertise, offer money and facilities to get you started. Your Chamber of Commerce is the place to check for further information on this idea.

Industrial banks are usually much more amenable to making business loans than regular banks, so be sure to check out these institutions in your area. Insurance companies are prime sources of long term business capital, but each company varies in its policies regarding the type of business it will consider. Check your local agent for the name of the directors of another companies to invest in your business. Look for a company that can benefit from your product or service. Also, be sure to check out the public library for available foundation grants. These grants can be the final answer to all of your needs if your business is perceived to be related to the objectives and activities of the foundation.

Finally, there is the Money Broker or Finder. These are the people who take your prospectus and circulate it with various known lenders and investors. They always require an upfront or retainer fee and there is no way they can guarantee to get you the loan or the money you want. There are exceptions to every rule and I have known Money Brokers to take a piece of the action such as shares or a percentage of your company and/or sometimes ask to be on the Board in return for finding the funding.

There are many very good Money Brokers and there are some that are not so good.   They all take a percentage of the gross amount that is finally raised for your needs. The important thing is to check them out and find out about successful loans or investment plans they have arranged and what kind of investor contacts they have had before you put up any front

There are a lot of things that go into creating success. I don't like to do just the things I like to do. I like to do things that cause the company to succeed. I don't spend a lot of time doing my favorite activities.

— *Michael Dell*

I have found no greater satisfaction than achieving success through honest dealing and strict adherence to the view that, for you to gain, those you deal with should gain as well.

— *Alan Greenspan*

money or retainer fees. There are many ways to raise money from selling stock to garage sales. Don't make the mistake of thinking that the only place you can find the money you need is through the bank or finance company.

Start thinking about the idea of investors to share in your business as silent partners. Think about the idea of obtaining financing for a primary business by arranging financing for another businesses that will support the startup, establishment and development of the primary business. Consider the feasibility of merging with a company that is already organized and with facilities that are compatible or related to your needs. Give some thought to the possibilities of getting people supplying your production equipment to co-sign the loan you need for startup capital. This is truly the age of creative financing.

Disregard the stories you hear of "tight money," and start making phone calls, talking to people, and making appointments to discuss your plans with the people who have money to invest. There is more money now than there's ever been for new business investment. The problem is that most beginning "business builders" don't know what to believe or which way to turn for help. They tend to believe the stories of "tight money," and set aside their plans for a business of their own until a time when startup money might be easier to find.

The longer that you put off the process of looking for the money you need to invest, the harder it is to get going. If you truly have a viable business plan and have done the test of reasonableness on the idea and it comes up positive, there will be people willing to invest. Be determined to succeed and you will make it happen.

Navigating Points:

Don't overlook the possibilities of the small business investment companies in your area. Look them up in your telephone directory under "Investment Services." These companies exist for the sole purpose of lending money to businesses which they feel have a good chance of making money. In many instances, they trade their help for a small interest in your company. Many states have Business Development Commissions whose goal it is to assist in the establishment and growth of new business. Not only do they offer favorable tax incentives but they also give business expertise, offer money and facilities to get you started.

Chapter 25
Performance Milestones

Performance Milestones are the objectives your company has established to measure the progress of a given products' progression towards completion. The more complex the product, the more milestones and feedback mechanisms have to be in place to not only track the progress but identify potential problem areas and modify the plan accordingly.

There are many software programs on the market to assist you in this effort and I would suggest you purchase the one that is compatible with your operating system. If your plans call for multiple access, purchase the networking version of the program. If you do not use an automated version of a Program Management tool, use a written version. Whatever you do, use some method to identify and track the progress of your project.

The reasons vary from believing a tracking system is absolutely necessary to being forced by your customers or investors to use one. No matter how much trust you may have in an individual's ability to perform as stated, something can, and usually does, go askew that requires an adjustment to your schedule. By monitoring the progress on a daily or weekly basis, you track the progress and keep the integrity of the project foremost.

Industrial banks are usually much more amenable to making business loans than regular banks, so be sure to check out these institutions in your area. Insurance companies are prime sources of long term business capital, but each company varies in its policies regarding the type of business it will consider. Check your local agent for the name of the directors of another companies to invest in your business. Look for a company that can benefit from your product or service.

A schedule can save you face as well as hundreds, thousands or millions of dollars and especially if you are working in tandem with one or more other companies to develop a product. Accidents, personnel leave of absences, personnel termination's, technology changes, regulatory requirements, parts shortages and test site availability are a few of the things that can affect or delay a project. If communicated on a project schedule, resource shortages that can cause delays will be identified before they occur and all parties work together much more closely to reach the common goal of a timely product release. Penalties for delayed release, lost customers and morale deterioration can happen when schedules are not being met.

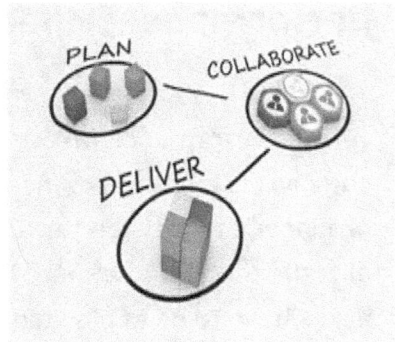

In order to create a project schedule, a project facilitator or manager should be appointed that has the responsibility for gathering input from all departments, generating a schedule and updating that schedule until the project is completed. After the first draft of the schedule is done, a meeting should be held to discuss the reality and modify it accordingly. This process may have to be done several times in order to get a draft that everyone agrees to. An inexperienced Project Manager may take at face value the input given. Never have I seen a project schedule that everyone agreed with. Sales and marketing are overly aggressive in identifying the size of the market and how soon sales can be made. Engineering is either overly optimistic or, at the other end, never wants to give a date for completion because of the unknowns.

It is the function of the Project Manager to bring together an agreement of all departments on milestones and the prerequisites necessary to begin or complete a given task before the next can begin. The Project Manager has to be part psychologist because during meetings, agreed to dates will be missed and new ones will be requested as well as suggestions on how to make up for lost progress. Your peers are in the meeting and no one likes to lose face so your task is to explore why the schedule was missed and what resources are required to get them back on schedule.

The communication in meetings involving the milestones should be communicated back to the employees, to your channels of distribution, end users - if you go direct, trade journals if you are using a teaser campaign to announce the progress of your product and other need to know entities.

These questions on Performance Milestones will aid you in identifying what is important for you to track in order to release an on schedule product.

- What are the top five key success factors for your new product?
- Examine your industry, not all products have the same success factors. Consider:
- Window of Opportunity. This is the time that marketing has told you that you have to enter the market and achieve a market share before competition.
- Hole in the Market. Where and what is the need that your product will fill?
- Is technology available?
- Can I make it cheap enough to make a decent margin?
- Can I get my product to distribution to take advantage of

the opportunity?

- Do I have the necessary funding?
- Do I have the resources?
- Can I meet the standards of the market?
- Can I get a flagship reseller to distribute our product?
- Can I adhere to ISO or other standards required for me to be successful?
- What is the combination of performance and positioning factors that will determine the success and profitability of your new product?

Ask yourself these questions and vary them based on the idiosyncrasies of your product.

- Are you positioning yourselves with resources that can maximize your channel to market potential?
- Are you entering a market with the window just beginning to open or starting to close?
- Will technology and volume allow you to continue to produce and enhance your product into a family of products?
- Will your patents and copyrights force manufacturers requiring like functionality to come to you for OEM, private label and or licensing for product rights?
- Can your product cross over to new markets nationally and internationally?
- Are you entering a market where you might awake a sleeping giant that could develop a next generation product with existing channels and keep you from reaching a reasonable level of market share?
- Are you positioned to meet supply and demand and not locked into sole sourced products that could potentially

Navigating Points:

Performance Milestones are the objectives your company has established to measure the progress of a given products' progression towards completion. The more complex the product, the more milestones and feedback mechanisms have to be in place to not only track the progress but identify potential problem areas and modify the plan accordingly.

shut your production down?

- Do you have adequate support systems to handle pre and post sales as well as warranty support?
- Does your accounting system integrate with your material planning systems and sales order entry?
- Are you positioned to allow for your major customers to dial into check inventory status or place orders if required?
- Does your business plan depict an optimistic or conservative forecast of revenue? If the conservative comes true, does this meet your minimum objectives for profitability?

1. **What will the marketing strategy be for your new product?**

    Let's differentiate marketing from sales and address the marketing strategy issue. The marketing strategy is the presales market identification where you perceive that there is minimal competition, a new technology break through, a fad that is right for the times, a window of opportunity or simply a product need.   A marketing strategy is one that ideally has you targeting a rifle shot into a market segment that you know has a need if you can supply the product. This rifle shot is ideal because you can readily identify the customers and distribution channels that would sell your product and research the potential, the cost to produce and bring to market, revenue forecasts, competitive issues, re sources and development time.

    A marketing strategy is one that says if you don't own one, you are not with the in-crowd. Another strategy

In order to create a project schedule, a project facilitator or manager should be appointed that has the responsibility for gathering input from all departments, generating a schedule and updating that schedule until the project is completed.   After the first draft of the schedule is done, a meeting should be held to discuss the reality and modify it accordingly. This process may have to be done several times in order to get a draft that everyone agrees to. An inexperienced Project Manager may take at face value the input given. Never have I seen a project schedule that everyone agreed with.

says that with our product, you enhance your existing product, improve output, and reduce costs or gain market share or entry into new markets. Other strategies tell stories about improving your standard of living or help you look or feel better.

The rifle shot strategy does not always hold for all products and services and many times you have to focus your energies on other markets in order to determine if there is a sufficient market to justify the expenditure to develop and deliver products through channels or direct to the end user.

The strategy is dictated by the amount of money you have allocated for marketing.   What resources are available to assist you in the marketing effort? Resources could be potential investors, consultants, university marketing departments, regulatory bodies, and large corporations looking for new products, emerging markets such as the Internet, trade associations, direct mail, trade shows, trade journals and telemarketing.

The "Marketing Strategy" comes after your test of reasonableness and should be written down or plotted on a project management grid with dates for completion, results and go or no go checkpoints. Don't wander aimlessly down a path of no rewards just because you wrote it down. Alter your efforts if results are more favorable in another target market. Many times you will uncover market demands through your research that will cause you to alter your development and thought process because there is a larger market, a quicker way to bring the product to market or any number of other reasons. Always be on the lookout for new ideas that can enhance marketability, improve performance and bring in bottom line revenue.

The marketing strategy should be aimed at researching the potential markets for your product, costs to develop, costs to manufacture, sales delivery methods and support costs. Once you determine that your idea is viable and right for a given market, you need to develop ownership of your idea and product with key potential channel distribution partners. Channel partners are distribution arms that purchase from you and sell to other distributors and/or sell direct to the end user.
Once you have developed ownership of your product with potential buyers and distribution, you can start the process of forecasting sales that are required for raising capital if you don't already have access to the necessary funding.

2.   **What are the current or anticipated strengths and weaknesses of the product when compared with ex--isting products?**
Your product does not have to be the best in order to be successful but you need to understand where your product should be targeted in order to give you the best opportunity to capitalize on your strengths. Your strengths could be price to performance. So many products are over engineered with capabilities beyond

the scope of what any single person could use. By add -ing all of this functionality, your price limits the market and the features place another limiting factor on your plan because it is too complicated to use by the majority of your targeted market.

When you design your product with performance mile-stones, remember your "Window of Opportunity". Make your Performance Milestones realistic in order to attract the maximum market. Many products can be de-signed with a life cycle that affords enhancements ei-ther by adding other peripheral equipment, replacing or upgrading components. Think of your market, the tech-nology, the competition, and your resources to develop and deliver and be proactive.

3. **What plans do you have to capitalize on your strengths?**
Identify your strengths. Strengths are existing distribu -tion channels, a name that stands for quality, a quality customer base, your personnel, location, catchy slogan or theme, excellent pre and post-sales support. All of these are strengths and each should be used to capture or keep markets for your new products.

When preparing your milestones, keep in mind the strengths of your company and don't forget quality if you want to be known for quality. In your advertising and sales campaigns, capitalize on what you are known for and modify to accommodate for other market seg-

Navigating Points:

Let's differentiate marketing from sales and address the marketing strategy issue. The marketing strategy is the pre-sales market identification where you perceive that there is minimal competition, a new technology breakthrough, a fad that is right for the times, a window of opportunity or simply a product need. A marketing strategy is one that ideally has you targeting a rifle shot into a market segment that you know has a need if you can supply the product.

ments.

4. **Have you addressed the vulnerabilities of your prod-uct?**

Vulnerabilities can be categorized in a number of ways and here are a few for you to keep in mind as you devel-op your product delivery milestones.

5. **Sole source parts**

If you can't find multiple vendors for the raw materials and parts to manufacture your product, you are vulner able to possible shortages and price increases which can delay your entry into the market, production schedule, increase your price and shrink your margin.

6. **Old looking, second generation**

If your product is not packaged correctly it can be per -ceived as not being state of the art.

7. **Lack of distribution**

If you do not have adequate distribution/sales partners in place or a direct sales force, your forecasts are not worth the paper they are written on and you will have a trickledown effect throughout the company. The trickle down effect comes from not having the revenue to sup -port your business plan. Possible delays in paying ven -dors, layoffs and a subsequent down turn in morale are but a few of the things that can occur if you do not have your distribution in place.

The Experts Speak Out...

You only have to do very few things right in your life so long as you don't do too many things wrong.

– *Warren Buffett*

The noblest search is the search for excellence

– *Lyndon B. Johnson*

The man who does not work for the love of work but only for money is likely to nei-ther make money nor find much fun in life.

– *Charles M. Schwab*

8. **Competition**

    Competition can knock you out of the market quicker than anything. If you are competing with the big boys and they perceive that you have a product that can have universal appeal and that you could erode or penetrate their market sales demographic, they will be breathing down your neck in ways you could not have imagined. Even if you have copyrights and patents, variations in technology can be made to produce a look alike product and if the competition has an established name, their customers will usually stay with them as opposed to go -ing with a new vendor for a perceived same product. Your objective in this circumstance is to be a second choice as much as it might hurt your ego even if you know that your product is better.

    All of these points should be carefully researched and you should have contingency plans in place in order to be proactive if they occur.

9. **What are the main competitive advantages you have with the new product?**

    During your brainstorming sessions, you should deter mine what your competitive advantages are and incur -porate them into your product and promote them in all of your promotional and product fact sheets.

10. **What are your performance review checkpoints?**

    Performance review checkpoints can be categorized in many ways and here are a few suggestions to consider. Major performance review checkpoints can be catego

-rized as a step or point in time where one item has to be completed or at least will cause no complications for following steps. There are risk takers that have concur-rent events taking place in order to meet deadlines and if the product is not technology bound where one piece of technology has to be working before the other can begin, you will have a minimal risk.

Major checkpoints can be funding, personnel, facility, equipment, marketing strategies and the execution, sales plans and the execution, promotional campaigns, department goals and objectives, product testing, regulatory approvals, your first sale, and celebrations to acknowledge work well done.

What is your market? If it is for children, is it simple and targeted at the correct market for maximum sales penetration? Does the product meet federal guidelines for breakage, paint chipping, etc? Is it packaged attractively to draw attention if it is on the shelf along with hundreds of other products?

Performance review checkpoints can be categorized in many ways and here are a few suggestions to consider. Major performance review checkpoints can be categorized as a step or point in time where one item has to be completed or at least will cause no complications for following steps. There are risk takers that have concurrent events taking place in order to meet deadlines and if the product is not technology bound where one piece of technology has to be working before the other can begin, you will have a minimal risk.

11. **Describe the major go/no go check points that would trigger a major re-evaluation of the products viability in the market.**
Major trigger points that would cause a re-evaluation of product viability could be:

- Downturn in economy
- Technology break through that makes your product obsolete
- Competition enters the market and relegates you insig-

nificant

- New regulatory requirements that you are not prepared to meet
- Testing determines that your product does not work as described, it is too complicated, to simple, etc.
- Cost of goods rises significantly and you are priced out of the market
- You sole sourced raw materials and a bigger client relegated you to when available status and you can't manufacture your product to meet the demand.

There are many other trigger points that could cause you to re-evaluate your products viability in the market so think of what could cause a re-evaluation and be proactive in your planning.

12. **How do you maintain accountability for each mile stone?**

Empower your people to be responsible for their area of development. Most of all get your key managers to take ownership of the project plan. Explain the market, the opportunity, the deadlines, and the competition. Ask your people for input as to resources, equipment and time to complete their piece of the equation. Plot out serially the events and input the information that each of your managers have given you and then hold a meeting to review the plan.

If the time to develop is too long with input from each manager on the plan, you can usually come up with a compromise that each can manage and buy into. By

Navigating Points:

Major checkpoints can be funding, personnel, facility, equipment, marketing strategies and the execution, sales plans and the execution, promotional campaigns, department goals and objectives, product testing, regulatory approvals, your first sale, and celebrations to acknowledge work well done.

What is your market? If it is for children, is it simple and targeted at the correct market for maximum sales penetration?

getting approval for each step from the key managers in a group meeting, pride of ownership is developed as no one wants to be the cog in the wheel that causes a breakdown in the process.

It is important that you schedule weekly meetings with all of your managers to update the plan and recognize possible problems that could cause delays. Be con-science of managers who are reluctant to give input and stay late and/or working weekends. Bring that manager out in the open with non-threatening statements to find out what the real problem is.

13. **What other alternative is there if milestones are missed?**

There is always the notion that with more money, per-sonnel and equipment, we can make up for lost time and get back on schedule; not always true. If a mile-stone is missed because of a lack of materials money will not get the materials any sooner. If key personnel are leaving for any reason, it may take weeks to find replacement person-nel and then you may have the issue of train-ing and bringing them up to speed. A natural disaster can displace your whole company and cause major delays.

Alternatives that you can be proactive about are identifying schools that provide trained personnel for specific jobs that require spe-cial training. Identify potential sites that could off-load manufacturing and that has the same standards that you require. Identify alternative funding sources if investors can't come up with the required funding as needed per your plan. Key personnel at your competitors that may be discontented and would make a move for the right reasons.

14. **What strengths do you have in both the company and products and how can you leverage them to build a competitive advantage in the products commercialization?**

   During your marketing phase you should have defined what strengths you bring to the market and build a plan to leverage them through distribution and maximize your direct sales force resources.

   Your competitive advantage can range from being the least expensive to the most costly and with features and benefits that range from minimum to all encompassing. You may want to piggy back on another product that has wide appeal such as a piece of software that operates under the Windows operating system. You may want to make a smaller or larger version of a toy or fad item.

   You may have national distribution that affords the luxury of instant market availability. Planning to deliver, promote and train key personnel to sell and support the product is crucial to your success. If you have a track record of delivering products that require strict regulatory compliance, you can leverage your reputation and alleviate any fears that buyers may have about your product not meeting the regulatory requirements.

Chapter 26
Qualifying and Establishing Test Sites

Test site qualification proves the validity of your market research. It proves validity by having test sites accept your product for testing and also assures your management that what you said during your market research about having quality test sites is true. The importance of quality test site representative of your target market is crucial to bringing your product to market in a timely, accepted and trouble free manner.

Encourage and expect constructive criticism on the various attributes of user friendliness, documentation, features and benefits. Listen to the comments of the test sites, make the appropriate changes to accommodate the market and you will definitely have a better chance of success than if you did not have quality customer test sites.

Pride in your company and in your product is transferred to the test site. Understand that the test site does not have the pride of authorship nor does it understand the development effort that went into your product to make it perform as it does. The test site is interested in what benefit the product will give them. If they are a reseller, they are interested in the market demand, price, quality and support. The consumer is interested in benefits, enjoyment, friendliness, time, cost savings, price and support. Remember, a test sites' input is not personal, take the input as constructive and, if you listen, they will recommend and purchase the product as related in your

Navigating Points:

Empower your people to be responsible for their area of development. Most of all get your key managers to take ownership of the project plan. Explain the market, the opportunity, the deadlines, and the competition. Ask your people for input as to resources, equipment and time to complete their piece of the equation. Plot out serially the events and input the information that each of your managers have given you and then hold a meeting to review the plan.

If the time to develop is too long with input from each manager on the plan, you can usually come up with a compromise that each can manage and buy into.

market research and subsequent sales process.

Development will test each component and assembly will test the product in every known way that they think the end user will use the product. This is bread board testing or alpha testing. The next level is beta and, depending on the amount of testing, there will be various versions of beta testing up until final release of the product.

For example, if the item is a Frisbee that is stamped from a mold or a Hula Hoop, the test sites may be a playground full of children. The product may have to be environmentally safe, be approved by a government regulatory body for various safety reasons and you will have to test for all of these criteria in your own environment. After you, the consumer and government regulatory bodies are satisfied that the product is safe for the target market you are ready for the next step. You invite the market to test your product, show them how it works, pass out the product and watch what happens. It is entirely possible that new uses for the product will emerge and that this will open up new markets that you have never before thought about. Children will abuse, use and give you input as in no other form of testing.

Other products may require a different set of standards. If it is a consumer electronics product with keys or membranes to press, jigs will have to be made to emulate thousands or millions of key depressions at different angles and forces. Stress tests for cold, heat and vibration may have to be done in order to meet the requirements of entering your target market. You will need drop tests of the product and package. Will the product splinter or have the keys drop off, will it burn or melt. Each of these issues is important in having your product approved by the government regulatory bodies and they are very stringent. Be prepared to have several prototypes available to be destroyed by the testing companies and consumer/distribution test sites that you have chosen.

Be prepared to deliver and administer a test plan to all of your test sites and thoroughly review the results for changes. If changes are required, weigh them related to cost, need of the market and Window of Opportunity. One of the biggest mistakes' companies make before releasing the product is to try to make every change possible. This is not possible, you will need to freeze the product at some agreed point and make that your baseline release. All subsequent releases will be enhancements and controlled based on the needs of the customer and changing market.

The following thirteen questions will help you through your thought process about the types of testing procedures you will need for your product.

1.   **What markets have you considered for beta test sites?**
       Markets for beta test sites should be representative of your priority target markets. If possible look at those markets that are periphery or synergistic to your target markets. If competition enters the market sooner than expected or if the market flattens out, you will have made inroads into other markets.

2.   What is the criteria for selecting the test site?

Criteria for selecting a test site should accomplish the function of educating the channel you are selling into, building enthusiasm and being a representative of the consumer of the product.

3.   What is the weighing criteria for each test site?

Weighing is not necessarily the same for each test site. Each site should have some commonality but also have specific areas of required feedback based on their role with your product. Weighing for a consumer will be heavy on ease of use and benefits. If it is for fun, how long before one gets bored with its use or is there a skill that has to be learned and can it never be perfected therefore having an unlimited use.

If it is a business application product, how does it benefit my business? Can I expect improved productivity, cost savings or larger market share? In your test plan for each test site have a list of testing criteria that you expect each test site participant to follow and ask for specific feedback on each item. In many instances you may want to observe the sites interaction with the precut and make your own determination on the various test site criteria.

4.   What are the most important test site criteria?

Define what it is that you want to test for? Examine the target market demographics. If the product is a toy,

The Experts Speak Out...

Far and away the best prize that life offers is the chance to work hard at work worth doing.

– Theodore Roosevelt

Where there is an open mind, there will always be a frontier.

– Charles F. Kettering

Whether you think you can or whether you think you can't, you're right!

– Henry Ford

You must either modify your dreams or magnify your skills.

– Jim Rohn

does it hold the child's interest, will it stand up to abuse, does the paint wear off? If it does break where does it break? Can the break cause bodily harm? If it is soft ware, what environment does it work in, is it compatible with Microsoft Windows for example? Is it easy to use? Is it fast? Can you cause it to fail? Is the documentation clear and concise?

Look at the product, the target demographics, what you want to accomplish and design a test plan to test thoroughly. Test the objective/obvious functions but also the subjective advantages that your product may offer the consumer.

5. **Are the test sites representative of the market condi--tions for commercialization of your product?**
Do not test the product in-house or have your friends test the product. These folks may be innately familiar with the use and operation of the product as a final commercial test for your product and you will not get objective input from this kind of test. Find representa -tive test sites or people who will be objective and thor -ough in comparing the documentation or written in -structions with the use of the product.

If you are selling through distribution, your channels will test the product internally and may even have lab environments similar to government regulatory agencies to determine if your product meets the stringent require- ments of the regulatory agencies. Two other tests are

Navigating Points:

Be prepared to deliver and administer a test plan to all of your test sites and thoroughly review the results for changes. If changes are required, weigh them related to cost, need of the market and Window of Opportunity. One of the biggest mistakes' companies make before releasing the product is to try to make every change possible. This is not possible, you will need to freeze the product at some agreed point and make that your baseline release. All subsequent releases will be enhancements and controlled based on the needs of the customer and changing market.

usually offered by your sales channels, internal product tests at the branch level with sales persons and customer service. They will establish customer test sites that have expressed an interest in your product.

Trade journal test drives are excellent methods to get editorials and evaluations of your product at no charge. If your product meets or exceed the specifications as advertised, the trade journal can be very favorable and in many instances give you an award of excellence, product of the month or year. You can then use this endorsement in other promotions.

6. **Is there an unusually significant concentration of ideal customers in your test sites?**
   Are all of your test sites customers agreeing to purchase the product as soon as it is available? I have found that in many instances, customers will agree to purchase and this forecasts great numbers. But no one wants to be f irst on the block and then not perform. Line up test sites that are very critical of products but when they do approve their history has proven out that they will make commitments and get behind a product in a big way.

   Large corporations with national and international distribution or retail outlets that have longer sales cycles negotiate harder but once approved volume usually occurs and when it comes time to bring out a new product the time frame for doing so is much shorter because of their track record.

Define what it is that you want to test for? Examine the target market demographics. If the product is a toy, does it hold the child's interest, will it stand up to abuse, does the paint wear off? If it does break where does it break? Can the break cause bodily harm? If it is software, what environment does it work in, is it compatible with Microsoft Windows for example? Is it easy to use? Is it fast? Can you cause it to fail? Is the documentation clear and concise?

7. **If the answer to six is yes, will your sales forecasts be skewed as a result and why?**

    As a manager listening to your Sales and Marketing Manager you need to determine the types of customers that have given you forecasts and what their track rec -ord has been in the past for living up to their commit -ment. If your customers are new to your product are they agreeing to establish a relationship to fill a hole in their product line until their current manufacturer deliv -ers a like product?

    If your product is brand new with no immediate compe- tition, you will have a better chance of establishing a solid relationship with new distribution than if you are taking market share from one of your competitors.

8. **What is your market share assumption for the market test?**

    Are you testing the niche market or the mass market? In some instances, if your product is full of features and requires extensive training to use, you may want to test the product in smaller markets. After you are convinced that the bugs have been worked out and the frustration level of your test market is lowered, move the product to the larger mass markets. This methodology is a luxu -ry only if you have minimal competition and a fairly large Window of Opportunity.

    Look to have a bell curve ramp instead of a hockey stick

curve ramp. The slower ramp can still be aggressive and with that slower ramp, you can control the release and manufacturing of your product.

9. **Are there other planning or forecasting assumptions that you hope to capture from the beta test?**
    Various markets can be tested in other than the target to gather input and interest. You can extend the appli cation of the interest and results into market research for other than your target market. If there are other fea tures that need to be added in order to penetrate other markets, you can determine the value during the testing phase. Marketing can take the test results and launch a marketing campaign into other markets and this will as sist in your future planning and forecasting.

10. **What aspects of your implementation will be tested during the test trial?**
    Depending on the product, you should try to test all phases of the implementation process. If your product is a rack mounted, cellophane packaged toy, your test of implementation is how well the product is received by the target audience.

    If your product requires training and is a standalone, you would want to monitor the installation process, training process, end user ease of operation, how well the product solves the problem for which your product was intended. You can also test for the various support issues that may be required for your product.

11. **How will you test the channel to make sure that your distributors are partners with you?**

This can be difficult in reality. You can sign corporate contracts for commitments, participate in co-op advertising and promotions, participate in distributor trade shows, be invited to train sales people and your product still may not sell like you envisioned.

If your product does not sell as advertised, you will get very frustrated and search for the way to make it happen. What usually occurs if your product is not totally unique is that the competition has mounted a counter attack directed at your product entry. The sales force is trained on their product, they feel comfortable, the customers are comfortable and they don't have to learn about your product and put themselves at risk by selling something new.

Usually salespeople have quotas and if your product does not help them significantly achieve this goal, your product will only be sold when requested. You can counter this mentality by working with the distributor to establish quotas for your product and where you will offer additional startup incentives for sales. You need to get the attention of the salesperson to sell you product since they are selling a competitive product even if it just appears to be a look alike.

The salesperson and customer may not perceive the differences in your product and you may have to volun-

As a manager listening to your Sales and Marketing Manager you need to determine the types of customers that have given you forecasts and what their track record has been in the past for living up to their commitment. If your customers are new to your product are they agreeing to establish a relationship to fill a hole in their product line until their current manufacturer delivers a like product?

If your product is brand new with no immediate competition, you will have a better chance of establishing a solid relationship with new distribution than if you are taking market share from one of your competitors.

teer to attend sales meetings and explain how your product offers greater benefits than that of the competitor. You may have to go on buddy calls with the salespeople to the customer sites and give the first few demonstrations so they will become more at ease with your product.

Just because you have a contract doesn't necessarily guarantee anything; now the job really begins. You begin the process of identifying inside champions, putting your support mechanisms in place and hiring good people that have the vision of success the way that you have viewed it during the development process.

12. Can you test product pricing?

Product price testing is usually done in the marketing phase of product development. The business plan reflects the startup costs including development, marketing and sales. Offsetting the cost side of the ledger is the revenue which is the margin you expect to receive on sales. As you ramp up sales, you offset the costs as you work towards breaking even and ultimately profitability.

You also test product pricing through direct contact with potential customers for feedback. Usually you get your base line price from your target market. If the consumer will purchase the product for $10.00 and you es-

Navigating Points:

Usually salespeople have quotas and if your product does not help them significantly achieve this goal, your product will only be sold when requested. You can counter this mentality by working with the distributor to establish quotas for your product and where you will offer additional startup incentives for sales. You need to get the attention of the salesperson to sell you product since they are selling a competitive product even if it just appears to be a look alike.

timate that it will cost you $5.00 to build and $100,000 to develop and your overhead is $20,000 per month, how many do I have to sell if I need to break even in 12 months?

You will need to sell 34,000 to break even over the next 12 months and recover all of your development costs. The rub comes when you do not have the sales force to physically sell 34,000 units and you don't have the channel partners in place that sell to your target demographic. Your channel partners also have to make a decent margin or mark up and that now cuts into your gross margin. Now the decision is one of raising the price beyond what the consumer said they were willing to pay for your product. You have to determine, what is the maximum ceiling price for your product? Can you raise the price another $1-$2.00 and still secure your target market share? If you go through channel partners, you will have to raise your end user price or reduce your margin in order to make it worthwhile for your channel partners to sell your product.

13. **Can you test product positioning?**
Product positioning can be based on several criteria. Benefit and feature should be key in positioning your product with your customer or distribution channel. How does your distribution channel perceive that your product be positioned? Are they using your product as a loss leader, a market leader, a product that compliments their own or a line of products or enhances the capability of a product?
Understand how your product will be positioned so you can capitalize on the positioning with promotions, attack like sales channels to sell your product and also look to new channels that would position your product in different market segments.
Other forms of positioning are where your product will be positioned in

the store or on the shelf. If your product is perceived to be in high de-mand and attracts customers into a store your product will probably be positioned in the front with its own display or in a place where it is easily visible.

Chapter 27

Testing

Testing can make or break your products successful entrance into your target market. Thousands of companies have wasted millions of dollars on products because they did not thoroughly test their products prior to making them ready for sale. Testing comes in many forms. The test of reasonableness is probably the first test that anyone takes even if they do not recognize it as a product test. The reasonableness test is your thought process about an idea that will do something unique, fun, save time and money or increase productivity.

Brainstorming usually follows the reasonableness test and this is where you bring in your friends, colleagues or people that you trust to give you an honest opinion on your idea. You are testing the validity of your idea beyond your own thought process. I usually brainstorm in a conference room or a place that has a white board and easel pads and sometimes a tape recorder to write down thoughts and ideas. Sometimes my ideas turn into another product through this brainstorming process; these sessions are always productive. Almost everyone likes to be asked to participate in a brainstorming session on a new idea or product. This process gives ownership to the organization and the people that participated in this process usually continue to give you feedback long after the brainstorming session.

You will find yourself testing the market for feedback on your idea and how to enhance it to fill the needs of other synergistic markets or maybe not so synergistic markets. You will test the idea through contacting potential resellers and end users of the product. Testing is a continuing process of asking for and receiving feedback on your product through its inception and life span.

The following fifteen questions were created to help you assimilate the parameters for your product testing. I have given the question and followed it with ideas to get you thinking about the various processes associated with the testing process.

1.	**What are the design parameters for your product prototype?**

The parameters can be on a napkin or produced on a sophisticated CAD computer; it depends on the com plexity of the product. A prototype is designed for the audience that you wish to have test your product. A big mistake that most companies make is in not building a prototype that is close, if not exact, to what the real product will be. I have seen products go to laboratories for testing only to get thrown out for not complying with the mandatory requirements of testing for the par ticular agency. Get the instructions and read them closely. The lab gets hundreds of products a year and if you do not comply with the set instructions you will have to continue to come back and until you do. This process wastes time, an incredible amount of money and can do irreparable damage to the moral of your company and cause delays in bringing the product to sale and distribution.

The design parameters should be set for the process

Navigating Points:

Product positioning can be based on several criteria. Benefit and feature should be key in positioning your product with your customer or distribution channel. How does your distribution channel perceive that your product be positioned? Are they using your product as a loss leader, a market leader, a product that compliments their own or a line of products or enhances the capability of a product?

which your product will tested. Evolution of the product can take the form of paper to cardboard, plastic or wood to the various high strength metals and sophisticated electronics to make it work as designed. When you take a product to a lab or customer for testing it'd better be right. Inside champions are necessary and can be cultivated internally to help you with getting your product approved in a specific channel or customer. When it comes time to test the product, their job is on the line and you'd better have a product that will stand up to the rigors of live, in use testing.

2. **What will your prototype look like and what will it do?**

A prototype can, and probably will, take many forms and shapes before it reaches the final testing environ ment. Your alpha or internal development tests will sometimes break down the product into components with each component being tested. After completion, the components are assembled into a single product that hopefully will function as designed. Ease of use and esthetics are important before making the product available for outside testing. Before you give the prod uct outside for testing, a concise set of testing parame ters should accompany the product and you should closely monitor the product and observe how easily the tester can open the box, assemble if necessary, read the instructions, observe body and facial language and fol low the instructions for use and testing.

3. **Can you use the prototype for market testing and cost estimating?**

Brainstorming usually follows the reasonableness test and this is where you bring in your friends, colleagues or people that you trust to give you an honest opinion on your idea. You are testing the validity of your idea beyond your own thought process. I usually brainstorm in a conference room or a place that has a white board and easel pads and sometimes a tape recorder to write down thoughts and ideas. Sometimes my ideas turn into another product through this brainstorming process; these sessions are always productive. Almost everyone likes to be asked to participate in a brain-storming session on a new idea or product.

Prototypes are built for cost estimating as well as market testing. The cost estimating process usually changes during the prototyping because a part does not work as advertised or, as you thought it would, in your product. You will have to find replacement components and the cost or size may be different than originally estimated. You should have an estimating process whether it is computerized or hand written. If the product is to be produced in mass quantities and involve many parts and assemblies to make up the end item, you will probably use a sophisticated Bill of Materials and/or a Material Requirements Planning program to keep track of the parts that make up the product.

An inventory package consisting of all of the various components that comprise your product is tied into a purchasing and/or accounts payable system to aid in the ordering of your parts. The description, lead time, cost per unit and quantity, substitute part and other factors are in this type of system and it makes it easy to estimate the cost of building a single unit or a thousand units because all of the costing parameters are readily available.

The prototype can then be used for market testing if it meets the standards that the regulatory bodies have in place or in use in your target segment of the market if it will perform as per the specifications. The prototype is named a prototype because there is a possibility that it may be changed after market testing for reasons of esthetics and ease of use.

4. What are the key features?

Key features should all be ready to be tested prior to being released to a testing lab or a customer test site. Be thorough in identifying the key features with easy to read instructions for use and assembly. All of the key features should be ready and functional in your proto type. There are exceptions to every rule, such as phased product development where separate and dis tinct modules or models can be tested without the oth er being in place or integrated upon completion for a complete test. Confidence is subjective at best and when you say that your product will be ready except for X, Y, and Z, apprehension sets in even if only slightly. Development is the time to work the extra hour to come in under schedule. If you request product testing assistance from within or outside prior to the scheduled completion, all concerned are more than willing to take ownership of the test and give positive feedback.

5. Can you test your customer's reaction to your product without making a prototype?

Yes you can. If your idea was not tested through inquiry and discovering needs, then brainstorming the ideas validity, you probably would not have taken the next steps to raise funds and develop the prototype. It is through the customer's enthusiasm that the marketing and development personnel get excited because this is their opportunity to author and promote a new prod uct.

6. Can you sell the product without having a prototype in

your salespersons hands?

Yes you can with these reservations. If you are an estab lished manufacturer or reseller, your customers are more likely to give you a letter of intent, contract or oth er form of agreement. If the product represents brand new technology, has mass market appeal and your cus tomers could be the first on the block to distribute the product, again, agreements can be negotiated to give them first right of refusal on quantities and price breaks if required on increased volume.

There have been many occasions where I have sold va por ware, smoke and mirrors, phantom ware or an idea. I had a good idea about the capability of the proposed product to perform and satisfy the needs of my custom ers and with past credibility, I was successful. The term that I chose to use is "timing the truth" meaning when my product was not readily available I gave my custom ers and prospects ownership of the product by getting them involved in the development process through an idea exchange and giving me market research answers of key questions.

7.   **How much testing will you need to do?**

Testing depends on the complexity of the product, the strictness of the regulatory testing bodies that may be involved, the cost of your product, the size of the mar ket, your distribution channels testing requirements and getting the MTBF (Mean Time between Failures) on all of the parts that you are using in the product.

Test time can be greatly reduced if the product plan is

frozen for development and the plan is agreed to by all of development, plugged into a Project Management scheduler and monitored on a regular basis. If the plan is like Jell-O and constantly moving, the product test may not ever get accomplished because you will not know what to test.

8. **Tests are done in four phases:**

    - The test of reasonableness to determine if the idea has any merit.

    - Bench and breadboard tests which are internal. Each developer has their own set of tests that test for heat and cold, shake and break, error detection and ease of use.

    - Alpha tests usually test the completed modules or components and also test the completed product.

    - Beta tests test the product in live customer environments. Depending on the product some customers may want to test the product for months to test for all of the variables and only time will tell if the tests covered all of the possible variables.

9. **Do you have all of the regulatory approvals required to sell the product?**

    First thing to do after checking patent and copyright registration is to find out what regulatory requirements are required for your product and determine from the regulatory agencies if they are approved by all of the possible resellers of your product. Also find out if they exchange approvals with other countries whom you

What Would John Do?

Can you test your customer's reaction to your product without making a prototype?

Yes you can. If your idea was not tested through inquiry and discovering needs, then brainstorming the ideas validity, you probably would not have taken the next steps to raise funds and develop the prototype. It is through the customer's enthusiasm that the marketing and development personnel get excited because this is their opportunity to author and promote a new product.

may choose to distribute your product to.

10. **Do you have or do you need other countries' regulatory approvals if you sell your product outside of the United States?**

The United States regulatory agencies can give you a good understanding of this but I would also work through my distributors that will be selling outside of the United States. Since they already sell outside, they will have had to get the right approvals.

11. **Have you scheduled government approved laboratory tests?**

Key to a timely release of your product is to schedule lab test time months in advance and if possible schedule two or three times if you anticipate problems or are sending your product through in modules. Be prepared to write off the products that you give out to test as these companies they will perform all of the damaging tests known to man.

Prior to giving your product over for test, request the testing criteria for your product and test for that criteria in your own company. If possible rent or find another company that would be willing to perform the tests on your product prior to releasing for government testing. The parameters for testing are varied but as an example:

• At what temperature will your product catch fire or melt?

• How high can I drop your product before it breaks?

Navigating Points:

The prototype can then be used for market testing if it meets the standards that the regulatory bodies have in place or in use in your target segment of the market if it will perform as per the specifications. The prototype is named a prototype because there is a possibility that it may be changed after market testing for reasons of esthetics and ease of use.

- If it breaks how does it break? Do parts fall off, are they sharp, and are they small or large and will it still operate?

- If electronic, ranges of operation will be measured for possible radiation, electronic emission, sound, etc.

Perform as many of the required tests as possible in your own shop and you will speed up the outside testing process and it will save you a great deal of time and money.

12. **Have you scheduled laboratory or customer tests with your major distribution channels?**

Timing is everything when dealing with your customers. The larger your customer channel is, the more testing is required and especially if they view the product as a possible flagship or trendsetter with new technology. If your product is viewed as a product to be in great de mand, testing can be preempted. If it is and also fills out a line or necessary because it is requested, you will get in the queue when all other priorities are filled.

13. **How will you test market the product?**

Depending on the size of the market, you and/or your channel may want to test the market in a specific region to make sure that you are employing the best method ology for promoting and selling the product. Only after getting all of the bugs worked out of the program would you launch it on a national basis.

There are books written on test marketing products. It is dependent on the demand, price and the money that you have available to test market your product. A few examples are:

1. Food and sundries are test marketed via the direct mail, telemarketing and sampling in grocery, department, malls and drug stores.

2. Selected demographic market segments are sent free samples with questionnaires to return for key information.

3. Free or low cost demo products are given to your channels for trial with customers for feedback.

4. Selected target segments are used for trial and error.

5. Trade shows and trade periodicals are used to test products.

14. What insight can you gain by prototype testing in your proposed distribution channels?

Tremendous product insight can be gained through this methodology. If your distribution channel has any real intent on selling your product, they will thoroughly market test your product in selected customer environments and gather feedback prior to launching an all-out campaign for your product.

15. What will producing the prototype tell you about the budgeted manufacturing costs?

If the product is hard, not soft. By that I mean hard as in something that you can feel as op posed to a piece of computer software. If it is hard, you will gather input as to how long you can expect to take to manufacturer the product in terms of labor, materials costs with specific quantities, manufacturing equipment, yield on manufacturing, rework considerations, warranty considerations, pre and post-sales support if necessary and the other overhead associated with running a company.

Chapter 28
Managing Expectations

Managing Expectations is often overlooked and only paid attention to when a crisis is happening or about to happen. The crisis could be an unexpected sale or how do we get the resources to ensure a satisfied customer. A crisis could be the unexpected departure of a key employee, shortage of raw materials, parts or inventory, cash running low, prospects going sideways, key employees getting sick or leaving, natural disaster, stock dropping or any number of things that management is expected to control. It is essential to minimize any hiccups understanding the financial position of your company and what the major milestones of each department are and in turn, communicating the results in a timely and non-confrontational or fearful nature. This is key to a smooth running company.

If you have investors or a Board of Directors that require timely reports on the position of your company, that is a forcing function to bring about a better understanding of the companies' operation. Financial reports such as profit and loss, receivables, payables, inventory, personnel head count, status of back orders, potential new sales, competitions position, key resources and anything that is required to communicate the status of your company to those that have a need to know are all required.

The following questions will assist you in better understanding management's responsibility relative to managing ex-

Navigating Points:

Timing is everything when dealing with your customers. The larger your customer channel is, the more testing is required and especially if they view the product as a possible flagship or trendsetter with new technology. If your product is viewed as a product to be in great demand, testing can be preempted. If it is and also fills out a line or necessary because it is requested, you will get in the queue when all other priorities are filled.

pectations.

1. **Who are the stockholders and what are their current expectations for the new product?**

Being involved with several startup organizations, and a few major corporations, I was responsible, in some cases, for all of the capital to begin the company and, in other cases, responsible for specific departments such as marketing, sales and customer service. In all instances, I was responsible for either the complete annual report or giving input on the status of marketing, revenue and projected revenue.

In the cases where venture capitalists raised money for a given product, it was important to keep them informed on a quarterly basis as to the status of marketing, product development, prospect development and how well we were budgeting our cash to meet the requirements of the business plan. The business plan was what the investors bought into based on there being a market with a wide Window of Opportunity and minimal competition. Most of all, we could make a generous profit if we were able to stay within the boundaries of our business plan.

As with most startup companies, business plans are fraught with unknowns. Unknowns such as technology not mature enough to deliver exactly as promised, resources not available when required, prospects vacillating and any number of steps that, when not taken in

The Experts Speak Out...

The most serious mistakes are not being made as a result of wrong answers. The truly dangerous thing is asking the wrong question.

– *Peter Drucker*

Why did I want to win? Because I didn't want to lose!

– *Max Schmelling*

To succeed in business, to reach the top, an individual must know all it is possible to know about that business.

– *J. Paul Getty*

To win without risk is to triumph without glory.

– *Pierre Corneille*

a timely manner, can cause untimely delays. The job of management is to keep the investor and employees aware of the delays and have contingency plans in place to carry the product to completion. In most cases, a venture capitalist firm or investor does not find it out of the ordinary to have to put more cash into a project to help it reach maturity. Usually in return for the cash, a dilution of stock takes place amongst the officers and the investors gain greater control.

All the stockholder wants is a good return for their money based on your original pitch on customer need, the ability to produce and the ability to sell to your chosen markets. If you are smart, you will develop a business plan with the knowledge that, if you do 30% of forecasted, you will be successful. Write the business plan with the 30% and if you exceed the plan, everyone is a hero. When you need to go to the well for a cash infusion for new products, you will have little if no resistance.

2. **How well do you expect to meet those expectations during the year?**

If you are a brand new startup, you probably have your hands full, with infrastructure, personnel, marketing, advertising and setting up a financial reporting system. You should have milestones projected on a project management reporting system and weekly, or sometimes daily, report the progress and adjust the milestones as required. If asked about the status of any project, you simply have to pull up the last project status. Without some type of reporting system that everyone can buy into and operate, you are headed down the path of confusion and costly wasted effort.

This type of automated or manual system is mandatory if you are operating a multi-faceted operation. You will be able to manage expectations and foresee delays or unexpected shortages or increased sales forecasts with a well-managed reporting system that all of your managers can contribute to.

3.   **What is your communication schedule to get key information to your stockholders during the year?**
Communication comes in many forms depending on the requirement. Some examples are:
- Annual reports which depict the profit and loss, new products, key customers, key officers and significant events that are deemed important.
- Route all forms of product announcements and key trade journal editorials
- If you attend trade shows, announce them so that your stock holders can attend and see the response that your products are getting at the show.
- If you have a Mission Statement and Theme or require input request it from those that have an interest in your products. Get ownership of your product from as many sources as possible. Each contact is a potential missionary for your product and you don't know who will contact you as a result of the communication.

4.   **What major events do you anticipate in with your new**

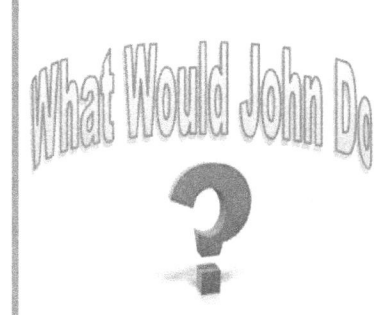

In the cases where venture capitalists raised money for a given product, it was important to keep them informed on a quarterly basis as to the status of marketing, product development, prospect development and how well we were budgeting our cash to meet the requirements of the business plan. The business plan was what the investors bought into based on there being a market with a wide Window of Opportunity and minimal competition. Most of all, we could make a generous profit if we were able to stay within the boundaries of our business plan.

products development during the year?

If you are a startup company, you may want to announce key technology breakthroughs or manufacturing steps completed. If you are a service company, you might want to announce technology availability along with materials and ways to access the materials such through the Internet.

If you are an existing company with imbedded products, you may want to announce the next generation being planned or enhancements to the current products. You may want to announce the acquisition of new products or key clients that are using the product. If you have acquired new distribution that gets you into other target markets or on the international stage, announce the alliance and what you expect the alliance to bring to the company.

Key editorials from major publications, regulatory bodies or consultants are significant in announcing goals met and can give your product immense credibility.

5. **What information systems will we use to fulfill your communications responsibilities during the year?**
    Information systems are thought to be automated and most companies use some sort of system with a word processor, graphics or Power Point to assist in com mu nicating to other media, internal employees, customers, prospects and investors.

Navigating Points:

If you are a brand new startup, you probably have your hands full, with infrastructure, personnel, marketing, advertising and setting up a financial reporting system. You should have milestones projected on a project management reporting system and weekly, or sometimes daily, report the progress and adjust the milestones as required. If asked about the status of any project, you simply have to pull up the last project status. Without some type of reporting system that everyone can buy into and operate, you are headed down the path of confusion and costly wasted effort.

Output from your internal system can be used externally with other media such as the Internet, a video house to make a video of your product, trade shows for hands on, trade journals, newsletters, direct mail, fax back, call centers, telemarketing, bingo card, direct contact and through your channels.

6. **If you find yourself in a worst case scenario, what are your communications plans?**

Worst case scenarios can be foreseen if you are using and updating a project management system on a regular re curring basis. Contingency plans should be established for: Possible downsizing and assistance in relocating personnel to other companies or arranging to contract, reduce hours, give different incentives for reduced direct com pensation.

Short of cash. Have a plan that will enable you to raise additional capital as opposed to the expense of losing control or liquidation of stock ownership.

Out of raw materials or stock to produce product to fill orders. Be prepared to delay all shipments or make a decision to try to fill those orders that offers the greatest long-term potential to the risk of losing other lesser value customers.

Natural disaster. Have a plan to immediately contact all customers telling them that you have this problem and informing them of the probable delay before you can continue begin manufacturing and fill orders.

Key employees leaving for any reason. Communicate via e-mail, your web and get press releases or fax messages to key customers and trade journals explaining the ramifications of the personnel loss and what you are doing to replace the person.

Competition announcing a product that looks, on the surface, as a replacement or a product that will make yours obsolete. Be prepared to counter with an enhancement, new announcement, inventory protection or price reduction. Be prepared to communicate in this order any major disruption in product delivery to your personnel, investors, suppliers, customers and prospects. You need to keep morale as high as possible amongst your key managers during times of delays so that they can communicate to their personnel.

The investors need to be kept informed as it is their money that is keeping your business afloat and you may need to go to the well several more times if unforeseen developments occur that delay your products release. Suppliers need to be kept aware of possible late receivables payments to ensure that you will have the materials to complete the development and manufacturing process. Customers and prospects need to be kept aware of any delays in product delivery as they may be planning training, advertising campaigns, testing and possibly enhancing an existing product.

If you find yourself in a best case scenario, how can you get additional resources to make it happen earlier to meet "The Window of Opportunity"?

This is an opportunity that many companies would like to be faced with. Not all cases can be dealt with by throwing additional money and resources at it to speed up the development and delivery process. The best case scenario is one that has you communicating the progress of development to your investors and customers and your customers agreeing to advance payment before delivery. Another scenario is that your investors are willing to raise more capital for a larger piece of the ownership in order to meet the "Window of Opportunity" earlier.

If the window is wide and your competition is not breathing down your neck or your customers are not clamoring for product. It would not be wise to dilute your ownership position for capital in order to move the product delivery up by a few days or weeks.

Resources should be identified both in personnel and manufacturing in order to manage an unexpected growth curve. There are many contract manufacturing firms that probably manufacture similar products with the same disciplines that your product requires and many even adhere to ISO-9000 requirements. If it is personnel you need and you're successful, people like to come to a winner so look to the competition or to temporary agencies.

7. **Will you have reward systems in place to recognize out standing achievement?**

Qualified cold calling is sometimes a necessary evil to generate leads and nobody likes to do it and that is why there are so many call centers and messages on your answering machine, voice mail or e-mail. A cookie that comes up while you are trying to do something on your computer is also a sign of cold calling. I would offer incentives such as a gas fill up, movie tickets or a dinner for two at a local restaurant. Try to get the spouse or significant other involved and make it a same day reward building to a weekly or monthly reward. You would be amazed at how fast leads can be generated.

Reward programs are dependent on the product, type of personnel and how competitive the industry is that you are competing in for resources. If you are a high tech company that requires degreed personnel with engineering backgrounds and are located in the Northwest, you will probably have to have reward systems in place in order to keep your personnel. The Northwest has Microsoft, Boeing and a host of other high tech companies that are in constant need of high tech, highly trained personnel. Reward systems can be flex time, money, time off, paid schools, new projects, new technology, promotions and trips. Some even like the fact that the manager buys them pizza or takes the time to talk to them and personally recognize their achievement.

8. **Are all of the milestones translated into action steps with resources and scheduled into your Rolling Four Quarter Work Plan?**
The key to "Managing Expectations" is to identify all milestones on a project flow that can be managed, used as a communication tool and be up

dated to report the progress or delays of a given step in the process.

Chapter 29
Vision Reinforcing

Vision reinforcing sets the tempo and style of the company and trickles down through each manager and to every employee. Taking ownership and pride in what you do is contagious and every manager should have a responsibility to periodically "Reinforce the Vision" of the company's objective.

Companies like Microsoft stress their vision for the future in computer automation and are synonymous with business and personal computer application processing. Saturn cars stress the care their employees take in doing their job to make your car of the best quality it can be. Fisher Price Toys stress the educational value and long life that their toys offered to the pre-adolescence. Companies strive for the Baldridge award for quality or the various seals of approval that are recognized for highest quality. Vision Reinforcing helps make quality happen and the truly successful companies not only have it but make a conscience effort to promote it on a daily basis.

Communicating the success of each department in achieving department goals is contagious. I always have each department manager give a brief talk on major accomplishments and recognize outstanding contributions on a monthly basis. Sales is what keeps us in business and I share the new sales, prospects and relate that sales would not happen if it were not for the effort and care of each employee in taking care of their responsibility to produce the best product that they possibly can.

Navigating Points:

Resources should be identified both in personnel and manufacturing in order to manage an unexpected growth curve. There are many contract manufacturing firms that probably manufacture similar products with the same disciplines that your product requires and many even adhere to ISO-9000 requirements. If it is personnel you need and you're successful, people like to come to a winner so look to the competition or to temporary agencies.

Vision Reinforcing is not only important to your employees but to your stockholders and investors as well as your sales channels, customers and future prospects. Vision Reinforcing comes in the form of how well you present your company from the receptionist at the front desk to the CEO. Vision Reinforcing should be a part of your Mission Statement and in the theme you use for all of your documentation and promotional materials. The message you deliver to your investors, trade journals, creditors and financial community have a bearing on how you are perceived and that is passed through to your product.

Competition will also view you differently and they will know that to compete, they have to raise their level of quality. It also makes your customers less vulnerable to the lures of competition. In summary, Vision Reinforcing separates your company from the pack and, if done correctly, or at all, everyone associated with your company will be better because of this effort.

The next seven questions are designed as an aid in helping you prepare to be proactive in Vision Reinforcing both internally and externally.

1. **What are your specific plans to meet the need of your supporters in terms of involvement and information?** Internal and external communication methodologies are vital to the success of today's business where almost everyone has a computer and access to the Internet via high speed links. Electronic mail is an easy way to com

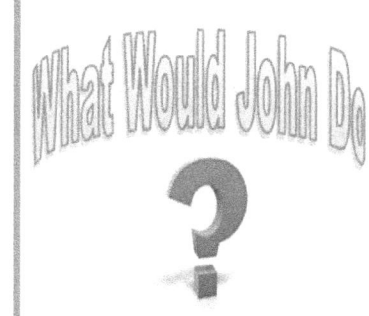

Reward programs are dependent on the product, type of personnel and how competitive the industry is that you are competing in for resources. If you are a high tech company that requires degreed personnel with engineering backgrounds and are located in the Northwest, you will probably have to have reward systems in place in order to keep your personnel. Reward systems can be flex time, money, time off, paid schools, new projects, new technology, promotions and trips. Some even like the fact that the manager buys them pizza or takes the time to talk to them and personally recognize their achievement.

municate the status of your company's key successes or strategies to your key supporters.   Instant feedback is also available from the same media. Some companies use fax broadcast, others newsletters, periodicals with editorials and voice mail to communicate information and solicit involvement.

Choose a method of communication that is in line with your budget and, if possible, use the media that the majority of your supporters are familiar with. Don't assume you are communicating correctly, periodically request information and then feedback. Also give feedback on the information that you received back from them to show that you listened and are taking action. In the future when you request input, you will again be well received where as if you did not respond, your response would be considered poor or nonexistent.

2.   **When talking to key supporters of your new product, what would you tell them in order to gain their personal support?**
This is an open ended question but designed to stimulate the process if you are looking for additional funding, help open new markets, attract key personnel or are having trouble delivering product or having manufacturing issues.

3.   **What are the groups of major stockholders that are essential to your products successful commercializetion?**
How you have your funding regulated for infusion into

your company could be critical to your success. Some times funding is authorized through completion of spe cific milestones meaning that in order to take the next step in the funding process, specific steps need to be completed.

4. **Are your stockholders and board members influential in the target markets that you have identified as key to your success?**

    Again, specific milestones might trigger their endorse ment into their company or other company's distribu tion channels. Are your stockholders major customers or resellers of your product? If the major stockholders have a vested interest in the distribution rights as well as the growth of the stock, your success could be de pendent on their endorsement.

    Is your stock privately held? How many Class A and Class B shares are outstanding and how many more are for sale? What is the dilution factor? What triggers the sales of more Class A and B shares?

    If you are privately held and are going for an IPO (Initial Private Offering) what are the prerequisites that are re quired in order to make your stock attractive on the public exchange?

5. **What is the downside for your stockholders and re sellers if we fail?**

    The downside to the stockholder is a complete loss of

the money invested, a resellers' downside could be a loss of credibility, customers' loyalty, customers' pur chases as well as the investment in product, sales train ing, advertising, support and the Window of Opportuni ty.

6. **In what ways does your company culture support the successful new product development effort?**
If you are small enough to make decisions rapidly, you have a better chance of capitalizing on the Window of Opportunity for new product introduction.

If you are a niche market product provider or have alli ances with large corporations, you have a degree of im munity to competition. As long as you target a specific market segment and do not encroach on the major mar kets, you will stay in good standing with your alliance partners.

If you are in a cash flush position, you do not have to go out for development money which may dilute your holdings and create another layer of decision before one can be made on a new product.

7. **What aspects of current corporate culture could be harmful to development or block your success?**
Are you decision making processes too slow to capital ize on the Window of Opportunity? This can especially happen in large corporations. Small corporations can act quickly and be proactive to market trends, new technol ogy and generally engineer new products quicker than

Navigating Points:

Choose a method of com munication that is in line with your budget and, if pos sible, use the media that the majority of your supporters are familiar with. Don't as sume you are communi cating correctly, periodically request information and then feedback. Also give feedback on the information that you received back from them to show that you lis tened and are taking action. In the future when you re quest input, you will again be well received where as if you did not respond, your response would be consid ered poor or nonexistent.

large corporations. Most large corporations have alliance partners that manufacture added value products because they understand the time it takes to develop products quickly.

The not-invented-here syndrome is sometimes deadly to a corporation's growth and in keeping or attracting new personnel. New technology may not be readily accepted until proven by many other companies which will delay your development of new products.
Not recognizing your competitors' strengths and getting blind-sided with new products that erode your market share can be a concern. Customers you thought were loyal to your company are, in fact, looking for the best product at the best possible price and could switch to your competitor. Do not think that customer loyalty will keep your customers. Remember that your customers may be distributors of your product and, as such, have an obligation to their customers to provide the best product with the latest technology at the best price. If you cannot continue to help your distributors stay abreast with the latest and greatest, the bottom line over rides loyalty.

The investors need to be kept informed as it is their money that is keeping your business afloat and you may need to go to the well several more times if unforeseen developments occur that delay your products release. Suppliers need to be kept aware of possible late receivables payments to ensure that you will have the materials to complete the development and manufacturing process. Customers and prospects need to be kept aware of any delays in product delivery.

8. **How can you remove the roadblocks if there are any?**
    Roadblocks are opportunities to excel and should never stop you. A pothole in the road can be patched and the road can be smooth once again. Roadblocks can be brought on by competition, economy, technology breakthroughs, distribution not ramping up as

quickly as anticipated, a bad review or editorial comment. All roadblocks can be converted to smooth riding if you plan and execute. Granted, all plans have the possibility of going sideways but if you plan and have a contingency plan for possible judgment errors, you will be in a position to be proactive instead of reactive.

An example of a roadblock is an inside champion for a competitor's product. I knew the key decision maker and he afforded me the opportunity to present my case to the other decision makers and, if I could convince this one decision maker that our product was superior and not smoke and mirrors, he would recommend our product. My ploy was to get him to take ownership of the problem our product could solve. I had him explain the problem which for us was an opportunity. He explained in detail what the problem was and how he would attack and solve the problem. What he did not recognize was through our discussions, I planted seeds of how the problem should be solved. He explained in detail, the solution that I had already provided him with. After he completed the explanation of the problem and proposed the solution, I reiterated that we had a solution for the problem and he was solidly in our camp and I won the order and their ongoing business.

Chapter 30
Senior Managements Role

Senior management's role sets the standard that all employees will usually follow. If management is very open and quick to identify and solve problems, most likely other managers will follow suit. If management is closed door and secretive, most likely, communications will be lacking from department to department.

Management can be effective depending on the product and/or type of product or service you are dealing with if they are conscious of the need for open communication. The most effective style of management is one that communicates the vision and enforces the vision by setting the example. Here's a story that shows how important this is, as president of a small company, I was bored one day and the trash can was full so I proceeded to empty the can in the customer service department. It happened that one of the service personnel saw me emptying the trash and they mentioned it to the customer. To this day that story is still told and some of my customers have come up to me at a trade show and said that I set a real example for the department and that my employees thought that it was a great gesture for me to empty trash cans. Something as simple as emptying the trash impressed the employees!

As Vice President of Sales and Marketing, I would call a companywide meeting of our 80 employees once a month. The purpose of this meeting was to give an update on the status of sales and prospects and each of the other department managers would than go over the accomplishments of their departments. Periodically, each of us would also recognize the contributions of key employees and award them a dinner for two at a local restaurant. This had a positive effect on everyone because they felt important. Management has to take ownership of ensuring that their teams feel like they are appreciated or you will lose them.

Other things that we would do to encourage teamwork was to have each department that was dependent on another's accomplishments or, as prerequisite before a project could be completed, have weekly or as needed meetings to ensure that the modules would link up properly. Imagine if two groups were building a tunnel or railroad track and each started at a different side and did not communicate. The tunnels and tracks wouldn't meet and there would be a great deal of rework in order to make the correction.

Communication is key and should be encouraged by senior management every step of the way as well as encouraged by other department managers and supervisors. Not everyone is a leader and most are followers and, if the truth be known, most like to be informed and feel that are an integral part of a team that is working towards a mutual goal rather than actually lead.

The following sixteen points are areas that a manager should be cognizance of in their company or department and should be encouraged to play an important role in.

1. **Developing and communicating the vision**

   The vision is most likely the CEO's or Presidents view of where this person sees the company in 1-10 years. The vision is founded on market intelligence taking into con sideration where your target markets are headed and what product you are bringing to the market to make life easier, offer more fun, do things faster, save time, conserve resources, create jobs or a myriad of other vi sions that all companies have for their products.

   Once you have a company, it is important to communi-cate your vision of the company and empower your people to make it happen. Communicating the vision is not only required when you hire a person but it needs to be re-enforced, sometimes daily, and it should be done formally on a periodic basis. Smaller companies' employees are more than likely going to work for a com-pany that has a visionary leading the way and is a good communicator of that vision. Smaller companies give a greater chance for recognition and the opportunity to excel and extend your boundaries of responsibility.

2. **Communicating the importance of speed.**

   Every manager wants the job done quicker and with ex cellent quality. Each customer would like to have the product yesterday. Loose cannons have their place and one should not discourage effort but, if speed of devel opment is done without quality control, the product may have to be restarted from the drawing board. En courage speed and quality as it pertains to your respon-

Navigating Points:

Roadblocks are opportunities to excel and should never stop you. A pothole in the road can be patched and the road can be smooth once again. Roadblocks can be brought on by competition, economy, technology break-throughs, distribution not ramping up as quickly as an-ticipated, a bad review or editorial comment. All road-blocks can be converted to smooth riding if you plan and execute. Granted, all plans have the possibility of going sideways but if you plan and have a contingency plan for possible judgment errors, you will be in a position to be proactive instead of reactive.

sibility. Encourage innovativeness and look for ways to speed up development. This effort can be accomplished through training, empowerment, new technology and department communication.

3. **Identifying and overcoming barriers to fuel product development.**

    So many companies beat their heads against the wall and don't ask for help when they run into a barrier. I used to be guilty of this to the extreme. I would stay up sometimes for 40 hours straight trying to figure out a problem and I would often collapse at my desk. I would get so frustrated that I would go into the rest room and cry and bash my fist into boxes or walls because I was so upset at myself for not being able to figure out the solution. I reluctantly would finally ask for help and low and behold it was usually a simple solution that was right in front of my face but, because I was so wrapped up in the problem, I would overlook the obvious.

    From this experience I learned to ask for help when I needed it and, as I became higher in the management rank, I would then encourage everyone, especially managers, to be especially aware of extreme hours being worked by individuals. I set in motion weekly or daily status meetings to identify and resolve problems (I call all problems opportunities) before they would get out of hand.

4. **Finding the right people for accurate and timely product**

The Experts Speak Out....

To succeed... You need to find something to hold on to, something to motivate you, something to inspire you.

— *Tony Dorsett*

Statistics suggest that when customers complain, business owners and managers ought to get excited about it. The complaining customer represents a huge opportunity for more business.

— *Zig Ziglar*

I wasn't satisfied just to earn a good living. I was looking to make a statement.

— *Donald Trump*

More managers try to hire inexperienced personnel to get the job done in order to save money, when in reali ty, if they would have paid for experienced talent the first time around it would save them money, the quality of work would be enhanced and the morale would be generally higher.   Intrinsic values are very important when hiring people into product development. Depend ing on your company, some might be driven to work for a company with great benefits and a long track record for steady advancement. Others might be driven by the technology or opportunity to excel, stock options, bo nuses, high pay or the opportunity for paid schooling, these are all intrinsic values for people wanting to work for a company and you need to be aware of them.

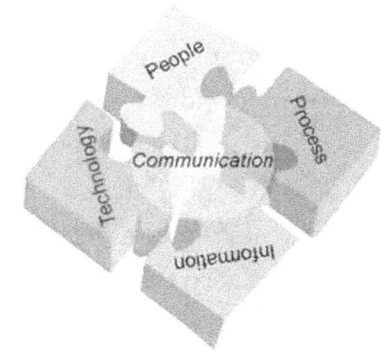

5.   **Staying informed**
Staying informed on the morale of your company by talking to key managers and periodically wandering through the company to get a pulse of how the compa ny is operating is always a great idea. Weigh your off-the-record evaluation with the project status meetings. So many times your managers will tell you what you want to hear and when a crisis arises, drastic measures have to be taken to right the ship. If your project meetings are accurate, you should have minimal ship wrecks but it is always a good idea to take the tempera ture of the company on a regular basis.

6.   **Empowering teams**
Empower teams and individuals to succeed and make it

okay to also fail. Great things can happen when people have the opportunity to fail. If you have hired good em ployees with the skills, attitudes and values commensu rate with what you want out of your employees, you have a much better chance of success than if you pigeon -hole personnel. Empower your people to think, give them guidelines and parameters and if that is not enough, leave the door open for further discussion to extend the boundaries. So many managers hire people with less skill than themselves. Good managers have confidence in their leadership abilities and hire person nel that are better than them in many ways and if you can do this, you will be surprised at the results.

7. **Emphasizing training**
Not all jobs require extensive training but all people like to feel that they have a special skill that makes their job important to the operation of the company. Emphasize training during off hours and be prepared to pay for the training if it aids in upgrading the skills of your employ ees.

8 **Minimizing bureaucracy**
Bureaucracy is a necessary evil so look to streamline the processes to get things done. Empower each depart ment to come up with a method that minimizes the red tape and reporting in order to get things done in an effi cient manner. Flex time is excellent for firms that don't manufacture but they often require personnel to spend great numbers of hours over a terminal to design or

I would stay up sometimes for 40 hours straight trying to fig- ure out a problem and I would often collapse at my desk. I would get so frustrated that I would go into the rest room and cry. I reluctantly would finally ask for help and low and behold it was usually a simple solution that was right in front of my face but, because I was so wrapped up in the problem, I would overlook the obvious. From this experience I learned to ask for help when I needed it and, as I became higher in the management rank, I would then encourage everyone, especially managers, to be especially aware of extreme hours being worked by individ- uals.

code programs. Getting ideas approved, improving cus tomer service and reviewing personnel are all areas where bureaucracy can be eliminated. Have a sugges tion box and encourage input. If you do have a sugges tion box, be sure to use the suggestions and publicize the ones that are implemented. You could even reward through money or recognition for the suggestions that worked. If you don't ever use the suggestions it will only work as detriment and morale will deteriorate.

Navigating Points:

Other things that we would do to encourage teamwork was to have each department that was dependent on an-other's accomplishments or, as prerequisite before a pro-ject could be completed, have weekly or as needed meetings to ensure that the modules would link up properly. Imagine if two groups were building a tunnel or railroad track and each started at a different side and did not communicate. The tunnels and tracks wouldn't meet and there would be a great deal of rework in order to make the correction.

9.   **Seeking ideas**

Always seek ideas and encourage an open door policy or a method for anyone to make a suggestion for any rea son. Recognition for ideas is critical for this flow to con tinue. If you do not recognize the ideas in some type of public forum, the ideas will dry up. People do not like to feel that they are being used and that only the company benefits.

Boeing solicited ideas for process improvement and de-pending on the dollars saved, the employee would re-ceive a percentage of the dollars saved over a given pe-riod of time. Many companies do this and/or a variation of this theme.

10.   **Identifying the marketplace needs**

Your personnel like to be informed on the status of their efforts as it translates to meeting the requirements of specific markets. As your product changes to meet the ever-changing market, inform your people of where you are taking them and encourage input on ways to keep your company ahead of the competition and increase market share.

11. **Establishing formal criteria for selecting projects**
There are many ways to formally select projects for de velopment, purchase a competitor or merge with anoth er company. Since the life blood of your company is in your product or service there should be sound market input and justification for selecting any new project. If you are a public company, you may have a rigid set of standards to adhere to in order to get approval for a merger, a buyout or developing a new project. If you are a privately held company you have much more lati tude from a regulatory standpoint but maybe more rigid purse strings.

Confidentiality may be critical until the final product se lection and/or negotiation is complete for a variety of reasons. When you can, you should inform all of your personnel of the selection and the rationale for the se lection. Rumors can start in the smallest company through the large conglomerates and each will have the same impact only with more or less dollars.

12. **Prioritizing projects and matching the project load to available resources**
Many managers tend to overlook the competitive in stincts of their people and only assign projects that they have specific training for or have had successes with in the past. A tactic that I have used very successfully when I did not have sufficient resources was to explain

the opportunity (not the problem) that we had and ask for input. You would be surprised at the volunteers who wanted to tackle the job. Depending on your organization, some people thrive on challenge and don't mind working the extra 10-50% to make it happen. They especially don't mind if it means opening up opportunities for training, recognition, meeting a deadline or being recognized as integral part of the team.

Throw out challenges and see what can be done internally without having to hire outside resources. An organization that runs lean and mean tends to be team and process oriented and always looking for quicker, better and less expensive ways to get the job done. With this attitude bred into your company, you will attract an employee that accepts challenges because they know they will be recognized for their effort.

If performing beyond the bounds of their job description offers rewards of increased bonuses, better benefits, high salaries or better 401K contributions, people will continually perform beyond expectations.

13. **Providing the resources to get the job done**
Resources always boil down to money and most business plans are overly aggressive in forecasting revenue. The result is having to go to the well for additional funds in order to support the effort until revenue is generated to offset the funding. Most entrepreneurs or engineers tend to think of what they can contribute to the total

Navigating Points:

There are many ways to formally select projects for development, purchase a competitor or merge with another company. Since the life blood of your company is in your product or service there should be sound market input and justification for selecting any new project. If you are a public company, you may have a rigid set of standards to adhere to in order to get approval for a merger, a buyout or developing a new project. If you are a privately held company you have much more latitude from a regulatory standpoint but maybe more rigid purse strings.

project and assume that everyone else has the same drive and will have the same knowledge in their area of expertise. I have found that this is seldom true but when it is true, getting the individuals to work as a team can sometimes be a bigger effort than the building of the product.

Resources need to be justified by each department and agreed to prior to beginning the project. You should have a meeting with all involved and each manager should be prepared to list the resources needed with required dates and then you need to look at whether you should purchase, borrow or lease the resource. Pride of ownership plays a big role with department heads and each wants control. If you set an example in the beginning and explain that the resource is expensive and underutilized, a sharing formula could be constructed where everyone has access and you don't need to duplicate the sometimes costly resource.

If specific talent is not readily available but a necessity in order to complete a given phase of the project, look to a contract house or specialty firm that will sell you the time or provide the capability for the needed period of time. This method eliminates the need to hire or train someone internally and then release them after the project is completed.

Resource planning and allocation begins with the marketing. If marketing provides proof of the requirement,

Throw out challenges and see what can be done internally without having to hire outside resources. An organization that runs lean and mean tends to be team and process oriented and always looking for quicker, better and less expensive ways to get the job done. With this attitude bred into your company, you will attract an employee that accepts challenges because they know they will be recognized for their effort.

the foundation is laid for all of the necessary resources. The size of the market, the opportunity, the margin and the competition are all a part of marketing and the result is funding for the product. If you do your job correctly, you will develop a business plan that can adequately fund the project with contingencies for delays or market changes.

14. **Making risk and failure acceptable**

Employees afraid to make a mistake for fear of a reprimand or firing tend to make an organization tight lipped with low morale and usually has a high turnover. If you fear for your job, you develop stresses, your health suffers, family life suffers and your quality of life in general tends to be poor. Make risk and failure commensurate with the job. If you are developing or engineering products you tend to have more of a trial and error to perfect the product. You have an understanding of the possible effects of making a mistake but if you are a good manager, you plan for errors and then if you come in under the deadline, you are recognized as a quality manager.

If you are manufacturing a product and forget to tighten a nut or solder a wire and the product gets by quality testing and is passed along to the consumer, you may have to reprimand or retrain since this type of position has the opportunity to accept failure more than someone in development or engineering.

15. **Insisting on quality**

There is no substitute for quality. Quality on the telephone, being cheerful and informative, accurate books, clean facilities, being on time, development, manufacturing marketing and sales and support are all areas where quality is important. Insist on quality stores and distribution and ensure that your salespeople and distribution are trained to best represent and support your product or service. Establish standards and don't waver. Quality is more relevant with ISO criteria being implemented and it covers all departments and processes. Not every product or service requires ISO standards but there are quality standards that each of you can implement and can become known for in your market.

As a manager you can set the example. If you are on time, keep the company informed, improve sales as you stay current with the market, provide a quality work place with appropriate benefits and these things will nurture quality.

16.   **Being a cheerleader and saying thanks**
Nothing spurs your company on like saying thanks. Everyone knows that the key managers had the vision and, if not for them, you would not be where you are. When you recognize your people for their efforts, you trig ger a sense of self-worth in the individual. Knowing that you are appreciate ed means a lot; make a point to have each manager talk to their people.

During our monthly company status report meetings, I would use Excel, Power Point and flip charts depicting our sales and projected sales, testimonials from customers and distributors as well as opportunities for improving the product or customer service. If it was about the product, I would complement the production and manufacturing, if it was support, I would recognize the support department and so on. I would also make it a key point

Chapter 31
Product Certification

Product Certification is a company philosophy that carries through from the CEO to the shipping clerk. Product Certification is based on more than the reliability of the product, it also requires that your company can comply with the standards and regulatory requirements that your market dictates. If you can answer yes to the following questions you have the foundation of releasing a product to the market with the certification.

- Can you provide a quality product consistent with specifications and guidelines of the governing body controlling the release of the product to the consumer?
- Do you have control of the product? Do you have product control and release procedures for alpha, beta and customer use?
- Has market research been thorough so that your target market justifies the expenditure to produce the product to the specifications and volume necessary to be profitable?
- Can you sell the product with trained and informed sales people?
- Do you have the appropriate business licenses and are you prepare to negotiate license and contract agreements?
- Can you quote the customer a consistent price, take an order, fill the order, ship the product and correctly bill the customer?
- If your product is not readily customer installable, do you provide quality installation manuals and/or on-site or telephone installation support?

- Can you professionally receive, and promptly respond, to customer problems and requests for help?
- Can you support the product consistent with contract commitments and company standards?
- Is "Product Certification" Required for my Product?
-

Navigating Points:

Important Questions to Ask…
Can you provide a quality product consistent with specifications and guidelines of the governing body controlling the release of the product to the consumer?
Do you have control of the product? Do you have product control and release procedures for alpha, beta and customer use?
Has market research been thorough so that your target market justifies the expenditure to produce the product to the specifications and volume necessary to be profitable?
Can you sell the product with trained and informed sales people?

All products require some level of Product Certification whether you are NASA and building a space ship to fly to the moon, building a Hula Hoop or making a bench for your patio. All products go through the reasonableness test from the individual dreaming up the idea to their discussing it with friends and peers. The mistake that most new entrepreneurs and new companies make is in not certifying the validity of the idea with the demographic most likely to purchase your product.

In many instances, the idea is thought to be the "best idea ever" and friends and family are advised of this breakthrough and, because of the enthusiasm of the person presenting the idea, moneys and life savings are poured into the product only to find out that there really is no market for the product.

This book is meant as an aid for the entrepreneur or established business to review what they are making before embarking on an all-out fund raising effort to build something that has a limited or no Window of Opportunity.

Chapter 32

Product Certification Guidelines

This last chapter is chalk full of information that your company can not live without. If you are an entrepreneur just embarking on a new business with limited capital the degree to which you act on each of these steps will be limited to the funds available. The most important steps for me in my pursuit of starting up a new business or developing a product were:

Can your idea be patented?

If your idea is already patented, don't lose heart, the company that patented the idea may never have ever developed the idea into a product for a variety of reasons. Call the parties and discuss a release of the patent, royalty arrangement, partnership or merger or geographic exclusivity. If the idea didn't take off, there is a reason, find out what that reason is and act accordingly.

Is there a market for your product?

Call product managers at retail or wholesale firms that would distribute a product like yours and ask for their advice. These people are deluged with calls so be patient and keep calling. Go to a store in your local mall and ask the store manager what they think of the product and ask for a reference to the main distribution outlet for the product manager that would evaluate and recommend merchandising your product.

Can you make a profit with this product?

Take the time to write a business plan and ask the advice of other small successful business owners or, some that were not so successful, to review and offer advice. Your local Small Business Administration Office and bank can also offer suggestions and give you guidelines. Many universities and col-

leges will advise you for no or minimal fee and there are courses offered on business plan development and how to get funded. The most common error that new businesses make is the lack of budget to promote and sell a given product. If you are manufacturing a product, the most overlooked area is the engineers over confidence in meeting product testing deadlines. Look at IBM and Microsoft, they are sometimes 18 months late on delivering a new product. The average small business can't afford a delay of that magnitude and it is the major reason for the demise and merger/acquisition of good idea companies without the capital to withstand the lack of experience in bringing a product to market.

Confirm the demand for your product in the market place

If you are delivering a service associated with food, training, consulting and not associated with manufacturing you still have to do a good job on market research before you can begin the selling and revenue process. Take a delicatessen for example, are there other fast food chains or delis in the local area? What would make yours special? Are you kosher, fresher, offer better service…just what makes you so special? Examine the local area and call on prospective businesses to survey what type of food they would like in the area. Will you specialize in breakfast and lunch or are you an all-day delicatessen? Can you cater to businesses? Find out what the locals would like and incorporate the findings into your business plan and look at the startup cost and how long it will take to show a profit.

Perform the test of reasonableness against your idea

Before anything else, talk to and ask for advice from those with experience about your product. Weigh the odds of making it happen with your product against the odds of failing. Only then should you take the next steps to detail marketing, searching the Patent Bureau, securing funding and incorporating. Are you trying to compete with the big boys with a

Navigating Points:

All products require some level of Product Certification whether you are NASA and building a space ship to fly to the moon, building a Hula Hoop or making a bench for your patio. All products go through the reasonableness test from the individual dreaming up the idea to their discussing it with friends and peers. The mistake that most new entrepreneurs and new companies make is in not certifying the validity of the idea with the demographic most likely to purchase your product.

product or service? If you are, you'd better be sure that you have a niche that could be profitable to you and that the big boys would neglect because they deal in volume.

How do you plan on selling your product?

Will you hire direct sales people, work through manufacturers' representatives, national distribution companies, telemarketing, catalog, direct mail? Have you thought about compensation and the cost to get your product to the sales organizations? What about the markups? Will your product support a one or two tiered mark up before the consumer purchases the item? For example, a marking pen costs $1.00 from off shore in packages of four if you purchase in quantities of 10,000. You now have to sell the marking pens at $3.50 per box in order to make your business profitable and you have to sell 15,000 per month. Now, what is your methodology in bringing your product to market? If you have a traditional two tiered distribution, you need to calculate what the cost will be to the consumer and determine if the product is salable at the quantities that you have projected.

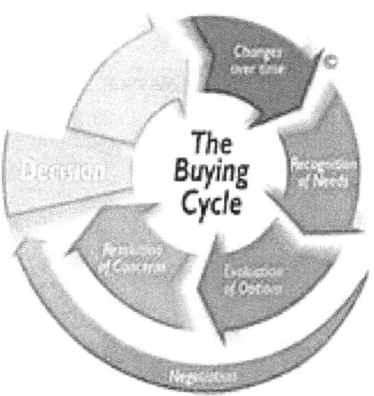

If you sell to a major distributor at $3.50 and they put a markup of 50% on the pens, the cost to their customer is $5.25. Their customer is a retail chain that adds a markup on the pens of 30% and the cost to the consumer is now $6.83. Ask yourself if your pens can sell at that price or should you be looking at new channels to distribute your pens. This is where the marketing phase of business comes to play. A major distribution warehouse would calculate the various mark ups and tell you that that the pens would be too expensive to the consumer with the methods of merchandising that you have for this product.

Product Certification is based on many tests of reasonableness if you are a startup company with an idea or an established company developing a new product. Product Certification will be based on input from:

- Market research from potential distributors and end users

- Product definition from the inventor or Product Management

- User Documentation

- Configuration management

- Pricing

- Testing

- Product entry

- Billing

- Commissions and compensation

- Promotional considerations

- Distribution and sales support

- Lead tracking and follow up

- Installation and warranty support

- Problem management

As your product is being readied for distribution to the customer, I have included for your review and use where applicable, Product Certification Checklist. This checklist can be as simple as a reminder, a to-do list or as a Certification Data Package. I have included a series of materials with steps to take to ensure that you have taken the necessary steps to enter your product successfully into a market place.

Product Certification Checklist Guidelines

When the Product Certification Checklist is completed, the output will demonstrate that your company has researched, and is fully prepared to deliver a product or service that is commensurate with the goals and objectives of your company. Product Certification will be based upon the review and evaluation of material from the areas of:

Navigating Points:

If you are delivering a service associated with food, training, consulting and not associated with manufacturing you still have to do a good job on market research before you can begin the selling and revenue process. Take a delicatessen for example, are there other fast food chains or delis in the local area? What would make yours special? Are you kosher, fresher, offer better service...just what makes you so special? Examine the local area and call on prospective businesses to survey what type of food they would like in the area. Will you specialize in breakfast and lunch or are you an all-day delicatessen? Can you cater to businesses?

- Senior Management team

- Product Marketing

- Sales

- Finance

- Engineering (Hardware and Software)

- Support (Technical and Customer)

- Advertising

- Documentation

As the product is readied for sale, the certification materials identified in the accompanying checklist will be accumulated in a Certification Data Package (CDP).

Product Management is encouraged to discuss certification requirements with the Quality Assurance group as early in the project as possible in order to avoid any unnecessary delays in readying the product for release. The product manager is responsible for notifying Quality Assurance when development is initiated. It is recommended that weekly meetings be scheduled with all involved parties present to discuss and update the status of the development process. It is also recommended that a project reporting package be used to initially create and update through the weekly meetings the status of the development process. It is crucial to your success that all responsible parties in the development process adhere to this process in order to avoid the inevitable, "It's not my fault" or "I didn't know I was supposed to have that ready" kind of statements that can bring the team to its knees and cause insurmountable delays.

When the product is ready for certification, the material in the CDP will be reviewed by Quality Assurance and the certifications decision will be made. If the product meets the standards given herein, it will be recommended for unconditional certification.

The most common error that new businesses make is the lack of budget to promote and sell a given product. If you are manufacturing a product, the most overlooked area is the engineers over confidence in meeting product testing deadlines. Look at IBM and Microsoft, they are sometimes 18 months late on delivering a new product. The average small business can't afford a delay of that magnitude and it is the major reason for the demise and merger/acquisition of good idea companies without the capital to withstand the lack of experience in bringing a product to market.

If minor problems with some of the certification steps are identified, the product may still be conditionally certified provided an acceptable plan and schedule for correcting the problems are submitted. However, conditional certification is valid for only a fixed period of time. If the problems are not corrected in a given period of time, the conditional certification would expire and the product could possibly not be certified. If the problems are corrected in an acceptable manner, the product could be recommended for full certification.

Market Evaluation

This section concerns the steps to determine if the product has any merit before a great deal of time and money is spent. This section should be completed by all businesses but the steps are especially true for a startup company developing its first product.

Reasonableness Test

This is simply a test that shows that the person with the idea has done some preliminary research to determine that the idea is marketable and if it can be produced at a price that a customer would purchase it. This document should contain a description of what the product is, who the target audience is, and an estimated price the customer would pay as well as and explanation as to how you would sell it and if there is any competition.

1.0   Market Identification

This is an extension of the Reasonableness Test but substantiated with some target customers input on their acceptability of the product, if it performed well and if the cost was justified. The market could be a toy or a sophisticated piece of computer hardware. Go to the potential reseller if you don't have the sales channel and also the end user. If you go to the reseller, be sure to have a non-disclosure signed to protect yourself against pirating your idea.

If money is not a real issue, you may want to have an independent marketing firm evaluate your idea and give you an unbiased opinion. If the opinion is favorable, the report would be excellent input for your business plan and aid in the fund raising. Other sources for independent appraisal are your local universities and colleges.

1.1 Competitive Research

Without a doubt you don't want to recreate the wheel and enter into a market that is saturated with compete tors that have close to the same product that you have an idea for. Big companies can lower their price on a like type of product and the customer that you thought you had locked in will purchase

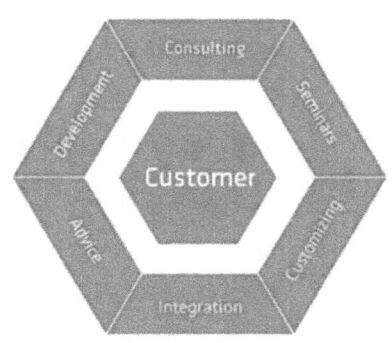

The competitor's product can go for the lesser dollar even if it does not have all of the features and benefits that your product has. Be real unique, have a complimentary product that can serve as an add-on to a major manufacturer to help them sell more products, go after a niche market that can be profitable but that the big boys don't want or can't afford, look to private labels where a major company puts their name on your product and sells it or uses your product as an OEM product that integrates into their product line.

Find out who your potential and real competitors are and try to determine if there is a need that will not be filled by the competition. If you have fad products that are here today and gone tomorrow can you manufacture it fast enough to make the Window of Opportunity. If the product has a long development cycle, is your Window of Opportunity long enough to develop and bring to market before it is obsolete?

1.2 Patent Search

Is your idea patentable? If it is, maybe somebody else has thought of it and patented it ahead of you. If they

have, all is not lost, they may not be in business any more or the patent may have run its course and you can still move forward. If the idea was patented but never developed, this could be a win-win situation.

If the company that tried to market the product was unsuccessful, find out why that was. Was the idea before its time, too costly or too close to a competitor's product that is entrenched in your target market?

1.3 Patent Application

1.4 Name Search/Registration

Naming your company and your product is sometimes very important because it conveys what you are doing. Where ever you are going to do business or even think ing about doing business, you should do a name search and if there is no other company by that name, register your business name. You should also check to see if there are other businesses that are national in scope and sound like yours. If your name sounds like Hertz, Avis or Timex, you will be getting calls and continually have to reroute calls which is a big nuisance.

2.0   Startup Requirements

2.1   Business Plan

Whether you have the personal capital or have to go after venture capital, Small Business Administration, bank or other avenues to raise funds to get your busi ness started, you will need a business plan. Included in this book is a copy of the Stanford Business Plan and a Performa for N years to explain the capital required for items in the plan as well as a sample income statement which projects when the revenue will become a reality.

2.2   Funding Requirements

Navigating Points:

If minor problems with some of the certification steps are identified, the product may still be conditionally certified provided an acceptable plan and schedule for correcting the problems are submitted. However, conditional certification is valid for only a fixed period of time. If the problems are not corrected in a given period of time, the conditional certification would expire and the product could possibly not be certified. If the problems are corrected in an acceptable manner, the product could be recommended for full certification.

Before a business plan can be written, an essential element of the plan is the funding requirements of the project. This is the essential element of the business plan and will take most of your time. I suggest that you use Excel and be prepared to make extensive modifications.

Estimating the funding of a project is underestimated 99% of the time. Why is it so difficult to estimate the funding of a project? Having been through six projects from the beginning, the elements that all had in common were in underestimating how difficult it was to get regulatory approval since three were computer or telephone related. In one instance a project was delayed 2 1/2 years and required that the investors give a total of 20 million dollars when it was estimated to take only 12 million.

All of the projects were underestimated in terms of the marketing and sales time required to establish name recognition and revenue generation. A high tech product requires sometimes a year and a half to get the sales channel signed up. The larger the company the more manufacturers they have knocking at their door and you have to get in the queue for testing, market evaluation, pricing, private labeling, support, warranty, co-op advertising, trade show participation, pre and post-sales training and buddy calls to your customers prospects and customers. If you didn't plan for this time and expenditure to get a sales channel established, it can totally consume your reserve capital and cause you to rethink and reallocate your funds to keep the doors open.

Advertising and promotions are vital to any products success and how you allocate your advertising dollars is critical to your success. You need to target your audience and not shotgun and when you do get leads, follow up on them immediately and don't let them atrophy.

Funding, advertising...all of this affects your bottom line and if you underestimate it can be just as damaging as if you overestimate. Setting your budgets for actual anticipated need is kay to a successful venture. I have been involved in many projects where the folks in charge truly didn't account for all their needs. If you make poor assumptions your business will be over before you get started.

Issues such as sole sourcing of parts and shortages of parts can close your doors so try not to sole source parts because if you are not a large purchaser of a particular component, a major supplier could consume the inventory and leave you high and dry.

If you are manufacturing off-shore, and the dollar loses, your cost of sales could sky rocket causing you to raise your price to distribution and reduce or lose all of your sales.

2.3 Potential Funding Sources

If you are an entrepreneur and not independently wealthy, you will probably have to go to the venture capital market for funding. These firms look at products and invest very sparingly or, at best, one in twenty five. When they do invest, be prepared to lose up to 50% of your company and, in some cases, considerably more.

If your funding requirements are less than $250,000 and you have a short product development time before revenue is generated, you could expect to keep 80-100% of your company and work out a repayment on a monthly, quarterly, yearly and percent of the profits depending on the requirements of the lender and how good of a negotiator you are.

Partnerships, friends and family are also sources of revenue. Friends and family are good if you have a no lose scenario. In most instances when you bring in friends and family, you are asking for heartache, lost friendships and even enemies if you lose their money and have no method for repayment.

2.4 Company Structure

Company structure is important for both long and term growth and attracting key personnel as well as keeping the confidence of your investors. Company structure is varied due to advantages in taxation, and how and who you do business with. Discuss with your bank, venture capital firm, SBA, CPA or look to other like types of busi nesses and pattern your company after them.

2.5   Employee Benefits

Depending on your company structure, your benefits can be a great expense. The more expensive your labor, the more comprehensive your benefit plan will be. Where you conduct business can also play a great role in your benefit plan. If there is a good source of labor and, depending on whether labor is white or blue collar, average benefits may suffice. If there is a shortage of labor, your benefits may have to be excellent to attract and keep your employees.

Product Information

3.0   Program Document

This document includes the rationale for embarking on the development of the product or service. Rationale examples are the availability of technology at an afford able price to meet an emerging market requirement, minimal competition, synergistic opportunities, easy access to distribution channels, technical and labor re sources available, margins and funding required until revenue is generated.

Also include the potential obstacles such as access to distribution, development time, Window of Opportuni ty, competition, size of the market, margin erosion, life of product or family, support and maintenance require ments and access to personnel resources and manufac turing.

3.1 Product Development Plan

This plan gives a high level look at what is planned for the product. Will the product be enhanced or is it a lim

The Experts Speak Out...

Leadership is a potent combi nation of strategy and charac ter. But if you must be with out one, be without the strat egy.

— Norman Schwarzkopf

A meeting is an event at which the minutes are kept and the hours are lost.

— Unknown

You are not your resume, you are your work.

— Seth Godin

Beware of any enterprise requiring new clothes.

— Henry Thoreau

ited opportunity? If the product is to be enhanced with mid-life kickers, give a brief description of where it is going, how it will get there, where the market, timing and cost to develop are.

3.2 Request for Certification

Depending on whether a product is the first or an evolutionary stage of development, an initial request for certification will be submitted for the product and included in the CDP. The request will also provide the details of previous certifications of the product.

4.0   Product Documentation and On-Line Media

Documents going to the prospect or customer will comply with a given standards that have been published. In some instances our standards may be those of a regulatory body and all of your customers adhere to them and will request that you follow them if you wish them to sell or use your product.

All documents will be approved by Marketing and Sales before certification. The product producers are encouraged to discuss documentation needs with your publications manager early in the project. The publications manager could be a designated person with good English skills, an outside contracting house that specializes in documentation or your own inside publications manager depending on your size and requirements.

In any case, your standards should be published so that all persons writing documentation will use the same standard for continuity and evaluation.

4.1   General Information Manual

This document contains the agreed to set of documents that a given product will have before Product Certification can be completed. It is essential that all requirements be reviewed for compliance with our published standards for documents. All of this information should be available on the internet so develop standards and help is easy to retrieve when your customers or prospects access your web page for FOQ, information or help.

Items that will require approval depending on the type of product are:

- General information Manual
- Warranty Card
- Packaging
- Bar Code for Inventory and Receiving
- Private Labeling
- Rebate Information
- Survey Information
- Promotional Materials
- Press Releases
- Tutorials
- User Guide
- User Reference
- Troubleshooting Guide
- Systems Administration Guide
- Installation Guide
- Quick Reference Guide or Card
- Trade Show Kiosks
- Logo and Trademark Usage
- Stationery

- Video and Audio Transcripts

- Pictures

This is a sampling of the types of documents that could accompany the delivery of a new product or service. I have listed a few of the most common documents on the certification checklist and if more are required, write them down and assign responsibilities accordingly.

5.0 Approval Statements

Approval Statements are assurances that what you are providing to your customers are accurate information and convey the correct message. Four steps are involved before a document can be released for insertion with the product.

Publications writes the material in a manner consistent with the publications standards. The appropriate departments sign off on the material to ensure that the material conveys the correct message.

Test sites use the materials from an end user perspective to make sure that the material is easy to read and serves the purpose that it was written for.

5.1 Quality Assurance approves the materials for product distribution.

It would be very rare that a document would go through each step just once before being released for product distribution so be prepared for rewrites. What may seem simple to you may be very complex for the end user to comprehend. End user simplicity is key to your products success so listen to your ends user and react accordingly.

6.0 Configuration Management

Configuration Management refers to the identification, control, release and concurrence of hardware, manufac

Navigating Points:

If you are an entrepreneur and not independently wealthy, you will probably have to go to the venture capital market for funding. These firms look at products and invest very sparingly or, at best, one in twenty five. When they do invest, be prepared to lose up to 50% of your company and, in some cases, considerably more.

If your funding requirements are less than $250,000 and you have a short product development time before revenue is generated, you could expect to keep 80-100% of your company and work out a repayment on a monthly, quarterly, yearly and percent of the profits depending on the requirements of the lender and how good of a negotiator you are.

turing, software development and documentation. For certification, a configuration management plan will be documented and implemented and copies of all perti nent designs and software will be archived off site on a ecurring basis concurrent with the release of new or en hanced products. Major customers will require a plan f this nature to be implemented as a part of our disaster recovery plan.

6.1 Hardware plans, software code and all related doc-umentation will be assigned a product name and num -ber with a version or release number.

These numbers and names apply to all products and will ensure all releases are current and if a recall should oc cur, you can identify what product was defective. Cus tomers and distributors alike will recognize your profess sionalism and it is sometimes a good ploy to start with a release number other than 1 because people in general do not want to be the first to purchase a product.

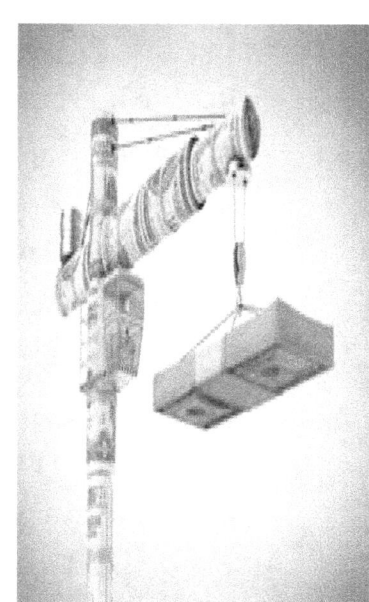

In some instances the customer which may be one of your channel partners will also give your product a different name and number and you will have to main-tain a library to cross reference your product name and numbers with theirs. Major customers many times will have this schema written in the contract to assist in sup-port of any product they carry and support in case of a major recall or disaster.

7.0   Pricing

Before product certification is complete a price sheet will be published and approved.

7.1   Price Verification

Pricing is the element that directly falls to your bottom line. You have one chance to get it right and that chance is on initial release. You can always lower your price but it is very difficult to increase your price once it has been released.

Prior to establishing your products pricing, take into consideration the following questions:

- What is my cost to manufacture? Cost of parts, labor, personnel, equipment, facility and utilities.

- What is my yield? What yield do I get from my manufacturing process? How much actual product do I receive after I do my rework and throw out my failed parts?

- Am I unique in my product offering?

- Do I have direct competition that will affect my pricing?

- How open is my Window of Opportunity before competition enters?

- If I am unique and my product is in high demand, do I have enough resources to meet the demand? What is my backup plan? Do I have secondary sources for special or unique parts and what is my lead time?

- What is the cost to sell the product?

- Does the product require a direct sales force?

- Can the sales force be call center based or do I have to have in-house personnel calling?

- Does my sales force have to make a technical presentation and if so, what type of sales people will I have to employ and at what cost?

- Does my product require massive sales channels to be successful? If it does will my product support multiple mark ups and still be viable to the consumer?

- If I have to develop sales channels, what channels do I go after and how long should I expect them to develop

Navigating Points:

Reasonableness Test

This is simply a test that shows that the person with the idea has done some preliminary research to determine that the idea is marketable and if it can be produced at a price that a customer would purchase it. This document should contain a description of what the product is, who the target audience is, and an estimated price the customer would pay as well as and explanation as to how you would sell it and if there is any competition.

before I can expect revenue?

- What type of tools do I have to develop in order to train their salespeople or promote my product in their sales channels? Can I develop train-the-trainer products and send them to my channel for training?

- Do I have to provide incentives or spills to their sales people or to their customers to move my product? How much and for how long should I offer the incentive?

- Did I allow enough time and money to develop the channel before revenue can be realized?

- Do I need to have a direct support hot-line? If yes, does the support line have cover all of the United States during prime time?

- How many support people will I need and what do I do about holidays?

- What is the cost of the telephone to support the product?

- Can I charge for support via a 900 line after the warranty is over or can I charge initially for support?

7.2 Separate or Shared

Consider a shared environment if your product is in a startup mode and the volume is going to be low. You could negotiate equipment and personnel time from a firm that has contract personnel to fit your needs or you might be able to find a firm that has the capability and willingness to contract manufacture and/or assemble your product until you can justify the expenditures.

7.3 Expansion Considerations

If your business has potential for growth, does your location have options for growth? Consider your lease options for more space or if you are very profitable, it may make sense to sing a facility for the tax incentives and

I have learned over the years to work with the best resources possible and that doesn't always mean brand new resources. There are hundreds of companies that fail every year who need to liquidate their assets. This means that a door is open for other new businesses to obtain what they need at great prices. Do your homework...it could save you money.

depreciation an owned facility can offer.

Consider your location relative to your product requirements, personnel, market, taxes and expansion. It is very difficult and expensive to uproot your business and move to another location, so think about your facility requirements.

8.0 Capital Equipment

8.1 New or Used

9.0 Used as an option

New or used equipment is an issue of pride and image. If the equipment if used is capable of performing the task required? New equipment is always nice to have, it smells good, it looks good and it gives the appearance that you are very successful or very foolish. Sometimes you can find nearly new equipment at auction, out of business sales or demos from the manufacturer. Placing ads in appropriate trade journals or contacting brokers are good methods for locating good used equipment. Someone coming to your company does not know if the equipment is new or used so I would recommend used equipment if it is priced right, under warrantee and can offer a life cycle consistent with your requirements.

New equipment is great but if you are the first to use the product, you may be the first to experience the failures and be the guinea pig for the engineers to get their on-hands product warranty experience.

If you are the first purchaser of new equipment, you should consider negotiating a referral discount for the manufacturer bringing in new prospects to reference your use of the equipment.

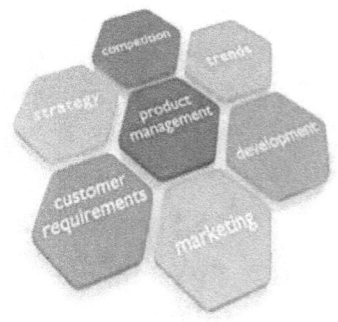

If you anticipate expansion and will require additional pieces of equipment, consider incorporating in the equipment contract a discount if purchased in the next months or years

Owned

Owned is for the well-funded or established business that can use the depreciation and gain the tax advantage that purchasing can offer.

Rented

Renting is usually done from an established business that has excess capacity and you rent the equipment and maybe the personnel for N hours or months. Renting offers a startup the luxury of having equipment at his disposal without the leasing or purchasing obligations. The owner of the equipment will warrantee the equipment, take care of the utilities and facility.

Leasing

Most of your expensive equipment is leased with an option to purchase. Again, it depends on the requirements of your business and your state of profitability or mindset about leasing or purchasing capital equipment. Leasing capital equipment is much like leasing a car. The original manufacturer of the equipment does not usually lease but has authorized brokers that they will refer you to for leasing.

The broker will negotiate a price with the manufacturer based on the leasing requirements and will give that price to the customer. If the customer accepts, the manufacturer receives their price and the leasing agent makes a monthly profit on the price of the equipment for the life of the lease. At the end of the lease, the customer returns the equipment or pays the residual for full ownership.

9.0   Approvals Required

9.1   Almost all products require some type of ap

The Experts Speak Out...

A man should never neglect his family for business.

– Walt Disney

Sometimes when you innovate, you make mistakes. It is best to admit them quickly and get on with improving your other innovations.

– Steve Jobs

The successful man is the one who finds out what is the matter with his business before his competitors do.

– Roy L. Smith

-proval and you should understand the approval process in detail before the startup of any manufacturing process.

Contact your state or federal licensing bureau for all licensing requirements to do business with your product or service.

10.0 Testing

10.1 Development Testing

Understand the testing requirements of your product or service. If you are making a toy ensure that the toy has the attributes that make it attractive to a demographic or market segment. The next step is to ensure that you can pass the federal and state approvals required to bring your product to market. If it is a high tech product such as sound equipment, many levels of federal approvals are required to meet sound, emission, fire, breakage and power. Many of these tests require very sophisticated pieces of test equipment that are very expensive and used for only minutes. Without the tests, your product is not salable so be prepared to purchase, borrow or lease the appropriate equipment to meet your guidelines and time frames for testing.

Prior to your own in-house testing, you should ask for the federal test specifications so that when your product reaches the test lab for federal approval, you will be close to having the product test compliant. Almost never does a product pass testing on its first acceptance in the test lab so be prepared to reschedule or lock in times at specific intervals. Test labs can get backlogged with product testing and this could cause delays in delivering product to the customer that you never anticipated.

10.2 Reliability Testing

Navigating Points:

Consider a shared environment if your product is in a startup mode and the volume is going to be low. You could negotiate equipment and personnel time from a firm that has contract personnel to fit your needs or you might be able to find a firm that has the capability and willingness to contract manufacture and/or assemble your product until you can justify the expenditures.

Reliability testing in many instances has to be done out side of the developers' office. Different than develop ment testing, you are testing the product for reliability. Prior to release, in-house tests should be done to max imize your chances for certification at a test lab.

Types of tests are internal lab tests that check for me chanical, electronic and end user friendliness. Soak tests are product tests where a product is placed in an environment for a period of time. Soak tests can be with your prospects or customers and have a given set of criteria the product is tested and evaluated against.

Depending on the complexity of the product or service, conduct your own in-house reliability testing. This may mean building jigs to drop the item or pounding the item thousands of times. The best methods for reliabil ity testing that I have found are with the people that are going to use the product. Develop relationships with your potential customers and enlist their support. Usu ally, if the product will benefit the end user, the poten tial purchaser will be more than willing to assist you in testing the product. During the testing process, observe the end users reaction to the documentation, use of the product and any hesitations or body language that could be positive or negative. Ask the end user to cri tique the product with a survey that asks constructive comments about the product or service.

Feed all of these comments back to product manage ment as soon as possible in order to update documen tation or correct product operating deficiencies.

11.0 Product Validation

Product validation is another form of testing but usually more complete than reliability testing. Validation testing is used to combine all of the elements of the product together to see how well the end user can use the product in an environment other than the developers.

The validator will evaluate the total product and its supporting documentation to ensure that is suitable for installation, using the associated documentation and training materials, marketability, and overall product quality.

The validator is to provide an independent evaluation of whether or not the product is ready for the market place. Also the validator is to determine if the product conforms to good business practices to ensure that there are no misleading statements or claims that can't be substantiated in or by the product. The validator is the first customer of the product and I recommend that an independent testing lab, consultant or other outside qualified source validate and make an independent and unbiased review of the product.

12.0   Sales and Marketing

12.1 Sales and Marketing are different disciplines.

Marketing includes all of the disciplines necessary to make the sales effort successful. Marketing will identify and understand the channel to market that can pur chase in volume to support the business plan. Mar keting will identify the competition, pricing, benefits, support, and advertising requirements as well as certify that the product has a wide Window of Opportunity with sufficient margins to support the development effort.

It will be expected that the marketing team and product management will make a presentation to senior management in graphic form and with supporting collateral materials in order to support the business case of the chosen product. Understanding that if you are a startup, you and your partners represent the marketing

Navigating Points:

Depending on the complexity of the product or service, conduct your own in-house reliability testing. This may mean building jigs to drop the item or pounding the item thousands of times. The best methods for reliability testing that I have found are with the people that are going to use the product. Develop relationships with your potential customers and enlist their support. Usually, if the product will benefit the end user, the potential purchaser will be more than willing to assist you in testing the product.

team.

Sales is the proof that marketing and development have done their job. Sales will generate the revenue required to support the business plan and allow for you and your investors to make a healthy ROI and pay your creditors. Sales will recommend the training requirements and tools necessary to identify and close the deals in a timely manner. Sales will identify new opportunities and bring them to the management team for evaluation and action.

All of the efforts of marketing will make the job of selling that much easier. The two teams will have a very close working relationship in order for the business to be successful.

12.2   Market Justification Plan

The marketing plan will include but not be limited to:

- Identifying the competition including pricing, strength of technology, imbedded base and customer loyalty, ability to price us
  out of the market and other potential Achilles heels.

- Recommended channel to market philosophy based on the channels ability to support and sell the product commensurate with the business plan.

- Pricing to support the tiers of distribution to sell to the end user including distribution agreements.

- Support including warranty considerations.

- Window of Opportunity available, product life, recommended enhancements and price erosion considerations.

- Promotion and advertising recommendations. This includes co-op advertising, trade shows, brochures, newsletters, focus groups and other media advertising required to get you name recognition and sales.

- Product theme. Is there a theme for the product that ties in the company with the family of products and concurs with your company's mission statement? Having a theme helps for short and long term product recognition.

Some key areas that need to be approved by the senior management team are:

12.3   Target Market

Misidentification of your target can be the demise of your company so be sure that all members of the senior management team agree on the market and how to gain market share to support the business plan.

12.4   Product Theme

This is a non-trivial exercise and is very time consuming and costly is done incorrect. This is a chance for all of the company personnel to participate in coming up with a theme for the product and ensuing family of products. More than likely, you will have to invest in a profession al advertising firm to assist you in coming up with a theme and logo that will tie in all of your products and advertising and promotional campaigns.

12.5   Product Brochures

More delays are caused by not having documentation and product flyers than anything else. Everyone thinks that documentation just evolves. It doesn't just evolve, it can't be finished until all of the testing is complete and a baseline is established for the product. The base line is the first release of the product to the field so that all the supporting materials can be scheduled to meet the release date for the product. Promotional and ad vertising materials are usually contracted out of compa ny and involve consultants, camera and video staff, talk

Navigating Points:

Sales is the proof that marketing and development have done their job. Sales will generate the revenue required to support the business plan and allow for you and your investors to make a healthy ROI and pay your creditors. Sales will recommend the training requirements and tools necessary to identify and close the deals in a timely manner. Sales will identify new opportunities and bring them to the management team for evaluation and action.

ing heads, story boards, artwork, color approvals, ed
iting proofs and finally the printing.

12.6   Advertising and Promotional Plans

Timing is critical with any advertising or promotional
plans so that it is not too far ahead of the release of the
product. Teaser campaigns are common but delays of
one year or more are not uncommon in delivering a
high tech product and your advertising campaign could
be very ineffective if it promises a product one day and
it is not released until 12 months later.

If you have distribution channels geared up for co-op
advertising, testing and training and you miss your
deadlines, you not only lose credibility but all of your
momentum and if you are a startup company, the incumbent will say "I told you so." to your customer and
you may not get another chance.

It is better to delay the product than to announce and
lose all momentum and credibility with your channels of
distribution. Other collateral material to consider are
newsletters which can highlight key personnel, testimonials, editorials from key executives, sales tips, technical
tips, testimonials from customers, gathering product
input from survey questions, a puzzle, announcing new
products and touting your successes.

12.7 Sales

The sales plan is comprehensive in all areas of explain
ing how the market will be covered to generate the re
quired sales to justify the business plan. Sales will work
very closely with marketing and product marketing to
ensure that adequate tools are available for your inter
nal sales people as well as your distributors. Elements
that sales will require and again, this is dependent upon
the product and how you are selling the product are:

12.8 Budget

More sales managers have left companies because they did not have an approved budget. In entrepreneurial companies where the personalities of the owners are engineers, they almost always overlook the time, effort and expense of establishing sales and channels of distribution. My experience tells me that this occurs because the engineer can see the benefits and features of the product because of this authorship and it is thought that everyone should be as clear on the benefits as they are.

Budgets are never as great as a manager would like but in the case of putting together a sales and promotional budget, it is difficult to see the direct rewards that purchasing a piece of capital equipment or hiring a programmer that can produce code. Get an approved budget, work the budget, report on the expenditures and successes and keep the senior management team abreast on the results of opening the sales channels.

12.9 Recruitment Assistance

Depending on the product, it may be required to have professional guidance in hiring the right personnel to sell your product. If you are looking for telemarketing personnel, having your secretary make calls during their spare time will not get the desired results. You will need people that are qualified and can close quickly. Many people are afraid, or not very good, at selling a product over the telephone and the expense of having a professional recruiter or contract house assist you in hiring the right personnel will be worth the extra up front expense.

If you are national or international in scope, one of the worst things that you can do is have a sales person in Seattle calling on accounts in New York or Georgia. There are exceptions, but you need to have people that talk the talk, have the right contacts to your sales channels and are successful and well respected by the client base that you are going after. If you have a product that you are selling locally that is a commodity and there are hundreds or thousands of potential businesses that could use your product or service, hiring local people to canvass has merit. This type of sales has a lot of rejection so a good motivator is required and incentives are necessary to keep the morale high. It is also good to have daily sessions with all of your sales people to discuss successes and objections.

The point of this section is to be aware that selling is an art and without the right personnel for the product, you could be wasting valuable time and money when you could have had a better chance of success if you seek advice.

12.10 Territory Coverage

Territory coverage is influenced by a great number of items not the least of which is money. You may have to cover the United States with a handful of people to sell established channels to distribute your product

Hopefully marketing has uncovered a requirement by the channel to pick up the product and it is a matter of hitting the road to make the contacts and move the sales cycles forward to meet your objective. If you do telephone sales, you need to have experienced telemarketers and invest in automatic dialers and automated call distribution systems with watts or other lines that can minimize your long distance expense. A great deal of thought needs to go into how you are going to cover the territory with a fixed budget to meet the business plan objectives.

12.11 Promotional and Sales Aids

Promotional and sales aids are required for your direct

Talk to your customer and find out what they expect by way of collateral material to promote your product and do the test of reasonableness. If the requests are excessive, the distributor will usually pay you the cost of printing the materials or, if they have the production capability, they will request the art work and files and do their own printing. If your customer would request the art work to print their own brochures, be sure to proof the materials before printing so that you can be assured that your customer has not altered the message about the product.

mail campaigns, trade shows and distribution channels. You should have a theme for your product or ensuing family of products for name and product recognition. There are ratios of product brochures necessary to sell a given product.

Talk to your customer and find out what they expect by way of collateral material to promote your product and do the test of reasonableness. If the requests are excessive, the distributor will usually pay you the cost of printing the materials or, if they have the production capability, they will request the art work and files and do their own printing. If your customer would request the art work to print their own brochures, be sure to proof the materials before printing so that you can be assured that your customer has not altered the message about the product.

12.12 Sales Tools

Sales aid requirements could include some or all of these depending on the product.

- Product flyers

- Product videos

- Demonstration equipment

- Product demonstration kits and dial in capabilities if required

- Product gives a way's

- Customer testimonials

- Independent research evaluations

- Product folders for hand-outs for seminars or proposals

- Your company profile

- Copies of trade journal ads

Navigating Points:

Budgets are never as great as a manager would like but in the case of putting together a sales and promotional budget, it is difficult to see the direct rewards that purchasing a piece of capital equipment or hiring a programmer that can produce code. Get an approved budget, work the budget, report on the expenditures and successes and keep the senior management team abreast on the results of opening the sales channels.

- Key internal personnel to contact for specific information

- Certification approvals

- Company visit capabilities

- Profit and Loss statements

- Credit reports

- D & B Reports or similar

- Resumes of key personnel

- Contracts and Distribution Agreements

- Non-Disclosure Agreements

- Letters of Intent

- Business Cards and other pertinent give a ways

- Projection equipment, computer equipment, white boards or other necessary visual aids

Items in this list should be available to your salespeople and distributors in the form of a prepackaged kit that can be carried with the salesperson to sell your product.

12.13 Training

Training could be as simple as a stick drawing showing the customer how to use the product or as detailed as a three month training school. Whatever the product, the training should be commensurate with the need for the customer to use the product for which it was designed.

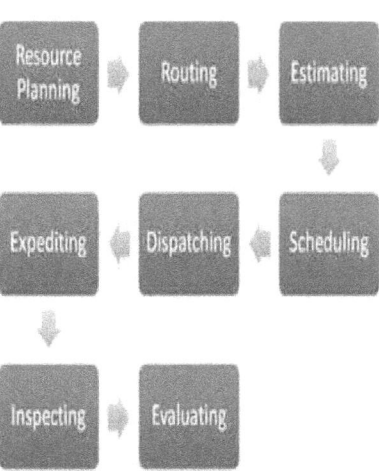

If the product has any potential danger such as transportation equipment, machinery or voltage, certification will probably be a requirement because of the danger and liability. If your product is a service, a computer application or a scholastic course, the grading should be objective but it may be subjective depending on the customer requirements. Sometimes managers send people to classes to learn as a reward for special achievement knowing full well that the person will never be required to use the knowledge. If the instructor gives the person a failing grade the reward turns out to be a demotivator.

Always test the validity of your course material with internal personnel and personnel outside of your company who can evaluate and give constructive input on how effective the material was in educating them on the use of the product.

Give consideration to the environment such as lighting, comfort of seats, warmth of room and having enough hands-on demonstration capability and presentation skills. The instructor can make or break the material. Usually a wide range of age and learning skills are represented in a given class so the instructor has to be cognizant of the speed that the slowest learner moves at in picking up the material and adjust the class so that all are moving forward but not to disrupt the class inordinately for one individual.

Try to vary your training aids so that boredom does not set in and you have to make a point to have your class interact with each other, the instructor and with the material in order to keep interest. If a student understands that they will be asked to do something on an interactive or random basis, they will be more apt to pay closer attention than if they are to just siting and listening.

If your clients are Fortune 5000 folks they may request you train in a specific format and you may have to adjust your materials accordingly to meet their needs.

If your clients have multiple locations, you will need to

Navigating Points:

Always test the validity of your course material with internal personnel and personnel outside of your company who can evaluate and give constructive input on how effective the material was in educating them on the use of the product.

Give consideration to the environment such as lighting, comfort of seats, warmth of room and having enough hands-on demonstration capability and presentation skills.

negotiate central locations for group training unless your margin justifies the travel expense for training. You should have a price for on-site training and in-house training if it falls beyond the bounds of reasonableness.

12.14 Production Plan

There is a plan from manufacturing that states that demonstration equipment or products will be available to meet the testing, presales and demand forecast for X number of months. This plan should be reviewed week ly against the forecast and adjusted accordingly.

I can't stress enough the need for sales to communicate to the management team the production forecast. A forecast is never accurate so you need to have enough product to meet the first three months and, as a trend develops, manufacture or order accordingly.

So much goes into a production plan in order to get ade- quate margins. Size of the order to get parts at the best price, lead time of the longest lead time part, schedul- ing of personnel and the manufacture and testing of the products.

Sales needs to be cognizant of the issues related to the MRP (Manufacturing Requirements Planning) and held accountable given that the product works as stat- ed with no long term delays or call backs or a com- plete down turn in the economy.

12.15 Lead Tracking and Follow-up System

One of the biggest faults that companies have is not having adequate immediate follow-up on leads that are generated by the salespersons, various advertising and promotional programs. Ensure that you have manual or an automated Lead

Tracking and Follow-up system in place to track the "Bang for your buck" scenario. Placing your dollars in media where the quality of leads results in real leads and not just collateral materials collectors that waste your time.

12.16 Field Prepared Statement

This is a statement from product management that all of the items in the CDP are complete and that the product is ready to go to market. In addition, a press release should be written and sent to all of the pertinent trade journals, customers, prospects and internal personnel.

13.0   Packaging

Packaging for breakage and shipment is part of the manufacturing and product management's role to ensure that EOQ (Economic Order Quantities) can be shipped to customers without fear of breakage and easy to receive and enter into inventory.

Many companies have a universal bar code reader that will scan a bar code and enter the product into inventory automatically. Be sure that your product conforms to your customers' bar code scheme or you could experience delays in the sale of your product because it was not entered into the inventory control system correctly.

Other things to think about are how the package is made for your customer. In some instances you may be requested to put a sleeve around the box with your distributors' logo.

14.0   Licenses, Contracts and other Agreements

There can be many types of agreements depending on how you are going to sell the product. I have listed a few with an explanation of how they would be used.

14.1   Agreements

Non-disclosure

This agreement is usually signed by a potential custom er so that extensive input to the development process can be given without fear that your proprietary infor mation will not be given to potential competition. After signatures, both parties are free to exchange infor mation which should move you closer to the sale.

14.2 License Agreement

License agreements usually have a volume commitment such as a software application that authorizes the dis -tributor the right to sell 10,000 copies and the distribu -tor makes the copies with your original. Your original version could be keyed so that when 10,000 copies are made a new license automatically is in place or you re-negotiate.

14.3 OEM Agreement

On Original Equipment Manufacturer Agreement is signed when a customer desires to integrate your prod -uct into theirs or sell it as an ancillary piece of equip ment to enhance their feature set. You could sell them the product intact, private label it, sell it in a kit where they assemble it, package or integrate into their product to their specifications.

14.4 Royalty Agreement

A Royalty Agreement is signed when a distributor/ channel partner might give you access to their cus-tomers and when a sale is made, you pay the distribu -tor a fixed royalty. The agreement usually goes the other way and when the partner sells a product, they give you a royalty. There is a lot of trust and paper work Involved in managing royalties and they can be all over the board.

14.5 Distribution Agreement

I can't stress enough the need for sales to communicate to the management team the production forecast. A forecast is never accurate so you need to have enough product to meet the first three months and, as a trend develops, man-ufacture or order accordingly.

So much goes into a produc-tion plan in order to get ade-quate margins. Size of the or-der to get parts at the best price, lead time of the longest lead time part, scheduling of personnel and the manufac-ture and testing of the prod-ucts.

The most common type of agreement is where the terms give the reseller the right to purchase your prod -uct in quantity and resell into specific territories. You will have to negotiate various disclaimers and outline warranty, pre and post-sales support, collateral materi als, training, co-op advertising, shipping and anything else that needs to be negotiated into the contract. Law -yers should be paid to review and validate the contract.

Be sure to stipulate volumes within time frames in order for your distributor to receive the discounts or exclusive -ty that you have agreed to in order to have your distrib utor sell into a specific territory. This is always a sticky issue when a new volume distributor comes on board and they are not allowed to sell into a territory where they have a store and are not allowed to sell your prod -uct because of an exclusivity clause in another part- ner's contract. Be sure to review this and have clauses that will allow you to enter into future agreements.

14.7 Manufacturers Rep Agreement

This agreement is for independent sales agents that rep resent a customer mix who can potentially use your product and can sell into a specific territory. The agree -ment outlines the commission structure, training and support that you will give the Rep to sell your product in a specific territory without you paying any benefits. The contract usually covers remote territories where major partners don't concentrate major sales efforts due to overhead to manage remote territories.

14.8 Employee Sales Agreement

This agreement outlines commissions, territory, quota, incentives and reporting requirements that you expect of your own internal and external sales people.

14.9 Letter of Intent

Navigating Points:

Be sure to stipulate volumes within time frames in order for your distributor to re- ceive the discounts or exclu- sivity that you have agreed to in order to have your distrib- utor sell into a specific terri- tory. This is always a sticky issue when a new volume distributor comes on board and they are not allowed to sell into a territory where they have a store and are not allowed to sell your product because of an exclusivity clause in another partner's contract. Be sure to review this and have clauses that will allow you to enter into future agreements.

This is one of the greatest closing tools and is used for trial closes and to raise money from investors. The LOI is great for forecasting, spreading good will, placing customers in the queue, locking in investors, taking owner ship of your product and helping keep the employee morale at a high level.

14.10 Extended Warranty

The razorblades that pay your overhead. Warranty con -tracts lock in your customers for X years beyond the normal warranty period. This type of contract gives your company credibility that you will support your product beyond the normal warranty period. Warranies add to the bottom line with little or no sales exper tise required and in fact the maintenance and support people can sell this when they are on line with the cus -tomer.

14.11 Nonstandard Contracts

Usually an addendum will suffice to make a standard contract acceptable to the terms and conditions of a customer requiring that something special be done to the product or have special terms added to the con -tract.

14.12 Contract Instructions

Anyone dealing with the safes end of the business should be aware of the types of agreements that are acceptable by your company and how to use them as -ploys or tools to close a specific deal. My philosophy is one that says try to work within the bounds of the standard agreements but bring all deals to the table for review.

15.0 Order Entry, Billing and Commissions

15.1 Internal or External Accountant

Depending on your company size, you may have an Ac counting Department or use the services of an outside accounting firm or bookkeeper. It is vital to have your accounting records intact for IRS, and the ebb and flow of the moneys necessary to keep a business functioning.

15.2   Selection of Accounting Package

Depending on your size, you may have a totally integrat -ed package that ties in all of your financial accounting, payroll, MRP, Order Entry and have a user friendly sys -tem for reporting on any piece of information. There are accounting packages on the market to fit any size business so explain your requirements including the personal computers that you currently use to a qualified salesperson and ask for a demonstration and references of like kinds of firms that use the package. If you use an outside accountant, ask this person for advice or hire a consultant to assist you in selecting the right package for your company.

If you do purchase a software package for your ac counting requirements, consider your growth expecta -tions over the next few years and make sure that your package has the capability to grow with you.

As simple as the demonstration may look in the store, ask if training is available. It would be a good idea to secure the services of person to assist you in bringing the system up and training the people who will be using the system. If you are a small company, your transact -tions may not require the sophistication of a PC based accounting system and manual record keeping might suffice.

15.3   Order Entry

A detailed statement on how orders are to be entered and processed will be included in the CDP. Orders should be entered into your automated or manual sys

Navigating Points:

Without Accounts Receiva-ble, your company can't sur-vive realistically. Your cus-tomer files with current names, e-mail, web page/ URL, titles, telephone num-bers, fax numbers, address-es, home office and branch offices, special notes on your customer such as non-standard terms or delivery, orders both past, current and future and salesperson are a few of the necessary items in your Accounts Receivable file.

tem immediately upon receipt in most instances. The lifeblood of most startup companies is orders and to ensure a timely delivery to your customers, order entry should be a number one priority.

Order Entry is the starting point for generating accounts receivable, collections, commissions, updating inventory and your MRP which includes accounts payable, sched -uling and receiving to name but a few applications that begin with order entry.

15.4 Billing/Accounts Receivable

Without Accounts Receivable, your company can't sur vive realistically. Your customer files with current names, e-mail, web page/URL, titles, telephone num -bers, fax numbers, addresses, home office and branch offices, special notes on your customer such as non-standard terms or delivery, orders both past, current and future and salesperson are a few of the necessary items in your Accounts Receivable file.

Your billing could be monthly or balance forward or by specific invoice. Each method has advantages and disad -vantages. Balance forward bills the customer their complete balance each month and your hope is that you receive a check for the balance and can begin anew each month.

Invoice billing allows you to track a payment to an in voice and will involve more paper work but you are usu ally clearer on what your customer is paying for because with balance forward, partial payments are the norm and you simply apply to the balance.

Considerations need to be given for late payments such as interest, how do you handle late payments if over your time limit, what about free samples and discount -ed items and under warranty items when returned.

I can't stress enough how important all of the details are. Yes, they can be frustrating and yes, there is a lot to consider but the bottom line it...leave out one of these details and your chance for success dwindles. Stay on top of each of the sections outlined in this book and the chances that your business will be successful increase.

15.5 Commissions

If you have salespersons and they are paid commissions, tracking commissions is essential to the well-being of the salesperson. The salesperson sells to be compen -sated and when a deal is clean and commissions are not paid and the reason is not communicated to the salesperson, much wasted time is spent by the salesper -son worrying and asking about why they were not paid in a timely manner. Commissions can be complex or simple so examine how your product is to be sold and enlist the support of your customers and ask how the competition pays commissions and also ask your sales people about commissions.

The norm is a percentage of gross sales paid monthly with bonuses paid if target sales are made monthly, quarterly or yearly. Sometimes, commissions are in creased as sales volumes increases. An example would be a salesperson with $500,000 quota. For the first $500,000, the commission is .01% and for the next $100,000 the commission increases to .015% and so on. Take the time to figure out how to pay your salespeople to get the most effort for their time.

15.6 Accounts Payable

The reverse is true of receivables in that you are paying for parts and services from your vendors. If you have an automated system, many of the Accounts Payables will be generated from the Order Entry process as it updates the MRP which can automatically generate orders to vendors for parts to build the products that you are manufacturing. Manual entry of other items such as soft goods and office use products which generate an order document for your vendor.

When the goods are filled and received at your door, you compare what was delivered to what was ordered

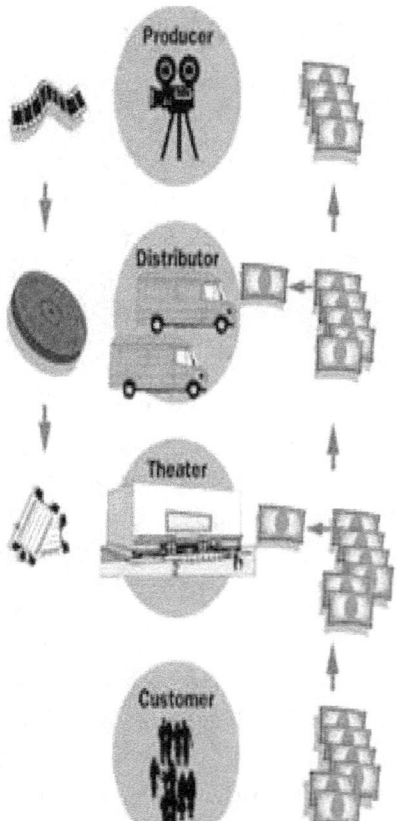

and note back orders and update your records accord
-ingly. You should also specify what type of freight carri
-er you desire, terms that you will accept if negotiable
with your vendor and when to contact you about when
a back order situation arises. In many instances, the cus
-tomer will automatically deduct .02% for prompt pay
ment and the vendor usually will not object.

15.7   General Ledger

The General Ledger is the posting of all of your mone
-tary transactions into one system so that you can see
what is being spent and what is being taken in. Your
profit and loss is noted, you can see trends in spending
and sales and compare departmental budgets to expenditures. The General Ledger can be totally automat
-ed which is called a Closed Loop. This is where every
sale, payable, payroll item, commission and expense is
automatically posted to its General Ledger has an item
number for daily, weekly, monthly, quarterly and yearly
reporting.

15.8   Inventory Control

Controlling inventory is critical to your success and your
customers' satisfaction. Without enough inventory to fill
your customers' requirements, your customers may
leave and seek out sources that can meet their needs.
With too much inventory, your cash is tied up in invent
-tory and other areas of you company will suffer.

There are times that you may wish to be heavy on in
-ventory such as a forecast of a shortage in a part, so
you may stock up X months' worth to meet future de
-mands. You may be faced with a price increase but if
you buy now, you can still purchase at the old price.
There are many extenuating circumstances and it will be
your job to balance the forecast to the real need and
track the buying trends accordingly.

There are times that you may
wish to be heavy on inventory
such as a forecast of a shortage in a part, so you may stock
up X months' worth to meet
future demands. You may be
faced with a price increase but
if you buy now, you can still
purchase at the old price.
There are many extenuating
circumstances and it will be
your job to balance the forecast to the real need and track
the buying trends accordingly.

Inventory Control can be a stand-alone system, manual or part of your MRP. Your size and complexity of the product will dictate, to a great extent, the type of sys-tem you will employ.

15.9 Payroll

Payroll for a small company is not too difficult but when you get beyond 20 and have employees residing in oth er states, the computation of taxes can be horrendous. I recommend that you use a company such as ADP that specializes in payroll and can provide you with all of the government reporting as it is required.

16.0 Product Distribution

16.1 Distribution Procedure

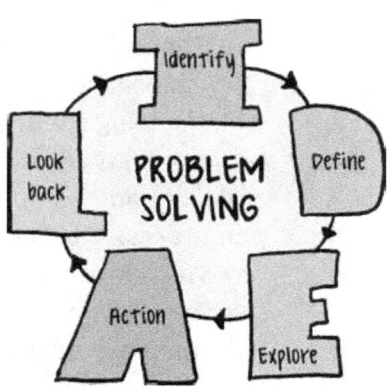

How am I going to sell and distribute my product? It sounds like a simple question and it can be if you are selling out of store front. If you are selling into channels throughout the United States or worldwide, the ques-tion is of a much greater proportion.

You need to think of the size of the container, what is my minimum and maximum number of items in a con -tainer, is there spoilage, do I have to worry about cus -toms and duties, what is the most economic method for shipment based on the type of product?

Other processes that have to be given consideration are the tracking procedures of your carrier and the receiv -ing process of your customer. Do they have a bar code that needs to be compatible with in orders for your goods to be received in inventory? Does your customer use your same product and model number or do you have to have a cross reference number for tracking.

16.2 Packaging Instructions

Critical for the well-being of your product in order for it

to arrive safe at your customers' warehouse are packaging instructions. Tests should be done at your facility to ensure that breakage will not occur under the most extreme circumstance and the boxes should be marked as fragile or this side up.

16.3 Packing List

The Packing List is usually on the outside or in the first container and it lists all of the products in this particular order and whether any were backordered or substituted. Substitutions can be made if pre-approved beforehand. The Packing List aids your customer in receiving the goods and noting any exceptions.

In many companies, the packing list is automated from the Order Entry and printed at the warehouse. The warehouse receives the document in the warehouse, given an order number and the products are picked. When the order is filled, the document is sent back physically or electronically with the exact quantities including backorders and substitutions noted and a new,   correct Packing List is sent to the warehouse for inclusion with the order.

16.4 Inventory Control

Just to note that the product distribution reflects a change in inventory and your system should be checked at timely intervals to ensure that what you think you have in inventory reflects an accurate count of what is really in inventory.

16.5 Warranty Statement

In each product, there should be a warranty statement that explains the terms and conditions of the warranty. This protects you and the distributor so that products will not be sent back for replacement unless they meet the requirements of the warranty statement. Conversely, the customer has protection if the product does not work as stated.

17.0 Installation

17.1   Installation Procedure

If your product requires an installation procedure, assembly instructions or how to use the product, they should be included in the product and easy to locate.

17.2   Installation Contract Required

If a contract is required, this is usually negotiated prior to delivery of the product with schedules so that the personnel using the product can learn from the contract installation personnel.

17.3   Installation Support Readiness Statement

This simply means that your company is ready to support the product commensurate with the business plan.

18.0   Product Support

18.1   Problem Reporting

Whatever your product, a reporting system should be in place that incorporates your internal identifications of problems, customer reported problems and a method of prioritizing and acting on the problems in the most expeditious manner.

Problems can be grouped and fixed and then released as a new release of the product and, in some instances, you may have to fix a particular problem for a customer to keep them online if your product is integral to product.

Management of problems requires a good release control procedure and the ability to say no to supporting releases that may be years old. Some companies support releases of products indefinitely and the support costs become so great that they can succumb to bankruptcy.

Examine your product for release management and determine when you should announce to your customers that you no longer support their release and you will give them a trade-in on the latest version or that they will have to live with the version they have and pay the hourly support cost.

Again, you may not to choose to support the product even on an hourly basis if your resources are working on a new product which will be worth 1,000 times more than working on the maintenance of an old release.

Considerations have to be made based on the customer's worth to your customer before any of these decision can be made.

John Parkin has decades of experience in the world of marketing. He has decades of experience building his own businesses and helping others seek out the right business path for themselves. In "Take it too Reality" John shares his vast knowledge in hopes that it will help others achieve success.

Often times these days books are written that are hard to follow. You grab a book that you think is going to guide you through a process only to discover that the person who wrote it really doesn't care if you actually understand it; this book is not like that at all.

This text is broken down into six sections. Those sections are entitled, Market Information Gathering, Business Case Development, Raising Money, Performance Measurement Criteria and Product Certification. As you can see, each section has been designed to walk you through the processes in the easiest, clearest way possible. I have also included thought provoking questions within each section to ask yourself and others regarding how to use your idea in the real world. The ultimate objective is to aid you, the entrepreneur, or you, the executive, in a way that will enable you to find out whether or not your idea has merit. If your idea has merit, the book will show you how to develop a business case, write a prospectus, raise money, develop and sell your idea.